The Heritage of War

The Heritage of War is an interdisciplinary study of the ways in which heritage is mobilized in remembering war, and in reconstructing landscapes, political systems and identities after conflict. It examines the deeply contested nature of war heritage in a series of places and contexts, highlighting the modes by which governments, communities and individuals claim validity for their own experiences of war, and the meanings they attach to them.

From colonizing violence in South America to the United States' Civil War, the Second World War on three continents, genocide in Rwanda and continuing divisions in Europe and the Middle East, these studies bring us closer to the very processes of heritage production. *The Heritage of War* uncovers the histories of heritage: it charts the constant social and political construction of heritage sites over time, by a series of different agents, and explores the continuous reworking of meaning into the present. What are the forces of contingency, agency and political power that produce, define and sustain the heritage of war? How do particular versions of the past and particular identities gain legitimacy, while others are marginalized? In this book contributors explore the active work by which heritage is produced and reproduced in a series of case studies of memorialization, battlefield preservation, tourism development, private remembering and urban reconstruction. These are the acts of making sense of war; they are acts that continue long after violent conflict itself has ended.

Martin Gegner is Visiting Professor at Universidade de São Paulo, Brazil, and director of the German Academic Exchange Service's (DAAD) centre in this city. His research interests lie in politics and sociology of urban heritage, cultural theory and political philosophy.

Bart Ziino is a lecturer in history at Deakin University, Australia. His research interests include memory and commemoration of war, and private experiences of Australian civilians during the First World War. Recent publications include *A Distant Grief: Australians, War Graves and the Great War* (2007).

Key Issues in Cultural Heritage
Series Editors: William Logan and Laurajane Smith

Also in the series:

Heritage and Globalisation
Sophia Labadi and Colin Long

Intangible Heritage
Laurajane Smith and Natsuko Akagawa

Places of Pain and Shame
William Logan and Keir Reeves

Cultural Diversity, Heritage and Human Rights
Michele Langfield, William Logan and Máiréad Nic Craith

Heritage, Labour and the Working Classes
Laurajane Smith, Paul Shackel and Gary Campbell

The Heritage of War

Edited by Martin Gegner and
Bart Ziino

Routledge
Taylor & Francis Group

LONDON AND NEW YORK

First edition published 2012
by Routledge
2 Park Square, Milton Park, Abingdon, Oxon OX14 4RN

Simultaneously published in the USA and Canada
by Routledge
711 Third Avenue, New York, NY 10017

Routledge is an imprint of the Taylor & Francis Group, an informa business

British Library Cataloguing in Publication Data
A catalogue record for this book is available from the British Library

Library of Congress Cataloging-in-Publication Data
A catalog record for this book has been requested

ISBN: 978-0-415-59328-1 (hbk)
ISBN: 978-0-415-59329-8 (pbk)
ISBN: 978-0-203-80920-4 (ebk)

Typeset in Garamond by
Saxon Graphics Ltd, Derby

Printed and bound in Great Britain by
CPI Antony Rowe, Chippenham, Wiltshire

Contents

List of Illustrations

Contributors

Joan Beaumont is Dean of Education, College of Arts and Social Sciences, The Australian National University. An historian of Australian prisoners of war in the Second World War, she is currently researching sites of Australian 'extra-territorial war heritage' including the Thai–Burma railway and the Kokoda Track, Papua New Guinea. Her recent publications include 'Contested Transnational Heritage: The Demolition of Changi Prison, Singapore', *International Journal of Heritage Studies* (2009).

O. Hugo Benavides is Associate Professor of Anthropology, Latin American and Latino studies, and International Political Economy and Development, and the Director of the MA Program in Humanities and Sciences at Fordham University. He has written three books and over twenty articles on Latin American culture and history which have appeared in academic journals and collections.

Judith A. Bennett is Professor of History at the University of Otago, New Zealand. Her research in the Solomon Islands produced a general history and a forest history. Her book *Natives and Exotics: World War Two and Environment in the Southern Pacific* was published in 2009. Currently, she is researching the children of Americans and indigenous women in the wartime Pacific.

Nguyễn Thanh Bình graduated in Architecture and Urban Planning in 1998 from Warsaw University of Technology (Poland), and completed his PhD at Deakin University, Australia, in 2010. He is a lecturer in the Architectural Faculty at Hanoi Architectural University, Vietnam, with research interests in public space and retaining heritage and traditional values in new Vietnamese architecture and urban landscape.

Esther Charlesworth, Senior Lecturer, Architecture and Design, RMIT University (Melbourne) is founding director of Architects Without Frontiers (Australia). Her research focuses on roles of design professionals in community development, particularly following conflict, natural disaster and other forms of social marginalization. Publications include two books:

Architects Without Frontiers: War, Reconstruction and Design Responsibility (2006) and *Divided Cities: Beirut, Belfast, Jerusalem, Nicosia and Mostar* (2009) co-written with Jon Calame.

Martin Gegner (post)graduated as Political Scientist from Freie Universität Berlin and did his doctorate in Sociology at Technische Universität Berlin. He worked as a researcher and lecturer at the Social Research Science Centre Berlin (WZB), at Humboldt Universität zu Berlin and as coordinator and lecturer of the World Heritage Studies Master's Course at Brandenburgische Technische Universität Cottbus, Germany. Currently he is Visiting Professor at Universidade de São Paulo and director of the German Academic Exchange Service's (DAAD) centre in this city. His research interests lie in politics and sociology of urban heritage, cultural theory and political philosophy.

Tony Joel is Lecturer in post-1945 world and modern european history at Deakin University and Research Fellow at the Alfred Deakin Research Institute (ADRI) in Geelong, Australia. A former German Academic Exchange Service (DAAD) scholarship holder, his main research intcrests are the politics of war memory and commemoration and the notion of Germans as victims.

Yasmin Khan teaches South Asian Studies at Royal Holloway, University of London. Her first book was *The Great Partition: The Making of India and Pakistan* (2007). She is currently writing a book about Indians and the Second World War.

William Logan is Alfred Deakin Professor and UNESCO Chair of Heritage and Urbanism at Deakin University, Melbourne, Australia. His recent research publications focus on urban and intangible heritage in Asia, world heritage, the heritage of places of pain and shame, and the links between cultural diversity, heritage and human rights.

Stephanie L. McKinney received her PhD in history, with a specialization in genocide and modern wars, from Claremont Graduate University, California. Currently, she teaches at several local colleges and works with organizations including Amnesty International, the Museum of Tolerance and the Josephson Institute of Ethics.

Anitra Nelson, Senior Research Associate in the School of Global Studies, Social Science and Planning at RMIT University (Melbourne, Australia), majored in Latin American studies and gained a BA with first-class honours in history at La Trobe University. Her research interests and teaching experience include the politics and economics of underdevelopment, community-based management and film studies.

Frank Schwartze is Visiting Professor and Head of the Department of Urban Planning at Brandenburg University of Technology Cottbus, Germany. For

17 years he has worked as an Urban Planner in development and planning projects in Germany and Eastern Europe, and is a consultant for international development cooperation.

Robert K. Sutton is Chief Historian of the United States National Park Service. As Chief Historian and as the former Superintendent at Manassas National Battlefield Park, he has encouraged Civil War battlefields to focus more attention on social, economic and political issues to commemorate the 150th anniversary of the war.

Bart Ziino is an Australian Research Council Postdoctoral Fellow at Deakin University, Australia. His first book, *A Distant Grief: Australians, War Graves and the Great War*, examined Australians' relationships with the graves and memorials of their dead of the First World War. He is currently a member of a team investigating Australian war heritage sites outside Australian territory.

Acknowledgements

The editors would like to thank the publisher and the series editors, Laurajane Smith and especially Bill Logan, who gave us the opportunity to publish this book within the series 'Key Issues in Cultural Heritage'. At Routledge, we are grateful for the interest, consideration and patience shown by Amy Davis-Poynter, Matthew Gibbons, Monica Kendall, Geraldine Martin and Lalle Pursglove.

Many of the ideas pursued in this volume were first presented and discussed in the 2009 workshop on 'Cultural Heritage and War', held at Brandenburg Technical University in Cottbus (BTU). We would like to thank all workshop participants and contributors to this book, including Stefan Disko, Adrian Henham and Sam Merrill. We are grateful to BTU and Deakin University, Melbourne, Australia, for co-financing, and especially to Juliane Gründel and Henry Crescini for technical co-organization of the event.

Martin Gegner wishes to thank Vanessa Domingues Silva for long-lasting indulgence, Klaus Zehbe, Regina Kirsche and Olaf Mittelstraß for trustful cooperation, the 2008–10 students of the World Heritage Studies Master's Course at BTU for many inspiring thoughts, and the International Association of World Heritage Professionals e.V., especially Andreza André da Rocha and Smriti Pant, for continuing intellectual exchange. He is also indebted to Christer Petersen for fruitful discussions, and to Bart Ziino for discussion, advice and patience with his co-editor.

Bart Ziino would like to thank Jenny Chapman for her continuing support, which makes endeavours like this possible. He would also like to thank Bill Logan for his guidance, Joan Beaumont for her intellectual rigour and Vilia Dukas for her editing assistance. He is especially grateful for his co-editor's honesty, dedication and forbearance across three continents and multiple time zones.

Series general co-editors foreword

The interdisciplinary field of Heritage Studies is now well established in many parts of the world. It differs from earlier scholarly and professional activities that focused narrowly on the architectural or archaeological preservation of monuments and sites. Such activities remain important, especially as modernization and globalization lead to new developments that threaten natural environments, archaeological sites, traditional buildings, and arts and crafts. But they are subsumed within the new field that sees 'heritage' as a social and political construct encompassing all those places, artefacts and cultural expressions inherited from the past which, because they are seen to reflect and validate our identity as nations, communities, families and even individuals, are worthy of some form of respect and protection.

Heritage results from a selection process, often government-initiated and supported by official regulation; it is not the same as history, although this, too, has its own elements of selectivity. Heritage can be used in positive ways to give a sense of community to disparate groups and individuals or to create jobs on the basis of cultural tourism. It can be actively used by governments and communities to foster respect for cultural and social diversity, and to challenge prejudice and misrecognition. But it can also be used by governments in less benign ways, to reshape public attitudes in line with undemocratic political agendas or even to rally people against their neighbours in civil and international wars, ethnic cleansing and genocide. In this way there is a real connection between heritage and human rights.

This is time for a new and unique series of books canvassing the key issues dealt with in the new heritage studies. The series seeks to address the deficiency facing the field identified by the Smithsonian in 2005 – that it is 'vastly under-theorized'. It is time to look again at the contestation that inevitably surrounds the identification and evaluation of heritage and to find new ways to elucidate the many layers of meaning that heritage places and intangible cultural expressions have acquired. Heritage conservation and safeguarding in such circumstances can only be understood as a form of cultural politics and this needs to be reflected in heritage practice, be that in educational institutions or in the field.

It is time, too, to recognize more fully that heritage protection does not depend alone on top-down interventions by governments or the expert actions of heritage industry professionals, but must involve local communities and communities of interest. It is critical that the values and practices of communities, together with traditional management systems where such exist, are understood, respected and incorporated in heritage management plans and policy documents so that communities feel a sense of 'ownership' of their heritage and take a leading role in sustaining it into the future.

This series of books aims then to identify interdisciplinary debates within heritage studies and to explore how they impact on not only the practices of heritage management and conservation, but also the processes of production, consumption and engagement with heritage in its many and varied forms.

William S. Logan
Laurajane Smith

The heritage of war: agency, contingency, identity

Martin Gegner and Bart Ziino

The political heritage of war has been the building of nations and empires. The cultural corollary has been the development of identities, as victors and as victims, soldiers and civilians, collaborators and resisters. If heritage can be understood as the selective use of the past as cultural and political resources in the present, then there are few fields more productive for understanding that process than the heritage of war. War mobilizes militaries, labour and material, but it also mobilizes identities, mentalities and emotions; it produces its heroes and its victims, and enduring legacies of trauma. The remembrance of war is then a fundamentally political process, in which the production of heritage is deeply implicated, as it shapes and sustains identities, provides legitimacy to political systems and underscores territorial claims. This volume investigates the production of war heritage in a series of contexts and time periods. It examines the agents of its production and contestation, and its transmission and adaptation to new cultural and political conditions over time. It seeks to expose and understand the centrality of heritage to reimagining and reconstructing communities and identities after war.

In this book are studies of the ways in which war catalyses, disrupts and reconstructs relationships between people and the memories, places and practices that define them. These studies of the heritage of war investigate those processes on a series of levels and in short- and long-term contexts. They utilize conceptions of cultural heritage as both tangible and intangible, and expose their fundamental intersections. *The Heritage of War* is not about the protection of heritage during war, though this remains incidental to its concerns. This distinguishes the approach of this book from a series of volumes that have addressed the difficulties of safeguarding tangible cultural heritage in wartime (Chamberlain 2004; Jansen 2005; Maniscalco 2007). The book is concerned with the production of 'new' cultural memory *by* war and its transformation into manifest and intangible heritage through the course of time *after* the war. Its central precept is to recognize the constant social and political construction of heritage sites by a series of agents, and over time. It is not simply the case that there are two or more sides to any story, but that heritage itself has a history: a history surrounding the creation of significant sites and practices; a history of management and continuous reworking of meanings into the present. In this volume we mean to get to the particularities of the production of the heritage of war in its local, national and transnational contexts, and to point to two key themes: that the heritage of war, like all forms of heritage, is not natural but contingent, and dependent on the work of those agents who bring it into being and sustain it; and that heritage sites themselves have histories that need to be recognized if we are genuinely to understand the processes of heritage as they work today.

The capacity for studies of war and commemoration to expose those processes is clear in the vast literature on memory and memorialization that has emerged over the past quarter of a century. Those in the field of heritage studies have been not only aware of its significance, but a key part of its emergence (Lowenthal 1985). Hence they have been willing to push beyond an understanding of heritage as fixed elements of the landscape, in which values are embedded, and to embrace a concept of heritage as the product of social, cultural and political processes that work selectively – sometimes in concert, but often in conflict – to fashion heritage in all its various tangible and intangible forms. This understanding of heritage acknowledges the agency of those people and communities who do the work of making meanings from the past, and it insists that heritage is not static but dynamic, and subject to contest and change. Heritage is constituted in the act of identifying what is appropriate to remember and preserve in light of experience. It is the process by which we compose pasts with which we can be comfortable, sometimes repressing those elements of the past that are difficult to assimilate, and sometimes confronting them. That process, then, is selective and constitutive: it has its purposes. As Eyal observes, 'There are many ways to remember, recall, recollect and memorialize, and there is nothing given or immutable about memory or its purpose' (Eyal 2004: 8–9).

Heritage is then a product of agency, contingency, politics, power and resistance. It is crucial, therefore, to understand and to investigate that process and the historical, cultural, demographic and political specifics that attend and influence the production and management of all heritage. In their important study, *The Politics of War Memory and Commemoration*, T. G. Ashplant, Graham Dawson and Michael Roper observed that war memory is constituted by a struggle between a series of agents of varying levels of power, in which particular memories and identities contend for public influence (Ashplant *et al.* 2000: 16). That struggle is conducted through a range of physical and intangible media that facilitate expression of memories in public. This is the space that cultural heritage occupies. It is a space that is not just fought over, but which is actively constructed and reconstructed to assert the primacy of personal, civic, religious, ethnic, cultural and national identities.

Agency

If heritage is the result of an act, then it must have its agents. This means we must recognize heritage as subjective, and acknowledge that there exist multiple perspectives on the past. Recognizing the agency of those who take part in the heritage process does not suggest an equal capacity to shape its products: the processes of heritage formation are inherently an unequal power struggle, in which the state – which generally governs cultural heritage protection frameworks – can be at odds with, apathetic about or indeed opposed to recognition of particular narratives of the past. There are two main approaches to understanding agency in this process. In one sense, heritage might be understood as a form of state-sponsored social control, a complex construction of social entities in defined geographical and historical places that are dominated by the narratives and representation of elite groups (Bourdieu 1984; Hall 2007). Here, the physical manifestation of war memorialization – especially state cenotaphs, monuments and cemeteries – uses distinct aesthetic strategies to represent a sanctioned interpretation of war experience. In Stuart Hall's phrasing (1992), they 'code' these artefacts in a way that makes the desired 'decoding' by the public possible. On the other hand, Jay Winter also alerts us to the multiplicity of groups developing their own usable pasts both in tandem and in competition with dominant stories (Winter 2001: 53–4). Rather than accepting a model of unqualified state power in shaping memory and heritage processes, he directs our attention to the agency of individuals responding to the trauma of war in asserting communal memories, to which the state responds.

There is of course a great deal of middle ground with which to come to a more nuanced appreciation of the production of heritage. Individual experience is always mediated by cultural narratives, and this complicates both state-centric narratives and those that emphasize the agency of private experience. Here the state is involved in constant reinterpretation of heritage, which allows for public connection and reconnection with sanctioned narratives of the past, and for those narratives to adapt in turn to the needs and demands of private citizens. Ashplant, Dawson and Roper observed a decade ago that we do not yet have a sufficient appreciation of the interplay between agents of memory in this process (Ashplant *et al.* 2000: 12). This remains an open project, and one especially for heritage studies to contemplate: we must analyse the interrelations between the processes linking individual, civil society and the state. And we need to understand the politics of war heritage as a continuing, uneven, contest and negotiation between state and private agencies.

Contingency

There is nothing inevitable about the production or identification of cultural heritage, no universal and unchanging set of values to inform its significance.

Nor does it exist by accident: cultural heritage is contingent on its historical, political and cultural contexts, and contingent too on the varied efforts of those agents of memory. Moreover, while the study of heritage is not so much about the study of the past as understanding the utilization of the past in the present, we need to recognize that heritage, too, changes over time. Its nature is constructed and contingent, rather than immutable; it is liable to be imbued and overlaid with new meanings and significance as political, cultural, demographic and economic contexts change. Kevin Walsh makes the point: 'Memories are not static; they develop and change with each generation and museums and other forms of representation must respond to and nurture this process' (Walsh 2001: 98). This is all the more important as beyond living memory tangible cultural heritage sites especially have the potential to acquire greater claims to authenticity. Such authenticity is constructed as authority within the discourse of war, and cultural heritage sites assume their role as places of authority for particular narratives of the past, and particular political orders in the present.

Cultural heritage practitioners in particular should be aware of their own agency in these processes, in that their work is not simply about preservation, but about governing the social and cultural meanings represented and transmitted at their sites (Smith 2006: 2; Ryan 2007: 1). Their task involves selection and interpretation of elements of the past for presentation to audiences who, while bringing their own cultural baggage to the interpretation of the past, remain less powerful than those with the capacity to make choices about what is presented and its manner of presentation (Ashworth 2008: 232). It is essential, as Langfield, Logan and Nic Craith have observed, that those undertaking such roles 'understand the broader economic, political and social context of their work' (Langfield *et al.* 2010: 3). While demanding this kind of awareness and sensitivity, we must also acknowledge the fact that site managers are often the last in a long chain of contingency and agency that brings a site within the structures of heritage interpretation and management. They, too, are constrained by the histories of activism and investment by other actors determined to define heritage places, and by the conflicts that may already have attended the site. In this highly sensitive field site managers must not only be good economic managers, but also historians, sociologists and diplomats. This volume therefore addresses itself not only to the academic community but also to practitioners. They are in the eye of the storm of highly contestable political processes, and this collection seeks to tease out those dynamics, and to understand the work of the agents of heritage and memory in representing critical elements of national, communal and personal pasts.

The challenge of Ashplant, Dawson and Roper's work has been to enhance our appreciation of the interplay between agents of memory and heritage, private and state. Their prediction that future research would centre on the interaction between the different agencies of remembering, and in particular the sites where it occurs, is close to the concerns of this volume. This book brings together a variety of contributors from different disciplinary backgrounds, whose work ranges widely across cultural, political and geographic boundaries and time periods. The authors, from Australia, Germany, New Zealand, the United Kingdom, the United States and Vietnam, have their individual backgrounds as anthropologists, cultural heritage professionals, geographers, historians, political scientists, sociologists and urban planners. The types of wars they discuss in the book are similarly broad, extending from colonizing violence, the world wars, civil war, ethnic conflict and atrocity. Finally, all of these authors take up the challenge to undertake analyses aware of the different sources and levels of power in any contest over the meaning of the past, and the forums in which they take place.

The book seeks to expose the ways in which cultural heritage has been produced over time: the life-cycles of enmity, pride and grief on different levels and in different places, and the constant personal and political adaptations of narratives of the past. Cultural heritage is a living and evolving phenomenon. In war, reconstruction and remembrance, we see it in some of its most dynamic and powerful forms, even generations away from the conflicts that fostered their significance. To this end, *The Heritage of War* is structured around three major interlinked themes: continuing contests over the wartime past between a series of agents, the production of identities through those contests, and the meanings of reconstruction after conflict.

Part I: remembering and representing war

Part I of the book examines the production and contest of multiple narratives around a series of wartime events and sites. Here, various agencies – state and non-state – express their particular claims to a site and its significance, and here we are better able to see the nature of the contest that accompanies all heritage, in which different narratives of the past must collide or negotiate. Understanding the processes of heritage production makes certain questions possible: can heritage exist that is inclusive of multiple and alternate narratives? The five chapters in this section explore representational strategies, and the inscription and re-inscription of war heritage that individuals, communities and governments conduct as they link events in the past to the present and future. These narratives of war are widely differentiated as between those engaged in remembering, including veterans, bereaved families and ethnic minorities, each articulating memories that justify their political claims to recognition. Contributors to this section are aware not only of such differentiation, but that these particular sites of war heritage have histories of contestation that continue to inform their uses and interpretation. Contestation at these sites is not just political, but historical. The meanings of heritage change with time and shifts in ideology, as well as in response to more immediate political and economic imperatives.

Further, the nature of war means that significant sites are not always within the sovereign territory of states interested in their management and preservation. Wars are rarely fought on neutral territory. This means that extraterritoriality becomes an inescapable factor in managing the heritage of war. This problem exposes some of the limitations of UNESCO's World Heritage Convention 1972, which has been criticized for enabling promotion of national identities through its procedures – sites must be nominated by national governments – as much as it speaks to the prospect of universal values (Long and Labadi 2010: 6). This procedure can lead to further enhancement of state power while disempowering minorities seeking to represent their own particular heritage. Also, the Convention's emphasis on shared values challenges us to find new modes of negotiation to define and protect sites beyond sovereign territory, but not necessarily of 'outstanding universal value'. To be fair, the Convention for the Safeguarding of the Intangible Heritage 2003 seeks to meet some of the criticisms levelled against the World Heritage Convention for its Western bias in the definition of heritage. Recognition of intangible heritage does at least force us to recognize the inherent dissonance within heritage. It queries the workability of reaching towards a 'shared story' (Smith and Akagawa 2009: 5), encouraging us to recognize the processes by which heritage is produced, and to provide spaces in which stories may be told in the presence of each other.

Joan Beaumont, in her chapter on the Hellfire Pass Memorial Museum in Thailand, asks how heritage that involves memories of different national groups can be represented: is it possible to transcend the national imperative and integrate different, often competing, memories in a single site? Beaumont investigates the modes by which memory survives below the level of state narratives, exposing the array of its private non-state agents, and observing the uneven negotiation between veterans' private memories and an Australian national memory of captivity under the Japanese, with its own particular structures and imperatives. This can be both affirming and problematic for individuals, but also creates problems for competing national memories of captivity and the war more generally. This heritage thus remains fragile and contingent on its economic and political benefit to the domestic population.

The fundamental question in William Logan and Nguyễn Thanh Bình's chapter on the former battlefields of Điện Biên Phủ in Vietnam is similar: can a shared heritage exist here, or are parallel stories more productive in defining a site of interest to more than one nation, and indeed to the former colonizer and the once colonized? They trace the significant cultural differences underpinning commemoration on the battlefield, differences in the agencies through which the battlefields have been marked, and also differences within the national communities that attach their memories of the battle to this place. Here again the agents of heritage are varied: a single veteran initiated a monument eventually officially sanctioned by the French state, while Điện Biên Phủ in Vietnamese sensibility is powerfully influenced by state agencies, which dominate the technologies of popular culture, and the national narratives that link the battle to other milestones in a centuries-long struggle for national independence. This is in part a study of the power of state agencies to produce a particular narrative of the past, not only through interpretative structures, but its intervention in traditional burial and remembrance practices, as it constructs war cemeteries for the dead and monuments to itself.

Similarly, Martin Gegner demonstrates the distinct 'recoding' that has occurred around Soviet and German memorials in Berlin since the Second World War. Gegner shows how these objects not only refer to particular events in time, but exist in the politics of their creation and use: commemoration of the Second World War in Berlin is infused not only with the politics of responsibility and guilt, but with the politics of the Cold War. Today, beyond the Cold War, these memorials are reinterpreted again by a wider public generating new meanings from the memorial landscape. Gegner brings fine-grained observation to the problem of what 'doing' heritage might involve for Berliners and visitors to the sites today. He identifies the problems of engagement when we recognize not only that sites are incapable of bearing any kind of petrified memory, but that those who visit them do not always recognize that they are encountering sites intended to bear those particular messages. Soviet cenotaphs, such as that in Treptower Park, once exclusive, are now unregulated and almost unrecognizable in the practices that surround them. Gegner uncovers not only contest, but the ways in which heritage is composed and experienced on-site and over time, and reminds us that agency is also a question of the reception of heritage, and not just its creation.

In her chapter on the politics of commemorating the Second World War on the islet of Tarawa, in the South Pacific, Judith A. Bennett deals not only with an extraterritorial war site, but with one in which multiple claims are made to the commemorative landscape by former belligerents, and the one-time imperial administration. Bennett examines the complicated politics of official war remembrance in Tarawa and shows how war memorialization is embedded in global and regional strategic interests. Here too the political and strategic interests of the Cold War and global security dominated the nature of commemoration of the Second World War. Bennett traces the changing contexts of war heritage, and their continuing and developing politics, in which indigenous notions of significance conflicted with those overlaid by the former combatants. In this we see more clearly that what is being managed here are values and meanings *symbolized* at heritage sites. As a new paradigm in global relations emerges in the crisis of climate change, Bennett expects further reinterpretation of the continuing legacy of the Second World War in the Pacific.

As Chief Historian of the United States National Park Service, Robert K. Sutton offers a different perspective in his chapter on the management of heritage in United States Civil War battlefield parks. Sutton played a key role in the regeneration of interpretative approaches to Civil War heritage over the past decade, and here points to the issues confronting managers of heritage beyond the generation that experienced the event. Sutton focuses on the internal dynamics of the interpretative and managerial process, and the responsibility of the National Park Service to respond to the changing historical and demographic contexts in which their work is situated. The continuing politics of this process are plainly highlighted in his discussion of the importance of acknowledging the institution of slavery as a major cause of the war, and the resistance that this recognition engendered among stakeholders attached to mythologies that have remained powerful for well over a century. While driven by core principles that have existed since the creation of the NPS itself, Sutton shows us heritage practitioners alert to the histories of their own sites, the politics of their storytelling, and the diversity of their contemporary and future publics.

Chapters in this section of the book affirm that the production of heritage is contingent on a wide range of actors, events and possibilities. The creation of meaningful heritage sites is subject not only to the conditions of war, but to the conditions – political, cultural and economic – that follow war. They are therefore liable to change, and we are obliged to pay attention to their histories and politics of representation. These are sites for the consumption of local and distant audiences, with multiple and conflicting perspectives. Thus, the idea of shared heritage is inherently fraught: there is no one story and nor is there value in rendering down competing versions of past events into a single past. The processes of heritage and memory take place within particular historical and cultural matrices that are difficult to reconcile, and which may ultimately be bonded more by delicately crafted interpretation and presentation of the past – and economic advantage – than developing a 'shared story'.

Part II: identities

Part II of the book explores the ways in which the heritage of war continues to be mobilized in the service of identities in conflict. This section ties an understanding of heritage as contested process to its key political outcome: the production, sustenance and marginalization of identities. Here we find narratives of inclusion and exclusion, drawing on a range of resources to constitute them, including language, political systems and cultural practices. The processes of heritage, as Sara McDowell observes, are intimately linked to our ideas of identity, as they help to produce the appearance of an unbroken narrative linking past and present: 'It is a process that draws on the past and which is intimately related to our identity requirements in the present' (McDowell 2008: 49). Thus, as much as the reverse may also be true, our conceptions of identity are critical to how we bestow meaning on objects and practices from the past.

The ways in which heritage affirms identity are not unmediated by the state or other powerful interests seeking legitimation for current actions and policies (Graham and Howard 2008: 6). In this sense one might argue that cultural heritage has tended to naturalize, rather than contest, national and group identities, and to make them appear seamless, organic and permanent. We must be careful, however, to recognize that identities are not simply constructs of the state. Remembering is an activity with all sorts of implications for personal and national identity: in the very act of remembering, people exercise a level of agency in producing their identities, rather than passively assuming them. In some ways this is self-evident. There are any number of examples of groups unreconciled to the political, social and cultural structures of the societies in which they reside, from ethnic and religious separatists demanding independent states, to myriad groups demanding recognition, equity and equality within their existing societies. All of these groups nurture their own identities, and all engage in the production of heritage to give those identities value and legitimacy. Thus, while heritage might be accused on one hand of ossifying the past, it can also represent contestation and demand negotiation between groups of varying levels of power. It has the potential to reveal the plurality of peoples, pasts, cultures and values within a single society, yet as chapters in this section show, that process is hardly smooth or uncontested.

Authors in this part of the book are concerned with the processes by which identities are formed, contested, appropriated and marginalized through the uses of heritage. If they take as their starting point the production of (or resistance to) national identities, then this is because despite the challenges of globalization, not only does the nation-state remain, but nationalism 'continues to shape the way countries interact with global processes' (Long and Labadi 2010: 5). Identities may be moving beyond or continue to fracture within nation-states, but the nation still remains the fundamental unit in the formation and sustenance of identities, and the critical point of contest with dissonant and dissident identities and heritage. Thus, it may be of little surprise that all of the chapters in this section relate to the experiences of post-colonial and post-imperial societies, in which the formulation of identities has been fundamental to a conscious nationalist project. These societies, as Sabine Marschall observes, 'tend to be preoccupied with issues of representation and defining a new identity, for which selected aspects of the past understood as heritage serve as inspiration or foundation' (Marschall 2008: 347). Wars, atrocities and anti-colonial struggle are central to their conceptions of identity, but memories of these events are also marked by dissonance, contest, and even ambivalence and erasure.

Hugo Benavides draws the longest perspective in the volume as he investigates the continuing resonance of the Incan past in modern Ecuador, and the production of historical narratives that feed current conceptions of identity. As a form of heritage, the Incan legacy has numerous expressions in landscape, literature and culture, and Benavides interrogates their roles in the continuing struggle over identity and the past in Ecuador. In examining the ambiguous representation of both Incan imperialist violence and Incan victimhood in the face of Spanish colonizing violence, Benavides argues that heritage is mobilized in modern Ecuador to maintain existing power relations between indigenous and non-indigenous citizens. It also perpetuates continuing feuds with Peru, which are represented as an extension of an ancient pattern. Benavides shows, through the dissident identity politics of the Confederación de Nacionalidades Indígenas del Ecuador, that identity formation is not a cynical process imposed on those without agency. The contest here is between a state narrative that posits a golden age of pre-Incan society in Ecuador as against a post-colonial politics in which an Indian (as opposed to Spanish) subjectivity can be revived and represented in historical texts and other forms of cultural heritage. The implications of this contest over identity in Ecuador Benavides explains as local in terms of the struggle for power in Ecuador, while at the same time criticizing a Western conception of indigenous heritage as ancient and passive, rather than active in the present with its own agendas.

Bart Ziino sees nationalist identity politics contending at the same site of war heritage: Gallipoli, Turkey. The centrality of this site to two different conceptions of national identity shows how fraught is the prospect of shared stories co-existing within the same heritage site. While expressions of shared heroism and suffering come easily, the politics of the Australian and Turkish identities that claim this place as their foundation point are very different: one a British settler society first seeking equality within empire, and increasingly differentiation from the metropole, the other a republican and secular society emerging from the end of empire, and today increasingly challenged by demands for recognition of Turkish society's Islamic foundations. Despite a rhetoric of confluence and sharing, events in the past decade have once again made clear the tensions that attend the production of heritage and identity at this site.

In Stephanie McKinney's chapter we see how heritage sites have a fundamental place in the reconstruction of identity after a major crisis. Here she investigates the Kigali City tour as a forum for the presentation of a state narrative of the Rwandan past and present, in which Rwanda's 1994 genocide is both an implied and a very real presence. Sensitive to the multiple audiences in the presentation of the genocide, McKinney argues that the active heritage work conducted on the tour – through both inclusion and exclusion – and at the Kigali Memorial Centre, may permit the 'complexities of victimhood' to be explored, as it might also permit of developing a Hutu identity beyond 'perpetrator'. The divisions fostered within the former colonial administration remain powerfully productive, and McKinney traces imbalances in the nature of commemoration and heritage work. While thousands of Rwandan victims remain nameless, interred in mass graves, memorials to eleven murdered Belgian (UN) soldiers have a role to play in diplomacy and a post-colonial Rwandan identity. Outlining active attempts to produce those new identities,

McKinney also points to the dangers of an identity politics based on attempted genocide, as cultural heritage is mobilized to counter Western perceptions and prejudices that would see the events in Rwanda as the product of an innate African barbarism.

Yasmin Khan explores the hidden layers of memory and commemoration of war in South Asia, showing how narratives of personal and national experience of the Second World War are marginalized and suppressed in favour of an identity based on anti-imperial struggle. Khan argues that memory of the Second World War has been doubly masked, first in its political subjugation to nationalist narratives of resistance to the British administration and subsequent conflict between the post-partition states of India and Pakistan, and second by its contextualization in a hyperactive, but still nationally defined, British culture of remembrance. The war is ignored as difficult to reconcile within nationalist narratives: what few objects exist to remind us of that experience, including imperial memorials both personal and public, are shown to be both wilfully detached from ordinary Indians and Pakistanis, and shunned by the two states as inassimilable with their peculiar histories of statehood. By analysing the different discourses referring to the wars in South Asia after 1940 Khan points to the continuing capacity of hegemonic power to shape public war memory and national identities.

Part III: the politics of reconstruction

The reconstruction of war-damaged cities occupies Part III of the book. Increasing attention has been paid both to the treatment of battlefield landscapes and to the issues of reconstruction. In recent years, attempts have been made to develop guidelines for the preservation of former battlefields, most particularly in the draft Vimy Declaration for the Conservation of Historic Battlefield Terrain (2001; also Leopold 2007). These are promising developments. Yet urban reconstruction remains deeply complex. Reconstruction after war is not simply achieved through the restoration of former landscapes, but occurs within a series of changing political, demographic and historical contexts. The identities and narratives of the past, examined in Part II, are central to that process, as the foundation both for conflict and for rebuilding and reconciliation. In the chapters in this section we see the reconstruction of meaning, social relationships and comprehension of experiences of conflict in the light of present conditions. Reconstruction is about building stable political conditions and communities, and this imperative has implications for the treatment of damaged cultural heritage sites and whole cities. As Jeffry M. Diefendorf observes, urban reconstruction 'is a process that involves contesting interests and groups, not a project with a clear beginning and end' (Diefendorf 1998: 13). This means that reconstruction must take account of the contexts in which identities are being reformulated and reasserted, and seek to produce usable narratives of the past to anchor social relations and identities in the present. In this we must recognize that the processes central to reconstruction are also those central to heritage.

Attempts to rebuild or reconstruct are also, therefore, attempts at narrative reconstruction, in which strategic forgetting is as important as the process of remembering. Such an understanding of reconstruction became increasingly important over the course of the twentieth century, as the nature of war itself was transformed. Elements of the built environment have become targets for the destruction of identities, as people themselves became targets for the destruction – or at least disruption – of cultural practices, religions and ethnicities. In the past several decades, wars have been increasingly characterized by asymmetrical conflict involving non-military and non-state actors, with a logic that involves destruction of civilian housing, places of worship and other cultural institutions. Reconstruction is then a process not just of the built environment, but a social and economic process which must produce consensus on the legitimacy of political systems, equity in access to housing and services, and a genuine engagement of domestic populations in planning and reconstructing the living environment, in both its practical and its symbolic forms.

This does not imply that faithful reconstruction is not a legitimate response to war's destruction. The built environment is constitutive of memory, and not just a place for its recall. Buildings and objects in the landscape become 'mnemonic devices for contextualizing the past and future' (Osborne 2001: 60). The destruction of that environment of memory 'can mean a disorienting exile from the memories they have invoked. It is the threat of a loss to one's collective identity and the secure continuity of those identities (even if, in reality, identity is always shifting over time)' (Bevan 2006: 13). The urge to reconstruct under these conditions is understandable: the restitution of a schematic of memory satisfies the demand to locate one's history physically. Of course the ways in which these sites of memory are reconstructed has the potential for both inclusion and exclusion, empowerment and disempowerment in the uses made possible, and in the narratives attached to the place. One cannot simply reconstruct historic centres in the assumption that doing so will produce some equilibrium, without approaching the issues causing and sustaining division (Charlesworth 2006: 6). Restoring buildings and associated land tenure has implications for restoring the political conditions obtaining before conflict, especially in the case of civil wars and ethnic conflicts. There is a burden of meaning here that is constantly accruing: faithful reconstruction cannot wholly return to what came before, nor can complete renewal erase the past.

Tony Joel's study of the debates surrounding reconstruction of Dresden's destroyed *Frauenkirche* after 1945 exposes the importance of historical and political context to the nature of reconstruction. Joel shows us how a series of agents contested the treatment of the ruined church for more than 40 years, their efforts shaped and confounded by political and economic conditions, as well as by developing ideas about authenticity and integrity in heritage practice. This chapter shows that reconstruction of particular buildings destroyed by war is not only symbolic; it is the materialization of political, social and cultural dynamics. Only in the emergent context of a unifying Germany was the debate finally resolved, and an acceptable narrative for the reconstruction process found. Despite the potential for forgetting, even faithful reconstruction is overlaid with new histories and 'updated cultural significance' (Thomson 2008: 71). Far from a simple restoration of the past and its meanings, Dresden's *Frauenkirche* continues to recall its own destruction and decades of political uncertainty and inactivity.

Frank Schwartze, in his chapter on Mitrovica in the former Yugoslavia, and Esther Charlesworth and Anitra Nelson in their investigation of reconstruction in Beirut, are concerned with the problems that emerge when agency in reconstruction is taken away from a broad base of residents, and when they are not engaged in planning or in the symbolic acts that accompany the process of reconstruction. Schwartze's study of reconstruction in a divided city in Kosovo shows how the process is contested not only by different ethnic groups but also by United Nations authorities. He shows that the population has not accepted the latter's idea of reconciliation symbolized by the reconstruction of a bridge that links two ethnically separated parts of the city. Schwartze's key point is that such processes of reconstruction and reconciliation have only 'exposed the limits of a joint cultural identity as a basis for a peaceful coexistence'. Successful reconstruction, including acknowledgement of land tenure and use, he argues, must be predicated on acceptance of different social realities. Only then will an appropriate symbolism emerge from reconstruction, rather than being imposed without addressing the continuing problems feeding division.

Charlesworth and Nelson are similarly concerned with the ways in which the privatized reconstruction of Beirut's Central District has meant the exclusion of traditional and popular heritage from rebuilding activities. The monopolization of reconstruction in the hands of powerful interests has produced a constricted and idealized interpretation of Beirut's five-millennium heritage, and inadequate urban representation of the social, religious and ethnic heterogeneity which had always been an outstanding characteristic of the city. Charlesworth and Nelson warn against such exclusive rights over the treatment of cultural heritage, arguing that a lack of democratic power has limited widespread engagement with Beirut's cultural heritage and ultimately endangered the possibility of building on that heritage as a means of reconciling former enemies in the long series of conflicts constituting the Lebanese 'civil war'. Rather than integrating people, reconstruction isolated people from their city. 'Beirut failed', they observe, 'because marginal groups were not empowered to participate in the reconstitution of their country and society.' The keys to successful reconstruction lay in engagement with heritage

– not simply as represented in the physical environment, but as an expression of a relationship with the past and with a place – and in the acknowledgement that heritage is a contestable process, involving multiple perspectives and multiple stories.

The authors of this volume all begin from the same premise: that multiple interpretations of the past compete for dominance in regional, national and global discourses. Wars are remembered in a series of contexts, stretching far beyond simple binaries of victory and defeat to encompass the new political realities that emerge from conflict. In this, the legacies of war are constantly contested and re-contested – they are a justification for entrenching particular power structures, and a font of identity-building politics. We must account for the ways in which those politics inform the production of cultural heritage now and into the future.

References

Ashplant, T. G., Dawson, G. and Roper, M. (2000) *The Politics of War Memory and Commemoration*, London: Routledge.

Ashworth, G. J. (2008) 'The Memorialization of Violence and Tragedy: Human Trauma as Heritage', in B. Graham and P. Howard (eds), *The Ashgate Research Companion to Heritage and Identity*, Farnham: Ashgate, 231–44.

Bevan, R. (2006) *The Destruction of Memory: Architecture at War*, London: Reaktion.

Bourdieu, P. (1984) *Distinction: A Social Critique of the Judgement of Taste*, London: Routledge.

Chamberlain, K. (2004) *War and Cultural Heritage: An Analysis of the 1954 Convention for the Protection of Cultural Property in the Event of Armed Conflict and its Two Protocols*, Leicester: Institute of Art and Law.

Charlesworth, E. (2006) *Architects without Frontiers: War, Reconstruction and Design Responsibility*, Oxford: Architectural.

Diefendorf, J. M. (1998) 'West Germany after World War II: Planning and the Role of Preservation Thinking', in S. Barakat, J. Calame and E. Charlesworth (eds), *Urban Triumph or Urban Disaster? Dilemmas of Contemporary Post-war Reconstruction*, York: University of York, 8–14.

Eyal, G. (2004) 'Identity and Trauma: Two Forms of the Will to Memory', *History & Memory* 16(1), 5–36.

Graham, B. and Howard, P. (2008) 'Heritage and Identity', in B. Graham and P. Howard (eds), *The Ashgate Research Companion to Heritage and Identity*, Farnham: Ashgate, 1–15.

Hall, S. (1992) 'Encoding, Decoding', in S. Hall, D. Hobson, A. Lowe and P. Willis (eds), *Culture, Media, Language*, London: Routledge in association with the Centre for Contemporary Cultural Studies, University of Birmingham, 128–38.

Hall, S. (2007) 'Whose heritage? Unsettling "The Heritage", Re-imagining the Post-Nation', in L. Smith, (ed.), *Cultural Heritage: Critical Concepts in Media and Cultural Studies. Vol. II., History and Concepts*, London: Routledge, 87–100.

Jansen, M. (2005) *War and Cultural Heritage: Cyprus after the 1974 Turkish Invasion*, Minneapolis: University of Minnesota – Minnesota Mediterranean and East European monographs 14.

Langfield, M., Logan, W. and Nic Craith, M. (eds) (2010) *Cultural Diversity, Heritage, and Human Rights: Intersections in Theory and Practice*, London: Routledge.

Leopold, T. (2007) 'A Proposed Code of Conduct for War Heritage Sites', in C. Ryan (ed.), *Battlefield Tourism: History, Place and Interpretation*, Oxford and Amsterdam: Elsevier, 49–58.

Long, C. and Labadi, S. (eds) (2010) *Heritage and Globalisation*, London: Routledge.

Lowenthal, D. (1985) *The Past is a Foreign Country*, Cambridge: Cambridge University Press.

McDowell, S. (2008) 'Heritage, Memory and Identity', in B. Graham and P. Howard (eds), *The Ashgate Research Companion to Heritage and Identity*, Farnham: Ashgate, 37–54.

Maniscalco, F. (ed.) (2007) *World Heritage and War: linee guida per interventi a salvaguardia dei Beni Culturali*, Naples: Massa Editore.

Marschall, S. (2008) 'The Heritage of Post-Colonial Societies', in B. Graham and P. Howard (eds), *The Ashgate Research Companion to Heritage and Identity*, Farnham: Ashgate, 347–63.

Osborne, B. S. (2001) 'In the Shadows of Monuments: The British League for the Reconstruction of the Devastated Areas of France', *International Journal of Heritage Studies* 7(1), 59–82.

Ryan, C. (ed.) (2007) *Battlefield Tourism: History, Place and Interpretation*, Oxford and Amsterdam: Elsevier.

Smith, L. (2006) *Uses of Heritage*, New York: Routledge.

Smith, L. and Akagawa, N. (eds) (2009) *Intangible Heritage*, London: Routledge.

Thomson, R. G. (2008) 'Authenticity and the Post-Conflict Reconstruction of Historic Sites', *CRM Journal* 5(1), 64–80.

Vimy Declaration for the Conservation of Historic Battlefield Terrain (2001). Online: www.vac-acc.gc.ca/remembers/sub.cfm?source=memorials/battlefield (accessed 30 November 2010).

Walsh, K. (2001) 'Collective Amnesia and the Mediation of Painful Pasts: The Representation of France in the Second World War', *International Journal of Heritage Studies* 7(1), 83–98.

Winter, J. (2001) 'The Memory Boom in Contemporary Historical Studies', *Raritan* 21(1), 52–66.

Part I

Remembering and representing war

Chapter 1

Hellfire Pass Memorial Museum, Thai–Burma railway[1]

Joan Beaumont

In Kanchanaburi province in western Thailand, a 240-kilometre road heads north-west from the major regional and tourist centre, Kanchanaburi, to Three Pagodas Pass, on the border with Myanmar (Burma). Just off the highway, 80 kilometres from Kanchanaburi, stands the Hellfire Pass Memorial Museum. This modest white building was opened in 1998 by the Australian government to serve as a memorial to the 60,000 Allied prisoners of war and perhaps 270,000 Asian labourers (*romusha*) who suffered and died while constructing the Thai–Burma railway during the Second World War.[2]

Behind the museum a flight of elegant wooden steps takes the visitor down a steep hill to the path of the railway itself and a dramatic cutting, Hellfire Pass (known locally as Konyu cutting) (Fig. 1.1). The rough faces of the cutting, 20 metres deep and about 100 metres long, tower above the visitor. Leaves from the deciduous jungle float silently down while the incisions of the drill bits driven into the rock by prisoners in 1943 are still clearly visible. On one wall at the end of the cutting a plaque commemorates the Australian surgeon Sir Edward 'Weary' Dunlop and other Allied doctors who cared for workers on the railway. Wedged into the rock crevices here and all along the cutting are Australian flags, Flanders poppies and small crosses placed as acts of remembrance by visitors. Just beyond the cutting a black shining plinth, installed by the Australian government in 2005, commemorates all who 'suffered' and died on the railway. Beyond this lies a walking trail of about 4.5 kilometres that follows the route of the former railway through more cuttings and across gullies over which wooden trestle bridges once stood.

Australian veterans, expatriates and government officials have developed this site of war heritage and memory over the past 25 years. More than 22,000 Australians were taken prisoner by the Japanese during their rapid conquest of South East Asia in early 1942. Of these, 8,031 died of malnutrition, disease, violence and exhaustion in the subsequent three-and-a-half years of captivity. Their story has become integral to the Australian national narrative of war and in a complex process of memory formation Hellfire Pass, where 400 Australians died, has become emblematic of the suffering and maltreatment of all Australian prisoners of the Japanese wherever they were interned.

Figure 1.1 Hellfire Pass (Konyu cutting).

The development of the Hellfire Pass Memorial Museum and its environs raises complex issues of war heritage that cross the boundaries of national memory. It is axiomatic that all memory in the public sphere is selective and contested, 'socially and politically mediated as well as historically and culturally embedded' (Kidd 1997: 157). The memory of war is particularly so, in that the commemorative practices associated with it commonly constitute 'a key element in the symbolic repertoire available to the nation-state for binding its citizens into a collective national identity' (Ashplant *et al.* 2000: 7). Given this entanglement of war heritage with nationalism, how can heritage that involves the memories of different national groups be represented? Can such heritage transcend the national imperative, integrating competing national narratives and cultural practices and creating a transnational memory?

When, as in the case of the Thai–Burma railway, atrocity is added to the mix the potential for heritage dissonance is even greater. Victims, perpetrators and bystanders all have competing memories of this difficult past. Who has the right to control and interpret its heritage: the national owners, the victims or all those associated with the site, including those for whom the past might be more conveniently forgotten?

This case study of Hellfire Pass suggests that 'ownership' of such a site of 'extraterritorial' heritage can be appropriated by individuals and the government of one nation, if the host nation accedes to foreigners exercising such agency. Australians were only a minority of the victims, yet it is they who have taken the initiative in developing Hellfire. The resulting commemoration of the site, however, is vulnerable to charges of selective and nationalistic representation and is inherently dissonant with local memories and cultural practices. Hence, the sustainability of such heritage is fragile, dependent upon diplomatic negotiation and a continuing perception on the part of the host country that the heritage development is to its economic and political benefit. As the Australian attempt to prevent the demolition of Singapore's Changi prison in 2004 showed, diplomacy has its limits as a means of protecting heritage in which meaning is asymmetrical between nations (Beaumont 2009). Hence, the sustainability of extraterritorial war heritage resides in the deeply problematic task of minimizing heritage dissonance by creating a memory of the past that is shared between the peoples of the host country and those outsiders who claim an interest in a land not their own.

*****

Japanese authorities ordered the construction of the Thai–Burma railway in 1942–3 in order to guarantee the supply of their forces in Burma, as sea lines of communication between Singapore and Rangoon became vulnerable to Allied attack. Stretching some 415 kilometres from Bampong in Thailand to Thanbyuzayat in Burma, the railway was constructed in only twelve months. A huge force of Allied prisoners and Asian labourers who were enticed or coerced by the Japanese worked from both ends and along the railway until they met at Konkoita, 37 kilometres on the Thai side of the border. The railway's route initially followed flat plains and the course of the River Kwai Noi in the south, while in the north it crossed coastal plains and foothills; but then it entered the rugged and inaccessible mountain ranges between Thailand and Burma. This topography demanded the construction of many large embankments, wooden trestle bridges and deep cuttings into rocky hill faces. Construction methods were often pre-industrial. Cuttings were excavated by hand, with steel tap drills hammered into solid rock and the holes thus formed packed with explosive. Earth and rock were broken up by shovels, picks and hoes. Massive embankments were built up by men carrying load after load of earth and rock in baskets or sacks. At the most frenetic period of construction in mid-1943, the so-called 'Speedo', shifts lasted up to 18 hours a day, with the darkness of the jungle lit up by fires and oil lamps – hence the name, Hellfire Pass, because of the hell-like appearance of the cutting at night.

Without adequate accommodation, food, clothing, footwear or medicine, and working for some months in the drenching monsoon, the workforce succumbed to malnutrition and disease: beri-beri, malaria, pellagra, tropical ulcers, dysentery and cholera. Many also fell victim to the gratuitous violence inflicted by their Japanese supervisors and Korean guards. By the time the railway was completed 20 per cent of the Allied prisoners of war and between 70,000 and 90,000 Asian labourers had died (Kratoska 2005: 242).[3] What was in fact a remarkable engineering achievement had been completed at the cost of 'a life for every sleeper', to use a phrase later popularized in Australian prisoner-of-war memory, even if something of an exaggeration.

Once completed, the railway served its purpose by carrying some 220,000 tons of military supplies, although increasingly its value was reduced by Allied bombing attacks (DVA 2002). The steel bridge over the River Mae Klong at Kanchanaburi, for example, was repeatedly bombed and several of its spans were destroyed in 1944–5. When the war ended, the railway fell into disuse and in 1947 the line and rolling stock were sold to the Thai government, with proceeds compensating those countries which lost rail stock to the Japanese (Thai–Burma Railway Centre 2005). The bodies of the Australian, British and Dutch prisoners of war who had died in the camps along the railway, meanwhile, were exhumed and reinterred in Commonwealth War Graves Commission (CWGC) cemeteries in Thanbyuzayat, Kanchanaburi and Chungkai (on the outskirts of Kanchanaburi). The bodies of the small number of US prisoners who had died on the railway were repatriated to the United States.

From 1949 to 1958, Thai railway authorities progressively reopened a 130-kilometre section of the line in the south, from Nong Pladuk to Nam Tok (formerly Tha Sao). While this section continues to operate today, serving the local community and tourists, the remainder of the railway to the north disappeared under agricultural land and the jungle, or was submerged under a major reservoir.

Yet, as the physical remains of the railway mostly disappeared, it secured a strong place in individual and cultural memory in Australia. This was partly because a large number of Australian families were affected by the loss of life in captivity (about 20 per cent of all Australian deaths in the Second World War) and the ongoing trauma of returning prisoners of the Japanese (Bomford 2001). It was also attributable to the production in the decade after the war of a plethora of memoirs and fictional accounts of captivity: fiction, such as Nevil Shute's *A Town Like Alice* (1950); and memoirs including Rohan Rivett's *Behind Bamboo* (1946), R. H. Whitecross, *Slaves of the Sons of Heaven* (1952), Russell Braddon's (semi-fictional) *The Naked Island* (1952), Betty Jeffrey's *White Coolies* (1954) and Jessie Elizabeth Simons' *While History Passed* (1954) – the latter two by nurses interned on Sumatra. Some of these publications were great commercial successes. Australians thereby became familiar with the narrative of captivity under the Japanese and, even more importantly, with a representation of prisoners as men and women who displayed under duress the qualities that were celebrated in the dominant national narrative of war, the Anzac legend – qualities such as resourcefulness, laconic humour, a capacity to survive against the odds and mateship (Beaumont 2005: 185–94).[4]

Possibly even more important in cultural memory, both in Australia and internationally, was the release in 1957 of the David Lean film, *The Bridge on the River Kwai*. Its plot, based on the novel by the French author Pierre Boulle, related only loosely to wartime events but its huge success (it won eight Academy Awards) popularized the Thai–Burma railway as the quintessential experience of captivity in the Asia Pacific (Hack and Blackburn 2008: 147–71). Thanks to the film, the town of Kanchanaburi developed a booming tourist industry around its wartime heritage. In fact, the steel bridge at this point of the railway bears no resemblance to the wooden trestle bridge depicted in the film and the river at Kanchanaburi was not called the Kwai during the war years but rather the Mae Klong. Kanchanaburi authorities, however, renamed the particular stretch of river which the bridge spans as the Kwai Noi and advertised the operating stretch of the railway as 'The Death Railway'. In a striking instance of displaced significance – that is, a site that lacks heritage authenticity being invested with a significant emotional power at the level of individual memory and popular culture – the bridge at Kanchanaburi has now come to stand for all those wooden trestle bridges built further up the line which were demolished progressively after the war (see also Beaumont 2009: 301–6).

This displacement occurred in part because other, more authentic heritage sites on the railway continued to be invisible to all but those with local knowledge of the topography. Hellfire Pass was one such site. Only in the 1980s was it rediscovered in the jungle and developed as a commemorative and heritage site. Its development typified that symbiotic interaction between individual and government agency that so often shapes memory formation at the level of national commemoration and ritual. At this time, ageing Australian ex-prisoners increasingly felt the need to find meaning in their personal life histories and to 'revisit' their often difficult memories of captivity. Encouraged by their families and a sympathetic mass media, many of them published their memoirs and diaries of captivity (especially Arneil 1980; Dunlop 1986). The more adventurous and fit veterans also returned to the sites of their wartime experiences. In 1983, following a visit to Hellfire Pass, Tom Morris from Victoria became committed to ensuring its development as a site commemorating both prisoners of war and Thais who risked their lives to supply them with medicines and food (AWM *c*.1995). With $25,000 secured from the Commonwealth Department of Arts, Heritage and the Environment in 1985, a survey of the more accessible parts of the railway was conducted by an engineer from the Snowy Mountains Engineering Corporation (SMEC) who happened to be working on a dam on the Upper Kwai Noi. This survey confirmed that Hellfire Pass would be a suitable memorial site. It was easily accessible from the main road along the Kwai Noi valley and had an inherent physical and historical significance (Australian-Thai Chamber of Commerce 2003: 2, 25; AWM 1985). The Australian-Thai Chamber of Commerce (ATCC), an organization established in 1977 to promote business relations between Australia and Thailand, volunteered to coordinate the project, working with the Bangkok-based representative of the SMEC and the Australian defence attaché in Bangkok.

After negotiations with the Thai government and the Thai Army authorities who control the land on which Hellfire Pass resides, the cutting was cleared of the jungle which choked it. Remains of the railway's construction were collected, and pathways, signage and an access staircase completed. The site was then dedicated in 1987 when a Return to Thailand (Hellfire Pass Memorial) Reunion trip – the term 'pilgrimage' had yet to gain currency – visited the cutting. Importantly the dedication took place during a dawn service on Anzac Day, the most important date in the Australian commemorative calendar that marks the landing of Allied troops at Gallipoli on 25 April 1915 (Anzac Day, as it happened by an extraordinary coincidence, was also the date on which Australians had started work at Hellfire Pass in 1943). A memorial plaque was unveiled by Weary Dunlop, the POW doctor who by the 1980s was acquiring iconic status in Australia as the embodiment of the self-sacrifice and compassion for mates that is integral to the Anzac legend (Ebury 1994; Hearder 2009). Hellfire Pass was now inscribed with the imported remembrance practices of Australia. It was in the process of becoming 'enclave heritage', that is, the location of the heritage of one people in the physical space of another (Ashworth and van der Aa 2002: 452).

Over the next five years 'improvements' to the site continued, largely through the efforts of individuals receiving modest injections of government funding: a grant of $31,000 from the 1988 Bicentennial fund and a further $15,000 granted in 1991 to assist with the building of concrete steps after a forest fire destroyed the existing wooden ones in 1987 (DVA 1997a). Somewhat to the irritation of Morris, who had initiated the Hellfire Pass project, another ex-prisoner from Victoria, John W. (Bill) Toon, assumed a self-appointed role of raising some $90,000 through selling stickers, books and 'relics' of the railway supposedly retrieved from the jungle (DVA 1996a).

In 1992 a Melbourne periodontist and military enthusiast, Ross Bastiaan, also placed near the cutting a bronze plaque mounted on a pedestal, displaying a three-dimensional map and a brief history of the railway in English and Thai languages. This was one of many such plaques that Bastiaan, a passionate amateur able to circumvent local and official opposition through sheer will and energy, would cast and position at battlefields of significance to Australians all over the world from 1990 on, in an effort to provide visitors with interpretative material that was otherwise lacking. Other Bastiaan plaques were to be placed in the early 1990s in Kanchanaburi near the bridge and outside the CWGC cemetery, at the railway terminus at Nam Tok where the Thai station master still maintains its polish, and at Three Pagodas Pass on the Thai–Burma border (interview with Ross Bastiaan, January 2010).

In 1994 this individual agency was overtaken by government intervention. A 'cross over' occurred, in which the national processes of remembrance created by the Australian state and its agencies reframed the memories of veterans and amateur enthusiasts. This transition can only be understood within the context of a wider memory boom that was developing in Australia and the Western world as the twentieth century and second millennium closed. Fuelled by a *fin de siècle* mood, a growing interest in genealogy, an anxiety about the loss of witnesses to the world wars as veterans died and by the affirmation of a traditional construction of national identity in a changing and multicultural society, the memory 'industry' in Australia generated a plethora of new commemorative activities. New war memorials were installed in Australia and on battlefields overseas. New rituals were created, such as the burial of an Unknown Soldier in the Australian War Memorial in Canberra in November 1993. New 'traditions' were invented, including in 1995 the Australian Football League Anzac Day 'clash' at the Melbourne Cricket Ground, an event which also embodied the growing and uneasy mix of commemoration and commercialization. Meanwhile every anniversary of note in Australia's chronology of war was marked by government attention and chauvinistic press coverage, the most notable instance of the former being the year-long Australia Remembers campaign launched in 1995 to commemorate the fiftieth anniversary of the end of the Second World War (Reed 2004).

This investment in war commemoration was bipartisan, though the Labor and Liberal (conservative) governments had different motivations. For Paul Keating, Labor Prime Minister 1991–6, the memory of the Pacific War affirmed his vision of an Australia that would jettison its imperial past and embrace republicanism and a dynamic future in the Asia Pacific region. As his biographer Don Watson says, 'The war washed through Keating's prime ministership like reflux' (Watson 2002: 182). He marked the fiftieth anniversary of the fall of Singapore, for example, by resurrecting the wartime accusation that Britain had betrayed Australia in early 1942. Captivity also resonated with Keating personally, in that one of his uncles had died on the 1945 Sandakan–Ranau death marches in north Borneo, an atrocity from which only six of about 2,400 Allied prisoners survived. Thus, for Keating, as for so many other Australians, family history was invested with meaning by being located in larger, more universal narratives (Winter 2006: 40).

John Howard, Liberal Prime Minister from 1996 to 2007, likewise was shaped by a family history of war since both his father and grandfather had served in the First World War. But for him the memory of war affirmed a more traditional Australian nationalism, valuing historic links with Great Britain and a unitary construction of national identity. At a time when Australia was becoming a diverse multicultural community, the values of Anzac could be invoked as 'what it means to be Australian' (*Sydney Morning Herald*, 17 May 2002). For Howard, also, the memory of war and the associated Anzac legend offered a tool for legitimizing Australia's commitment to current global conflicts. Whatever the public disquiet about Australia's involvement in the wars in Iraq and Afghanistan, the men and women of the

Australian defence forces serving in these theatres could be positioned as beyond critique, heirs to a revered military tradition, the new Anzacs (McKenna 2003: 167–200).

Hellfire Pass became incorporated into this state-fashioned memory of war in 1994. Keating attended the Anzac Day ceremony at Hellfire Pass, an occasion given particular significance by the fact that it included the interring of a portion of Dunlop's ashes following his death in July 1993. Another portion of Dunlop's ashes was buried in his home state, Victoria, while a third was floated down the River Kwai Noi from Home Phu Toey, a resort near Hellfire Pass managed by Thai businessman Khun Kanit Wanachote, who had become a close friend and admirer of Dunlop after meeting him in 1985. The plaque commemorating Dunlop and other POW doctors was also unveiled on this occasion. Apparently moved by the ceremony, Keating announced that he would 'do something about it', that 'something' being the construction of a memorial museum at Hellfire Pass (DVA 1994). Before leaving Thailand he raised the matter with the Thai government and in 1995/6 the federal budget included an allocation to the project of some $1.6 million.

The proposed memorial museum had obvious potential to become a contested space. The Thai–Burma railway has many of the characteristics of atrocity heritage embodying multiple and dissonant histories: those of victims, perpetrators and bystanders. Exposing the Japanese record of brutality was not in the Thai government's interest, given the importance of the contemporary economic and diplomatic relationship with Japan. The ambiguity of Thailand's association with the Japanese during the Second World War was also a complicating factor. Though formally this was an alliance which is represented in today's Thailand as an appropriately pragmatic response to the war (Arrunnapaporn 2007: 118–19), as the war progressed it acquired some of the characteristics of an occupation. Understandably there has been something of a national amnesia about the Thais' bystander role as war crimes were committed on their territory. The Thai military authorities with whom the Australian government negotiated permission to build the memorial museum made clear their preference that the displays should be presented 'in a spirit of reconciliation rather than dwelling on the circumstances of the Japanese occupation'.

> The Thais [they said] tend to take these relics of war in their stride, and places such as Hellfire Pass did not bear the same significance in their minds, [though] the Thai Government, the Thai people and especially the people of Kanchanaburi would welcome any measure that would attract additional tourism to the region. (DVA 1996b)

As David Lowenthal might put it, the Thai authorities wanted 'an embraceable past' celebrating some elements and forgetting others (Lowenthal 1997: 162). It was agreed that they would take responsibility for upgrading the road access and parking facilities at Hellfire Pass while the Australians would determine the content of the museum (*VetAffairs* 1995: 8).

The potential for contest over memory existed in Australia also. When Air Vice Marshal Alan Heggen, Director of the Office of Australian War Graves (OAWG) in the Department of Veterans' Affairs (DVA), announced the project, the ex-POW community expressed some unease. Was the memory of captivity to be sanitized? Were Japanese atrocities to be downplayed in deference to Japanese tourists? And would commercialization of Hellfire Pass eclipse its commemorative purposes? In Queensland, a state where there had already been protests about the level of Japanese investment in real estate (Hajdu 2005), ex-prisoners demanded that:

> somewhere in a conspicuous place within the memorial complex [there be] clearly displayed an image of brutality to prisoners of war by Japanese guards ... Truth must be clearly portrayed, even at the risk of offending the Japanese who should not be considered in any respect. (DVA 1996c)[5]

The Federal Ex-POW Association, meanwhile, recommended that within the memorial complex,

> printed in large, easy to read letters, both in English and Japanese, [it be stated] that Japan started the war in the Pacific region in December 1942 [sic] by her unprovoked and without warning, attack on the American Fleet in Pearl Harbour and on Singapore. Japan continued her aggression and destruction of human life throughout the Pacific and its Islands until her defeat in 1945 when she unconditionally surrendered to the Allies. ... Japan has never told her young people at home that it was Japan who started the war and she never will tell them. (DVA n.d.)

Some ex-prisoners also took alarm at what they took to be the implication in Heggen's announcement of the project that their work on the railway might be construed as contributing to the Japanese war effort (as, of course, it manifestly did) (DVA 1996d).

To defuse the situation Minister for Veterans' Affairs Bruce Scott met with ex-POW representatives while the OAWG set itself the challenge of telling 'the story in a factual and balanced way without over-emphasizing or under-emphasizing any aspect for the sake of sparing anyone's feelings' (DVA 1996e). The memorial museum, it was agreed, would commemorate not only those who worked on the railway but also prisoners interned elsewhere in the Asia Pacific region. Moreover, the content would be multinational; not with the intention of diminishing the Australian story but rather of providing balance and recognizing the role of prisoners of other nationalities and Asian labourers in the building of the railway (DVA 1997b).

This aspiration proved the next point of contestation: how to include voices other than Australians when this was an Australian-funded initiative? There were more British prisoners at Hellfire Pass than Australians and many Asian labourers had worked on sites nearby. Yet the voices of the Asians who were illiterate, without formal leadership structures and kept no records of their suffering, were lost in the past. Attempts to engage British ex-prisoners in the project meanwhile proved unproductive. Mostly this happened through the agency of another individual who had become passionately engaged in commemoration of the railway, Rod Beattie. An Australian gem merchant living in Kanchanaburi, Beattie had devoted countless unpaid hours in the 1990s to identifying the railway's route and the location of every work camp along its length in Thailand. Together with his Vietnamese wife, he had cleared the walking trail beyond Hellfire Pass using only a machete and chain saw and had unearthed many artefacts of the prisoners. Appointed by the OAWG to be site manager of the museum's construction, Beattie became progressively concerned with the question of what would be displayed in its interior.

Since Beattie was also employed as supervisor of the CWGC war cemeteries in Thailand, he had the opportunity to discuss the Hellfire Pass project with visiting British veterans, including senior members of the Royal British Legion. In 1996 he also briefed Prince Philip on the Hellfire Pass project when the Prince accompanied Queen Elizabeth II on a state visit to Thailand (DVA 1997c). From these contacts and Beattie's subsequent visits to the United Kingdom, a rather uncoordinated attempt to incorporate the British into the Hellfire Pass project developed. Beattie liaised with Buckingham Palace staff, ultimately to no effect. The British Legion made contact with the Australian Returned and Services League (RSL) and established a fund-raising initiative 'Project Remember' with the aim of adding to the facilities at Hellfire Pass or raising funds for a similar memorial to British prisoners and civilian internees. A second British association, the Kwai Railway Memorial (Three Pagodas Group), was formed in 1995 aiming to support the Australian initiative, perhaps by supplying books for a library. In April 1997 the president of the British Legion, Graham Downing, also visited Minister Scott in Australia, while informal approaches were made to the British authorities by the Australian High Commissioner in London and the Australian Chief of Army (DVA 1998a).

None of these discussions, however, led to any formal agreement and the British government, whose attitude towards prisoners of the Japanese had historically been 'at best ambivalent' (Flower 2008: 64), declined to contribute any funding. In stark contrast to the proactive role of the Australian government in commemoration, the UK Ministry of Defence stated late in 1997 that 'the cost of such memorials were [sic] usually met from private donations or public subscriptions and not from public funds' (DVA 1997d).

By this time in any case the OAWG, from which Heggen had retired in mid-1997 and been replaced by Air Vice Marshal Gary Beck, was committed to the view that the Hellfire Pass Memorial Museum 'was clearly an Australian

Government project designed to be international in scope working to a timeline … to be opened on ANZAC day and by the Australian Prime Minister' (DVA 1998b). The plans for the memorial museum were well advanced and the contract for the design of the memorial displays had been granted to Australian company Hewitt Pender Associates, which had already done considerable work for the Australian War Memorial, the pre-eminent site of the national memory of war in Canberra (DVA 1997a).[6] The work of writing the content for the museum panels was assigned to Australian historians.

The outcome was perhaps predictable. When the memorial museum opened in April 1998 it was condemned by a British historian of the railway, Sibylla Jane Flower, as an attempt by Australians to claim ownership of the memory of the railway to the exclusion of other nationalities. The displays in the museum, she maintained, were not only inaccurate and grammatically sloppy but failed to be international in their perspective. They did not do justice to the experience of British prisoners (of whom Flower's father was one). Rather the museum was 'built by Australians to honour Australians' (DVA 1998c).

The Australian government refuted this claim, citing the number of times that prisoners of other nationalities and the Japanese were mentioned in text panels and insisting that the memorial museum did indeed have an international perspective.[7] In its defence, it can be said that the major panel texts were in Thai as well as the English language (a decision made by Beck very late during the museum's construction) and that some of the paintings used in the displays were by British prisoner Jack Chalker. In addition, the time capsule buried near the ramp at the memorial museum's entrance contained letters and badges from not only Australian leaders and associations but also from the Royal British Legion, the USS *Houston* Survivors' Association, Buckingham Palace and the prime minister of Singapore. Yet, for all this, the memorial museum's displays had an indisputably Australian character. The narrative was unexceptionable but the photographs, the artistic images and the quotations from prisoners' memoirs were largely Australian. It was Australian cultural memory, captivity through Australian eyes and voices.

Moreover, the impression that the Hellfire Pass project was an exercise in 'honouring Australians' was confirmed by the ceremonies that accompanied the opening of the memorial museum. At the dawn service held in Hellfire Pass, Prime Minister Howard spoke only of Australian servicemen and women – understandably, since it was Anzac Day and an official pilgrimage of Australian ex-POWs was present. Howard's later speech at the Kanchanaburi cemetery, which houses British and Dutch as well as Australian dead, again eulogized the Anzacs, referring no fewer than seven times in a speech of fewer than 800 words to mateship. 'In the experience of captivity', Howard said, 'the Anzac legend found a new form.' Only in his speech at the opening of the memorial museum itself did Howard mention the 'thousands' of British, American, Indian and Dutch prisoners on the railway, the 'estimated quarter of a million *romusha'* and the Thai people 'who attempted to ease the suffering of our men'. In recognition of the last, Howard announced a donation of $50,000 towards a fund supporting medical student exchange which had been established in the 1980s by Dunlop and a local Thai businessman, Boong Pong, who had smuggled supplies to the POWs during the war years.[8]

*****

In the years that followed the memorial museum's opening the Australian authorities without fanfare made some adjustments to its displays. All the text in the gallery was reproduced in Thai and English, new panels explaining the role of the *romusha* were introduced and the foyer was redesigned to make space for an introductory video. The text on the panels, presented under chronological and thematic headings – such as 'Origins of the Railway', 'Laying the Railway', 'Sabotage', 'Hammer and Tap', 'Bridge Building', 'Organization', 'Equipment', 'Pay', 'Speedo!', 'The Prisoners of War Arrive', 'The Romusha Arrive' – now (2010) reads as 'internationalized' almost to the point of blandness. Although many of the visual images and quotations remain Australian and the entrance hall declares the Australian origins and funding of the museum, Asian labourers are given primacy in the dedication that concludes the introductory video. The treatment of the Japanese perpetrators is adroit, placating ex-prisoners without being offensive to (the increasing number of) Japanese tourists. Some panels acknowledge the issue of Japanese brutality but the audio guide (in English, Japanese, Dutch and Thai languages) attributes the savagery on the railway to systems of government, not people; 'human nature', we are told, 'is pretty constant but depends actively on political or social environment' (Fig. 1.2).

If the comments in the visitors' book at the memorial museum are a guide, it now succeeds in presenting a narrative that inspires empathy from visitors of many nationalities. The heritage consumers, as Ashworth would say, identify themselves with the individuals in the atrocities being related (Ashworth 2002: 364). This is consistent with the intent of the Australian government which always saw the facility as more a memorial than a museum, an interpretative centre which prepared visitors for the affective experience of visiting the cutting below. The DVA included the word 'museum' in the facility's title only because this appeared to have more traction with the Thai community (interview with Gary Beck, 4 March 2010). For Beck particularly this was not a space in which to profile physical artefacts and his insistence on this was, by his account, one of the reasons for a falling out with Beattie. Although employed only as site manager Beattie became intent on shaping the museum's contents according to his vision and when frustrated by DVA, funded and built his own museum in Kanchanaburi, strategically overlooking the peaceful CWGC cemetery. Here can be found the more traditional

Figure 1.2 Hellfire Pass Memorial Museum, opened 1998.

museology: artefacts unearthed from the railway, reconstructions of POW hospitals, data of deaths in pie charts and even a headstone retrieved from the jungle.

In a final episode in this contest over memory, Beck in 2005 made a further imprint on the Hellfire Pass landscape. Some years earlier the on-site Australian manager of the memorial museum, Terry Beaton, had placed a wooden cross in the Hellfire Pass to provide a focus for Anzac Day services. The DVA thought this singularly Christian icon to be culturally unacceptable, given the religious beliefs of both the Asian labourers who had died in such numbers on the railway and the local Thai population. Moreover, the Thai Army insisted that the cross be removed between Anzac Day ceremonies (Kelly 2005). Beck therefore ordered the installation of a new memorial, the shining black memorial plinth that now stands at one end of the cutting (Fig. 1.3). In attempting to shift the commemorative focus towards this memorial, Beck also arranged for some rails and sleepers in the cutting to be removed. The loose ballast around the rails was disposed of too, since it was considered a safety hazard for elderly visitors.

A public outcry erupted in Australia. Even though the rails had been placed in the cutting only in 1989, like the bridge at Kanchanaburi they were now invested with authenticity. According to Beaton (now relieved of his post at

Figure 1.3 Memorial to prisoners of war, erected at the end of Hellfire Pass by the Australian government, 2005.

Hellfire Pass) and various vocal ex-POWs, the rails were 'genuine', something 'that the prisoners had carried' and which had come to form 'Dunlop's headstone'. 'I think it's sacrilege to have pulled them up,' the indomitable Bill Toon, now 84 years old, declared from his Melbourne home. 'But the Government can do what they want.' An English tourist whose father had worked on the railway added, 'The granite is very nice but they were the real rails. The granite memorial means nothing. The rails meant everything' (*Sydney Morning Herald*, 7 June 2005).

Even more explosively Beck's new works were claimed to have disturbed Dunlop's ashes – and, it seemed, those of other veterans whose remains had been buried in the pass without the knowledge of the DVA (Silver 2005). The removal of the rails therefore was constructed in the Australian press as a 'desecration of a war grave' (Silver 2005; *Age*, 7 June 2005; *Age*, 8 June 2005). Beck fought back, pointing out that Dunlop's ashes had been buried, not scattered, in 1994 and that the cutting was not in any sense an official war grave. However, the 'shock jocks' of talk-back radio who had taken up the cause of the critics accused Beck of finding 'a new way to insult Australian war veterans' (Neil Mitchell, 3AW Melbourne, 7 July 2005). Having earlier in 2005 been ensnared in an even more controversial issue, the widening of the access road to Anzac Cove at Gallipoli, which unearthed human remains and damaged the heritage landscape, Beck was sent on special leave by his minister. He chose not to reapply for his post as Director of War Graves.

What will be the future of the Hellfire Pass Memorial Museum? The Australian tenure of the land was guaranteed by an 'endorsement in principle' by the Thai cabinet on 19 November 1996, and a draft and unsigned Memorandum of Understanding stating that development of the site would be conducted with the agreement of the Australian and Thai governments (DVA 1996f). These are not robust guarantees.

The heritage within which the memorial museum is positioned, that is the railway itself, sits awkwardly between national and global significance. It is improbable that it would ever qualify for World Heritage status. Certainly some sites of atrocity from the Second World War, such as Auschwitz-Birkenau and Hiroshima, have acquired transnational significance and it could be argued, in the case of the railway, that Western tourists have over time asserted a 'right of a global accessibility' to it as part of 'their' heritage (Graham *et al.* 2000: 238). But the railway would struggle to meet the requirement for World Heritage inscription of having 'outstanding universal value' or any of the six cultural criteria. Even if it were ever to be reclaimed in its entirety from the jungle in both Thailand and Burma (where access is currently restricted), the vast majority of its original infrastructure – the rails, the railway stations, the rolling stock and particularly the wooden trestle bridges so central to cultural memory – have been lost.

As it is, the Thai government has shown no inclination to nominate the railway for World Heritage status and its length in Thailand is not even listed on the Thai Heritage Registration List (Arrunnapaporn 2007: 36, 146–7; Ashworth and van der Aa 2002: 454). Thailand has a hierarchical system of heritage management, with national government controls applying only to heritage features of national significance, regional controls to those of regional significance, provincial controls to sites of provincial significance, and municipal to those at that level. Over the years the maintenance and development of the railway has been fragmented between a number of agencies: the State Railway of Thailand, the Kanchanaburi municipality, the Thai Heritage Agency and the Tourism Authority of Thailand. Only some of these are concerned with heritage preservation.

Hence the sustainability of a site managed by foreigners at one point along the railway is inherently fragile. It depends on tolerance by the Thai government and the Thai Army which controls the land. This tolerance, in turn, is contingent on there being economic, political and cultural advantages to the Thais, first, in the museum's continued existence and, second, in its being controlled by the Australian government. The Thai Army, for instance, has shown some interest in assuming management of the museum itself, perhaps because of its potential commercial benefit (though currently admission to the museum is free).

The OAWG manager of the memorial museum (2001 to the present), Bill Slape, is sensitive to these issues. He consciously seeks to maximize the economic value of Hellfire Pass to stakeholders in the wider Kanchanaburi province by increasing the number of tourists visiting the site. He has promoted Hellfire Pass in local media and magazines, placed brochures in Bangkok restaurants frequented by Japanese tourists and even managed to insert an article in an in-flight magazine on an international airline. Slape has also sought to embed the memorial museum in the local Thai agricultural community around Hellfire Pass. Conscious that the memorial museum is in the Thais' 'backyard' he has, with the assistance of the Australian-Thai Chamber of Commerce, provided IT equipment to local schools, installed water systems and rebuilt a local kindergarten. The number of tourists to the museum has grown steadily, reaching 90,000 visitors in 2008. Of these, significantly, 52 per cent were Thais. The next largest groups of tourists are Dutch, British, Americans and Australians, in that order (interview with Bill Slape, March 2009).

How many of these tourists actively seek out the memorial museum, driven by knowledge of its history or even a fascination with 'dark' tourism, is debatable. Kanchanaburi province is a popular destination with Thai and foreign tourists because of its scenic beauty and accessibility from Bangkok. Bus tours heading to the national parks further north find the memorial museum a convenient stop en route. The discovery of the memorial museum may therefore be accidental or subsidiary to the primary purpose of the tourists' travel, as much of heritage tourism is. Nevertheless, it does have the effect of extending knowledge of the POW and *romusha* experience within the wider Thai population.

The greater challenge, however, is to go beyond tourism and development aid and anchor the railway more deeply in Thai national and cultural memory. This is problematic at the national level, given the fact that Thailand has not integrated the Second World War into its narratives of nation building. Unlike Singapore, the Philippines and Burma it has not designated any national day to mark the Japanese intervention (Blackburn 2010). At the local level, in contrast, there are personal memories of the construction of the railway. Older residents of Kanchanaburi recall the Japanese presence and their families' supplying food to the prison camps. The Allied bombing of the bridge at Kanchanaburi in 1944–5 which caused civilian casualties also retains a strong place in local memory. For many years it has been celebrated each November in a *son et lumière* performance that tells the story of 'the bridge on the River Kwai'. Attracting thousands of tourists, the event culminates in a fireworks display invoking the experience of the bombing – and incidentally affirming the importance of entertainment in heritage.

The local experience of the railway is also reflected in graphic dioramas and extensive murals depicting the bombing and captivity in a private museum adjacent to the bridge, the World War II museum. A second museum located a little further up river at a Buddhist temple, the JEATH museum, meanwhile is constructed as a replica of a POW hut. It displays photos and memorabilia of Allied prisoners of war while its name JEATH also reflects a memory of the railway, being formed from the initials Japan, England, America, Australia, Thailand and Holland. Meanwhile, the bones of *romusha* discovered in a mass grave nearby in the early 1990s are on public display in the museum by the bridge.

At other points in the vicinity of the operating railway line there are also reminders of its history: bomb craters and bomb casings at the Tham Krasae station; a dramatic viaduct hugging a cliff at Wampo; and a Japanese locomotive at the Nam Sai Yok waterfall, for example. Prominent local businessman Kuhn Kanit Wanachote has also been actively involved in the production of memory and heritage, developing (in collaboration with an Australian ex-POW Keith Flanagan) a memorial park in honour of Weary Dunlop at his resort on the River Kwai Noi. It incorporates an eclectic mix of memorabilia, a statue of Dunlop, copies of Jack Chalker sketches, a recreation of a POW hospital and, most dramatically, a steam locomotive and trucks on a hill overlooking the site, with the phrase 'The Death Railway' spelled out in wooden sleepers below.

Yet little of this 'heritage' activity represents a memory of the war years that is shared between Thais and former prisoners of war. Rather the local and Western memories of the war tend to constitute 'parallel' narratives. Many of the most traumatic events in POW memory – the huge loss of life on the upper and inaccessible reaches of the railway near the border with Burma, for example – occurred beyond areas of Thai settlement. Hence there are few surviving Thai witnesses to them. Moreover, where physical remnants of the railway remain, they are often marginal to the commercial or leisure activities that also occur at that site. The viaduct at Wampo, for example, is visited as much for the Buddhist temple in the adjacent cave as for its war history, while at Sai Yok Noi, near the railway terminus at Nam Tok, it is the waterfall, not the history of the now invisible prison camps that draws tourists. As Apinya Arrunnapaporn argues, it is as if the Thais 'share the physical part of the heritage, but not the intangible values' (2007: 48).

Furthermore, the memory of the railway, which to Australians has acquired a semi-sacred quality, has been sanitized and commodified: here as elsewhere globally, 'death has become a commodity for consumption in a global communications market' (G. Palmer in Lennon and Foley, 2004: 5). Hence, even where Thais remember the railway there is, to quote Annette Hamilton, 'a new level of mass interpretation that stands between the personal and the official, authorized, accounts … [a site] where individuals can personally intersect with a commercialized version of "the past"' (Hamilton 1994: 93). At the bridge in Kanchanaburi even the name of the river has been commodified and market stalls selling war-related memorabilia of all kinds are more visible than the war relics. Gaudy T-shirts carry images of steam trains crossing the bridge. Various fridge magnets depict the bombed bridge. One bears a photo of emaciated POWs with the caption 'The Death Railway'; another carries the message 'Memory can make that moment last forever'.

Thais and Australians also recall the past of the railway in ways that are culturally contingent. For Australians the commemoration of war, though core to the construction of national identity, is still positioned within the aesthetics, discourse and iconography of Christianity and the British Empire. The cemeteries at Kanchanaburi and Chungkai are designed on the model of the Commonwealth War Graves Commission that is replicated with local variations throughout the world. They feature the traditional cross of sacrifice, the stone of remembrance and the biblical text 'Their Name Liveth Forevermore' (selected by that epitome of imperialism, Rudyard Kipling). Private tokens of remembrance left at Hellfire Pass meanwhile include crosses, Flanders poppies and Australian flags. What resonance do these symbols have with Thais? How can a largely Buddhist culture in which the dead are cremated comprehend the British and Australian way of death: the systematic exhumation of decaying corpses from up-country camps and their careful reburial and identification in CWGC cemeteries? And what do Thais make of 'pilgrimages' to these sites of memory by Westerners decades later, given that many who make these journeys have no direct connection with the building of the railway? As a Thai graduate student said to the author on a study tour in 2007, they simply 'don't get it' (Fig. 1.4).

These cultural differences could easily translate into heritage dissonance, should the railway be further developed for heritage purposes. For instance, any attempt by Western heritage practitioners to mark sites of mass death along the railway route, a macabre 'discovery trail', would be intrusive and could be 'read in quite a different way from that intended' by those developing the site (Tunbridge and Ashworth 1996: 28). Given Thai sensibilities about death it might even damage the tourist industry on which the local economy depends. Most of the resorts along the scenically stunning River Kwai Noi are located on the campsites occupied by POWs during the war when the river served as a supply route and source of water. The hidden and tragic past of these sites is currently unacknowledged, just as the 1965 massacre sites in Bali are invisible to the hordes of tourists who now visit that island. Do Westerners, seeking to reclaim their history, have the right to unsettle these 'structures of forgetting' (Byrne, 1998)?

It seems therefore improbable that the Thai section of the railway will ever be systematically reclaimed along its full length for heritage purposes (some of it is in fact irreversibly submerged under a reservoir). Nor is it likely that the publicly used sections of the railway will be interpreted in a manner that Western heritage practitioners and tourists might anticipate. The Hellfire Pass Memorial Museum therefore will almost certainly remain physically and culturally an enclave heritage. Even as more Thais come to understand the meanings of Hellfire Pass for foreigners, its heritage will continue to be

Figure 1.4 Two plaques in Hellfire Pass have acquired the character of a shrine through mementos being left by visitors. On the left is a 1994 memorial to 'Weary Dunlop'; on the right a plaque describing the history of the Pass donated by the Australian–Thai Chamber of Commerce in April 1987.

dependent on the same Thai tolerance, pragmatism and sense of mutual benefit that allowed it to come into being from the 1980s on. In the event of this tolerance eroding, then the Australian government will have only the strength of the bilateral relationship between Australia and Thailand, and possibly international public opinion, to resort to in defence of this delicately located transplanted site of memory.

Notes

1   The author acknowledges the assistance during the research for this chapter of James Rogers and staff of the Department of Veterans' Affairs, Canberra; Gary Beck, Canberra; Ross Bastiaan, Melbourne; Rod Beattie, Thai–Burma Railway Centre, Kanchanaburi; Bill Slape, Hellfire Pass Museum, Hintok; and Sibylla Jane Flower, London. Glenda Lynch provided exemplary support as research assistant. Department of Veterans' Affairs records in Australia have been made available to the author under Special Access conditions.

2   Given the lack or destruction of records, it is impossible to determine exactly the number of Asian labourers (predominantly Burmese, Thai, Malayan, Tamil and Indonesian) who worked on the railway.

3   Japanese sources place the number of acknowledged *romusha* deaths at 42,214 but another 92,220 Asian labourers were reported as having deserted, many of these probably to trying to escape cholera outbreaks, and may have died.

4   ANZAC is the acronym for the Australian and New Zealand Army Corps.

5   For further opposition, see Heggen's Report on Briefing to Ex-POW Association National Executive, 26 February 1996, DVA file 96022W; C. L. Wilson, Federal Secretary Ex-POW Association to Minister for Veterans' Affairs, Bruce Scott, 2 April 1996, DVA file 96037W.

6   The architects were an Australian firm with interests in Thailand, Woods Bagot; Rod Beattie was Project Manager on site; the interior design was contracted within Australia. The fragmented nature of the project management led to tensions, particularly between Beattie and OAWG.

7   There were 14 references to British POWs, four to Americans, five to Dutch, 19 to 'Allied' and six to Australians. There were 72 references to the Japanese (Hewitt 1998).

8   Howard's three speeches are held in DVA file 98481.

References

A Timeline of Thai Railways (2004) Online: www.2bangkok.com/2bangkok/srt/timeline.shtml (accessed 25 August 2010).

Arneil, S. (1980) *One Man's War*, Sydney: Alternative Publishing.

Arrunnapaporn, A. B. (2007) 'Interpretation of Atrocity Heritage of the 'Death Railway' of the River Kwai', PhD thesis, Silpakorn University, Thailand.

Ashplant, T. G., Dawson, G. and Roper, M. (2000) *The Politics of War Memory and Commemoration*, London: Routledge.

Ashworth, G. J. (2002) 'Holocaust Tourism: The Experience of Karkow-Kazimierz', *International Research in Geographical and Environmental Education* 11(4), 363–7.

Ashworth, G. J. and van der Aa, B. J. M. (2002) 'Bamyam: Whose Heritage Was It and What Should We Do about It?', *Current Issues in Tourism* 5(5), 447–57.

Australian Bronze Commemorative Plaques (2001). Online: www.plaques.satlink.com.au (accessed 30 August 2010).

Australian-Thai Chamber of Commerce (2003) *Hellfire Pass Memorial Thai–Burma Railway*, Bangkok: ATCC.

AWM – Australian War Memorial files (*c.* 1985) SMEC report by Jim Appleby, February. 563/003/051 pt 1.

AWM – Australian War Memorial files (*c.* 1995) Memo by Ken Bradley, Public Affairs Sub-committee, ATCC, Hellfire Pass Project Proposal, n.d. (July 1995?), 563/003/051, pt 1.

Beaumont, J. (2005) 'Prisoners of War in Australian National Memory', in B. Moore and B. Hately (eds), *Prisoners of War, Prisoners of Peace: Captivity, Homecoming and Memory in World War II*, Oxford: Berg.

Beaumont, J. (2009) 'Contested Transnational Heritage: The Demolition of Changi Prison', *International Journal of Heritage Studies* 15(4), 294–316.

Blackburn, K. (2010) 'War Memory and Nation-Building in South East Asia', *South East Asia Research* 18(1), 5–31.

Bomford, J. (2001) 'Fractured Lives: Australian Prisoners of War of the Japanese and their Families', PhD thesis, Victoria: Deakin University, Australia.

Byrne, D. (1998) 'Traces of '65: Sites and Memories of the Post-Coup Killings in Bali', *Australian Humanities Review* May. Online: www.australianhumanitiesreview.org/archive/Issue-May-1998/byrne.html (accessed 14 September 2010).

Dunlop, E. E. (1986) *The War Diaries of Weary Dunlop: Java and the Burma–Thailand Railway 1942–45*, Melbourne: Nelson.

DVA – Department of Veterans' Affairs records (n.d.) Clarrie Wilson and Harry J. Nesbitt, Australia/Thai Memorial Project. File 96069W.

DVA – Department of Veterans' Affairs records (1994) Alan Heggen, OAWG, to J. P. McCarthy, Australian embassy, Bangkok, 7 July. File 94334W.

DVA – Department of Veterans' Affairs records (1996a) Bill Toon, History of Hellfire Pass Project, n.d., February 1996. File 96022W.

DVA – Department of Veterans' Affairs records (1996b) A. Heggen, Report on Visit to Thailand and Malaysia, 20 April – 1 May 1996. File 96307W.

DVA – Department of Veterans' Affairs records (1996c) Queensland Report on Hellfire Pass Project to Federal Conference, n.d. (February 1996?). File 96022W, DVA records.

DVA – Department of Veterans' Affairs records (1996d) C. L. Wilson to Heggen, 5 February 1996, Memo Heggen to Beattie, 9 February. File 96002W.

DVA – Department of Veterans' Affairs records (1996e) Heggen to Beattie, 30 August. File 96069W.

DVA – Department of Veterans' Affairs records (1996f) Synopsis of cabinet meeting, 19 November. File. 96092W.

DVA – Department of Veterans' Affairs records (1997a) Media release, Hellfire Pass Memorial Project: Background Information, April. File 97045W.

DVA – Department of Veterans' Affairs records (1997b) Brief by Heggen for the Minister, 4 April. File 97028W.

DVA – Department of Veterans' Affairs records (1997c) Beattie to Duncan MacLennan, OAWG, 13 November. File 97097W.

DVA – Department of Veterans' Affairs records (1997d) 'UK Ministers Pressed to Rethink Burma Railway Memorial', AAP Diary, 3 December. File 97104.

DVA – Department of Veterans' Affairs records (1998a) Graham Downing, Project Remember, to Bruce Scott, Minister for Veterans' Affairs, 14 June; F. A. H. Champkin, Kwai Railway Memorial, to Gary Beck, OAWG, 7 September; Downing to Bruce Scott, 14 June; Bruce Scott to Graham Downing, 24 August. File 982302.

DVA – Department of Veterans' Affairs records (1998b) Beck to Peter Phillips, RSL National President, 27 July. File 981481.

DVA – Department of Veterans' Affairs records (1998c) Scott to Downing, 24 August; Beck to Champkin, 9 September. File 982302.

DVA – Department of Veterans' Affairs records (2002) *Hellfire Pass Memorial*, Canberra, Department of Veterans' Affairs.

Ebury, S. (1994) *Weary: The Life of Sir Edward Dunlop*, Ringwood, Melbourne: Viking.

Flower, S. J. (2008) 'British Memory and the Prisoner of War Experience', in K. Blackburn and K. Hack (eds), *Forgotten Captives in Japanese Occupied Asia*, Abingdon: Routledge.

Graham, B., Ashworth, G. J. and Tunbridge, J. (2000) *A Geography of Heritage*, London: Arnold.

Hack, K. and Blackburn, K. (2008) 'The Bridge on the River Kwai and King Rat', in K. Blackburn and K. Hack (eds), *Forgotten Captives in Japanese Occupied Asia*, Abingdon: Routledge.

Hajdu, J. (2005) *Samurai in the Surf: The Arrival of the Japanese on the Gold Coast in the 1980s*, Canberra: Pandanus Books.

Hamilton, A. (1994) 'Skeletons of Empire: Australians and the Burma–Thailand Railway', in K. Darian-Smith and P. Hamilton (eds), *Memory and History in Twentieth Century Australia*, Melbourne: Oxford University Press.

Hearder, R. (2009) *Keep the Men Alive: Australian POW Doctors in Japanese Captivity*, Sydney: Allen & Unwin.

Hewitt, T. (1998) Letter, 18 August. Provided by Sibylla Jane Flower.

Kelly, D. (2005) Draft letter from Minister of Veterans' Affairs, De-Anne Kelly, *c.* June. Copy provided by Gary Beck.

Kidd, W. (1997) 'Memory, Memorials and the Commemoration of War Memorials in Lorraine, 1908–1988' in M. Evans, and K. Lunn (eds), *War and Memory in the Twentieth Century*, Oxford: Berg.

Kratoska, W. (2005) 'Labor in the Malay Peninsula and Singapore under Japanese Occupation', in P. H. Kratoska (ed.), *Asian Labor in the Wartime Japanese Empire: Unknown Histories*, New York: East Gate Books.

Lennon, John and Malcolm Foley (2004) *Dark Tourism: The Attraction of Death and Disaster*, London: Thomson, 2004.

Lowenthal, D. (1997) *The Heritage Crusade and the Spoils of History*, Cambridge: Cambridge University Press.

McKenna, M. (2003) 'Howard's Warriors', in R. Gaita (ed.), *Why the War Was Wrong*, Melbourne: Text Publishing.

Reed, L. (2004) *Bigger than Gallipoli: War History and Memory in Australia*, Crawley, Western Australia: University of Western Australia Press.

Silver, Lynette (2005) Letter to De-Anne Kelly, 17 July. Copy provided by Gary Beck.

Thai–Burma Railway Centre (2005) *A Brief History of the Thailand–Burma Railway.* Online: www.tbrconline.com/default.asp?PageID=4 (accessed 25 August 2010).

Tunbridge, J. E. and Ashworth, G. J. (1996) *Dissonant Heritage: The Management of the Past as a Resource in Conflict*, Chichester: John Wiley & Sons.

VetAffairs (1995) Canberra: Dept of Veterans' Affairs, May.

Watson, D. (2002) *Recollections of a Bleeding Heart: A Portrait of Paul Keating PM*, Sydney: Knopf.

Winter, J. (2006) *Remembering War: The Great War between Memory and History in the Twentieth Century*, New Haven: Yale University Press.

Chapter 2

Victory and defeat at Điện Biên Phủ: memory and memorialization in Vietnam and France

William Logan and Nguyễn Thanh Bình

The noted Vietnam scholar Stanley Karnow ranked the 1954 Battle of Điện Biên Phủ as 'one of the great military engagements of history' along with Agincourt, Waterloo and Gettysburg (in Simpson 1994: xi). Certainly it is one of the twentieth century's most significant battles, effectively marking the end of French Indochina and, indeed, of Western colonization in Asia, although with the Vietnam War the United States sought to maintain that hold before it also capitulated. The two main belligerent parties in the battle at Điện Biên Phủ – the French and the Vietnamese – see the battlefield from different points of view (Figs 2.1, 2.2).

Figure 2.1 Vietnamese troops take the French headquarters, 7 May 1954.

Figure 2.2 Captured French soldiers on the 'long march' to prison, 1954.

Are these viewpoints irreconcilable? Can a 'shared heritage' be defined or are parallel stories the most that can be hoped for? Are the French able to see beyond their humiliation in the unanticipated defeat suffered at the hands of the Việt Minh, a coalition of Vietnamese nationalists and communists led by Hồ Chí Minh and his army chief Võ Nguyên Giáp? Can the Vietnamese forgive the French for imposing a harsh colonial rule on their country that necessitated the loss of so many lives in the struggle for national independence? The matter has been and, for some, remains delicate. As Chris Ryan (2007: 2) has observed, battlefields are 'complex phenomena located in the cultural politics of silence and absence as much as articulation and presence'.

This chapter seeks to see the battle site cross-culturally, highlighting its dual roles: as the place holding physical reminders of Vietnamese and French troops coming together in bloody combat but also as the place harbouring an intangible emotional heritage captured in memories and memorialized in another set of physical impacts on the landscape – war cemeteries and war memorials. The chapter shows that significant cultural differences exist in the memorialization of those who died at Điện Biên Phủ – between the Vietnamese and the French, Asian and European, the colonized and the colonizers, the victors and the defeated.

Of course, these binaries are too simplistic. There are also significant differences within each country in attitudes towards Điện Biên Phủ and its protection and memorialization based on different personal or family connections with the place, different memories and different understandings about the role of heritage in today's world. Moreover these attitudes are not fixed but are changing over time as 1954 and Điện Biên Phủ recede into the past and as other issues assume priority in life. This complexity needs to be recognized if the meaning and significance of the battlefield are to be understood and if light is to be shed on universal questions relating to war and its remembrance, such as: how does memorialization alter as the generations which experienced a particular war first-hand pass away? At what point do pain and grief die and old enmities disappear? When can states begin to reuse hallowed ground?

French memories and memorialization of Điện Biên Phủ

The French, the perpetrators of colonialism in Vietnam and instigators of the Điện Biên Phủ battle, have residual emotions in which pain at the loss of family and community members mixes with national loss of face. If it was not clearly seen before 1954 that French imperialism in Indochina was doomed, Điện Biên Phủ brought the realization home in the most brutal way.

Catastrophe at Điện Biên Phủ

The French authorities in Hanoi had selected the time and place for what was to be a final physical confrontation with the Việt Minh. Expecting a victory, the battle was timed to give advantage to the French negotiators at the international conference in Geneva that had opened in April 1954 – talks that were initially to deal with the situation on the Korean peninsula but that were scheduled in sessions on 8 May to move on to considering the future of Indochina. A small area of Mường Thanh plain was selected, in the middle of the remote mountainous area of western Tonkin, now north-west Vietnam, where the French military forces had set up an initial outpost in 1922. Here under Operation Castor French troops parachuted in and started work in November 1953 constructing a group of nine fortified strongholds on the rounded hills running along the eastern edge of the valley: Gabrielle in the north, Anne-Marie in the north-west, Beatrice in the north-east, Isabelle in the south, and an inner ring of Éliane, Claudine, Françoise, Huguette and Dominique. They thought that this construction of the Điện Biên Phủ base, being adjacent to the key Việt Minh supply line to Laos, would lure the Việt Minh troops into the north-west of Vietnam where they would be decimated by superior French technology and firepower (Fig. 2.3).

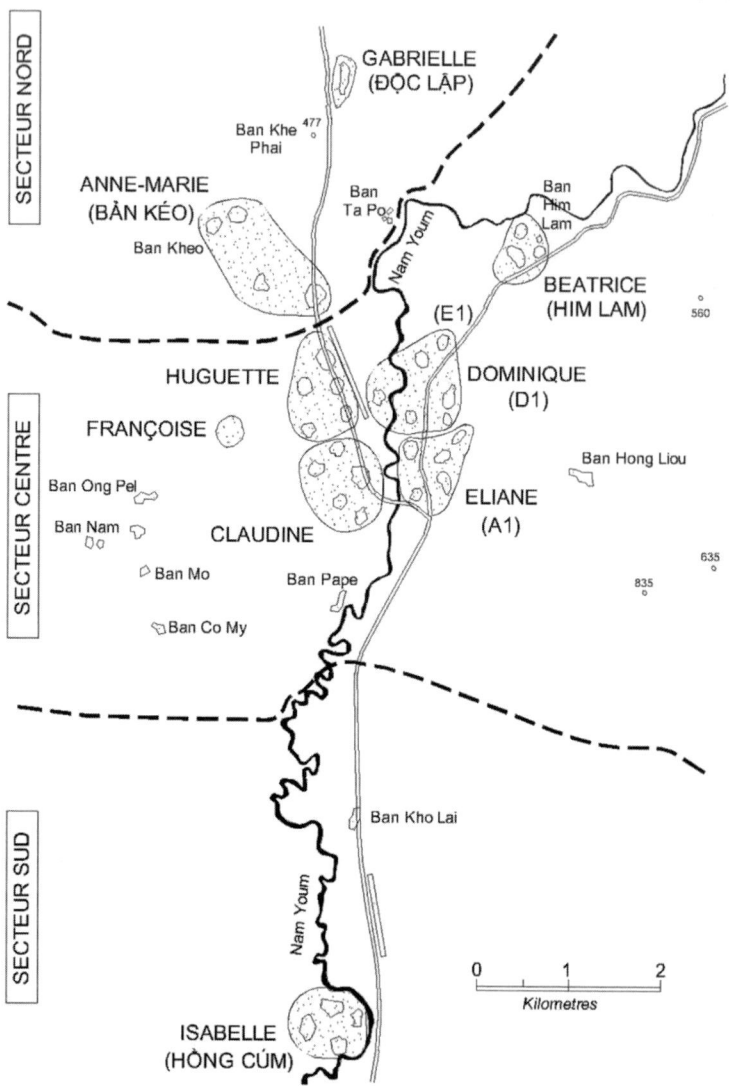

Figure 2.3 Map of the battlefield, 1954.

This was the 'Navarre Plan' named after its architect General Henri-Eugène Navarre and based on the hedgehog (*hérisson*) concept successfully used in an earlier (1952) battle at Nà Sản, east of Điện Biên Phủ. The French Army would establish a fortified airhead at Mường Thanh and airlift soldiers into a ring of armed positions. As it turned out, Navarre had made a massive strategic blunder and was totally unprepared for the guerrilla tactics adopted by the Việt Minh – the use of massive numbers of troops to drag artillery onto the ridges overlooking the valley and the mobilization of farmers to provide continuous food supplies to the battlefield. Over a period of 56 days and nights from 13 March to 7 May 1954, the Việt Minh infantry surrounded the valley, dug hundreds of trenches and attacked and destroyed all of the fortresses. Sixty-two French planes were destroyed and 30 canon, six tanks and 60,000 parachutes taken (*Le Courrier du Vietnam* 2004: 9). The French forces under Brigadier-General Christian de la Croix de Castries capitulated on 7 May 1954, only hours before the opening of negotiations on Indochina at the Geneva Conference.

The numbers of Điện Biên Phủ casualties are unclear, the French government refusing to give an official toll of deaths, wounded or missing in action. It is estimated that almost 11,000 French Union military personnel were garrisoned at Điện Biên Phủ, of whom 19 per cent were French regulars, 26 per cent Foreign Legionnaires of whom about half were German nationals (Mackenzie 2004), 19 per cent troops from French colonial Africa and 36 per cent Indochinese (including Hmong mercenaries) (Windrow 2004: 647).

It is further estimated that 2,000–3,000 French military personnel were killed in the fighting and 5,000–6,500 wounded (Simpson 1994: 169). The website of the Association Nationale des Combattants de Dien Bien Phu (ANC) (www.dienbienphu.org) indicates that 10,863 were captured. The prisoners were divided into groups of 50 and set on a 'long march' to jungle prisons and re-education camps near the Chinese border or in Thanh Hóa Province in central Vietnam (Simpson 1994: 170). Of these, according to the ANC, only 3,290 were liberated on 9 September 1954, the deadline for the release of POWs set by the Geneva Accord (www.dienbienphu.org). Some 7,573 were simply missing. It may be that more than 8,000 died in captivity, in which case the death ratio was around 60 per cent, 'a statistic to rival the very worst battles of the twentieth century' (Windrow 2004: 646–7).

Most of the prisoners were Vietnamese, Lao and Cambodian soldiers, however, and it was unlikely that the Việt Minh would have handed them back to the French authorities. Even so, there were still 2,350 French nationals and 2,867 Legionnaires unaccounted for (Advocacy and Intelligence Index for Prisoners of War-Missing in Action 2009). The anguish of French families and communities at the loss of their loved ones is understandable, made worse no doubt by the failure of the French political and military agencies both to foresee the disaster and to reveal the scale of the loss. For the French nation, Điện Biên Phủ was another symbol of acute soul-searching following on from the 1940 capitulation to Nazi Germany, the establishment of the Vichy puppet government and the collaboration with the Japanese in Indochina from 1940 to 1945. It foreshadowed the loss of Algeria, the Suez debacle and the rapid decline of French imperial power in the second half of the twentieth century.

Colonial nostalgia

Now, half a century later, it seems that for many French citizens it is time to move on. This seems especially true for the young, now more concerned with racism and related social problems in France, European unification and the transnational mobility and job opportunities that membership of the European Union provides, and universal concerns such as environmental sustainability and global warming (www.frenchamerican.org/cms/young leaders?nid=223). For others, however, the debacle at Điện Biên Phủ has been set aside and memories of colonial Indochina allowed to resurface with a mix of curiosity and pride. This restrengthening interest led to the reproduction by Éditions Kailash of the many novels written about colonial life and adventures in Indochina in the 1920s and 1930s, such as Pourtier's *Mékong* (1931, 1997) and Royer's *Kham, la Laotienne* (1935, 1997).

The fascination with colonial Indochina has been reflected in modern novels such as Catherine Cole's *The Grave at Thu Le* (2003), which revolves around an imaginary French family who lived in Hanoi but left after Điện Biên Phủ. In another publication Cole refers to meeting French psychiatrist François Lelord in Hanoi when she was researching her novel. She reports his view that a new post-postmodernist movement was forming in France, which he termed 'Nostalgie', a search ostensibly for 'something of themselves in their colonial past' but which is really a hankering after life in France, not the colonies, as it was in the 1950s – 'a kind of Jacques Tati place – uncomplicated but quirky – pre Algeria, Indochina, pre 1968 and the corruption of the '80s, certainly pre those pesky Muslim migrants who insist on wearing the veil' (Cole 2004).

A number of French television and cinema productions about Vietnam have reflected this nostalgia less critically (Biles *et al.* 1999). In 1992 Régis Wargnier's *Indochine* was released, for instance, with a plot focusing on a French plantation owner, played by Catherine Deneuve, who raises the child of Vietnamese nobility-cum-revolutionaries, a storyline that allows the 'mission civilisatrice' delusion of bringing peace and civility to the natives to be maintained. It was clearly not coincidental that the character played by Deneuve, who had been chosen in the 1970s as 'Marianne', the image of French womanhood for coins and medallions, was called Éliane, the name of the last French stronghold to fall at Điện Biên Phủ. In the film, events beyond her control conspire to undermine her hold on the plantation, the message being that the colonial intervention was misguided rather than fundamentally exploitative. The final scene is one of reconciliation between the protagonists on a terrace overlooking Lake Geneva, the sun setting in the background.

Jackel and Duverger (1993) comment that the film raises questions of cultural identity, of Frenchness and Vietnameseness, but it solves them 'through the recreation of a mythical and unproblematic colonial past based on an implicitly assimilationist model'. This was exactly the image that the French tourism industry began marketing when Vietnam opened up as an international tourism destination in the 1990s. By 1995 French arrivals reached almost 120,000, making France the largest source of tourists (PATA 1995: 62). Cultural products such as films and books clearly revived Vietnam in people's imaginations; they have also had a powerful influence on the meaning of heritage sites today.

Continuing grief

Nevertheless, for still many others, casting off the grief associated with Điện Biên Phủ has not been so easy. The need to revisit the battle emotionally is reflected in a continuing audience for books, films and television programmes and through tourism. The 1953 recollections of Geneviève de Galard were republished in 2003 and still appear on French bestseller Internet pages, clearly showing a continuing interest in de Galard's heroism – the 'Angel of Dien Bien Phu' – tending to wounded soldiers on the battlefield before being taken prisoner herself.

Another film that appeared on screens across France in the early 1990s – the docu-drama *Dien Bien Phu* (1992) – represents a less romanticized remembrance of Vietnam in the 1950s and a personal attempt by the director, Pierre Schoendoerffer, to come to terms with his own demons. Schoendoerffer was a veteran of Điện Biên Phủ, having been parachuted into the conflict zone, captured and imprisoned for four months. The film was apparently well received by audiences and critics in France but it had little distribution abroad. One of those impressed by the film seems to have been François Mitterand who, during the first official visit by a French president to independent Vietnam in February 1993, invited Schoendoerffer to accompany him on a tour of Điện Biên Phủ. According to one commentator (Simpson 1994: 180), the two men 'stood together at sunset at Dominique 2 while Schoendoerffer pointed out features of the now-peaceful terrain that had once been furrowed by shellfire'.

For veterans making pilgrimages back to places of pain and shame from their own past, it is often difficult to identify specific sites because the landscape has been transformed by economic development, changed settlement patterns and regrowth of vegetation. Under such circumstances the existence of memorials erected to remember those who fought and suffered in battle take on a special importance as the focus of the pilgrimage. However, construction of such memorials by any country is complicated when they are to be built outside the national territory. Building memorials within the territory of the former enemy is usually impossible, especially when political relations between the two countries involved remain cool. In the Điện Biên Phủ case France and Vietnam have been cooperating on the diplomatic front since 1973 and economically for 25 years, but, even so, resolving this issue of extraterritoriality needed considerable negotiation. For the French government to establish an official memorial at Điện Biên Phủ required Vietnamese government approval and no negotiations appear to have happened until as recently as the mid-1990s, angering veteran groups such as the Association Nationale des Anciens Prisonniers Internés Déportés d'Indochine (ANAPI).

Rodel's monument at Điện Biên Phủ

Instead, a French memorial was built at Điện Biên Phủ by one of the veterans, Rolf Rodel, acting as a private citizen. Rodel had commanded one of the Foreign Legion companies at Điện Biên Phủ and was wounded and captured defending Isabelle (www.dienbienphu.org). Not prepared to wait any longer for the French government, he obtained a small plot of land near the de Castries headquarters site and in 1994 constructed a simple memorial in the form of an obelisk within a walled enclosure (www.anapi.asso.fr/index.php) (Fig. 2.4). According to Nương Phượng Các, director of the Điện Biên Phủ Museum (interview, Điện Biên Phủ, January 2005), the memorial site was a gift from the Vietnamese government which recognized that Điện Biên Phủ was a place of pain for both countries.

In 1995, however, the French Defence Minister, François Léotard, presumably under pressure from ANAPI, asked Rodel to extend the memorial to 1,800 square metres, with expenses to be covered by the Ministry. By the time the extension was effected Léotard was no longer minister and Rodel was left carrying the cost. In September ANAPI met with President Jacques Chirac at the Élysée Palace and secured Léotard's promise to repay Rodel. ANAPI, with the help of other associations and donors, eventually paid Rodel fully. When Chirac visited Hanoi for the French-speaking world conference in November 1997 a side trip to inspect the Điện Biên Phủ memorial was included, with Rodel in tow. Rodel died in January 1999 before ANAPI could officially inaugurate the memorial. In June 1998 a maintenance agreement was signed between the French ambassador to Vietnam and the Lai Chau Province (www.dienbienphu.org/english/html/memory/memorial/ monum_dbp.htm). With the official inauguration in 1999 the memorial became an official French Republic monument, nearly 50 years after the battle. ANAPI now pays local people to maintain the memorial.

Further research is required into the reasons for this French reluctance to negotiate an official memorial at Điện Biên Phủ and to honour the dead and missing or even announce publicly their number. Indeed, other French government interventions were equally slow. It was not until 1989, for instance, that, after numerous campaigns by ANAPI, ANC and other groups and individuals, a law – the *loi J. Brocard* – was passed which recognized the

Figure 2.4 Rodel's monument at Điện Biên Phủ.

sacrifices made and accorded some rights to the survivors (www.dienbienphu. org). But it is in relation to the repatriation of the remains of Điện Biên Phủ's war dead that the French government seems to have been least successful, if not least active. Agreements between the two countries establishing protocols for such repatriation were signed in February 1955 and September 1986 (http://untreaty.un.org/unts/60001_120000/21/2/00040053.pdf). The second agreement led to the exhumation and repatriation in 1986–7 of more than 27,000 bodies from the Tân Sơn Nhất and Vũng Tàu cemeteries near the St-Jacques camp where the French military in South Vietnam had been located and from the Ba Huyen cemetery near Hanoi in the north. These were mostly French servicemen who had died during 1940–5 when Indochina was under Japanese control and in the Việt Minh war of 1946–54. It remains unclear whether any of France's dead from the Điện Biên Phủ battlefield and associated POW camps and military hospitals have been repatriated (www. memorial-indochine.org/3_en_memorial_projet.php). An American group, Advocacy and Intelligence Index for Prisoners of War-Missing in Action (AII POW-MIA) (www.aiipowmia.com/reports/exam5.html), claims that the French government paid Hanoi around $30 million over 20 years, via Hungarian banks, for the maintenance of French military graves and, in return, the Vietnamese periodically repatriated remains to France. If AII POW-MIA is to be believed, it seems that all these repatriated remains had been exhumed from French military graves and were already known to French authorities.

Pilgrimage to Vietnam, memorialization in France

Pressure from veterans' groups seems eventually to have led to a change in the French government's approach, especially in the 1990s, but diplomatic and economic factors were also important. With regard to the repatriation of remains, Task Force Omega Inc. notes that in 1971 the French Foreign Minister sought to finalize the problem of unaccounted-for POWs and MIAs from the First Indochina War (1946–54) by declaring them all officially dead and that, shortly after, in 1973, France resumed diplomatic relations with North Vietnam. Changes were occurring in Vietnam that made the re-establishment of official relations more urgent. Following the introduction of its *đổi mới* (renovation) policies by the Sixth Vietnamese Communist Party Congress in 1986, Vietnam was undergoing economic liberalization and its doors were opened to foreign investment. France, as in colonial times, wanted a share in trade and other business with Vietnam, a resource-rich country with a population of around 70 million in the early 1990s. At this time the French share of total foreign investment in Vietnam was running at only 5 per cent, behind a dozen or so other countries. Until 1994 the United States had placed an embargo on trade with Vietnam so that, for Vietnam, developing economic relations with other Western nations such as France was critically important.

When French tourists began visiting Vietnam after 1986, they comprised two main groups: the well-off, middle-aged 'globe-trotters' and the older, less affluent veterans, former settlers and their friends and families (Violier 1993: 54). Of course many French veterans are now, 20 years later, too old to make the journey back to Vietnam; instead, they continue to remember in France. Annual events and special anniversary celebrations and again memorials have become increasingly important and the official website of the Association Nationale des Combattants de Dien Bien Phu lists the local commemorative ceremonies at war memorials and the church services held in towns and cities across France between March and July each year. A special fiftieth anniversary commemorative ceremony was held at the Hôtel national des Invalides on 7 May 2004, at which President Chirac paid homage to those who fought and died there and presented 18 Légions d'honneur and a Médaille militaire (www.dienbienphu.org/commemo2004/index2.htm). Later in the day a mass at the Church of Saint-Louis des Invalides was celebrated in memory of the dead and missing in action and a wreath was laid at the foot of one of the monuments in the church – the Notre Dame d'Indochine.

There are now Indochina memorials scattered across France from Dijon to Brest and Dinan. The body of an unknown soldier from the Indochinese conflicts was buried at the Notre Dame de Lorette national cemetery near Arras in northern France in 1980. But it is the memorial at Fréjus on the Mediterranean coast of France that has become the main memorial site for French servicemen and women who died in Indochina. The memorial was established to deal with repatriations following the signing of the 1986 Franco-Vietnamese protocol. According to the memorial's official website, the city of Fréjus was chosen when it offered to donate a site; it had also been the site of a military camp for soldiers leaving for combat in the Indochina wars (www.memorial-indochine.org). The first stone was laid in January 1988 by Jacques Chirac, then Prime Minister, and the memorial complex was inaugurated by President Mitterand on 16 February 1993, just days after his visit to Điện Biên Phủ. The Indochinese connection is particularly reflected in the pagoda, monument and marine museum within the memorial complex. Within the cemetery there is an earlier Indochina memorial erected by a veteran's group in 1983, a wall listing all who died for France in Indochina, including Điện Biên Phủ, and a virtual wall for those wishing to access the memorial electronically.

Vietnamese attitudes towards suffering, death and memorialization

It is to be expected that the heritage values attributed to Điện Biên Phủ's cultural landscape by the victorious Vietnamese would differ sharply to the French. For the Vietnamese soldiers involved it was the site of a stunning Việt Minh victory over the colonial French forces. Although around 8,000 Việt

Minh soldiers were killed and 15,000 wounded (Simpson 1994: 169), the losses were quickly overlain by official messages of dedication and heroism. As Winphret Lulei, a Vietnam historian based in Berlin, noted, 'The image of thousands of non-combatants pushing bicycles laden with food and ammunition to the front is a lasting symbol of the conflict' (in *Outlook* 2004: 13).

For the Vietnamese, the Điện Biên Phủ spirit of self-sacrifice for the fatherland is encapsulated in the example of three martyrs – Bế Văn Đàn, Tô Vĩnh Diện and Phan Đình Giót – whose brave physical feats to help their comrades fulfil their common goals ended in their own deaths. These three are central to many stories about Điện Biên Phủ; they have become legends, part of the battle's intangible heritage and exploited in state propaganda aimed at drawing the Vietnamese citizens into the struggle for nationhood, national security and better living standards. Thus Điện Biên Phủ is now seen as a glorious milestone on the path to national independence and prosperity alongside the Bạch Đằng River battle of AD 938 when Chinese invading forces were turned on their heels (Taylor 1983: 269; MOCI 2000: unpaginated). This content is consistently reinforced through school syllabuses, stories in books, films and television programmes, picture collections and official commemoration ceremonies.

The Stories of People who Made History: Memories of Điện Biên Phủ 1954–2009 (Đào Thanh Huyền *et al* 2009), for example, records the memories of Vietnamese who had been involved in the battle as porters, nurses, doctors, journalists, soldiers or army commanders. While their most frequent memories are of the incredible hardship and constant fear that death could come at any moment, the contributors recall their past with excitement and pride. They express pain at having seen comrades killed, but none refer to the physical exhaustion and mental stress they no doubt experienced themselves. Of course, being an official publication, testimonies displaying other sentiments are likely to have been discarded. It is also possible that such memories were suppressed by those interviewed, downplayed as insignificant when compared to the overall victory.

Certainly alternative views have never been fully recognized and absorbed into the official picture of the battle. Although General Giáp had noted this battle fatigue and demoralization around mid-April 1954, the public admission of what he called the 'new phenomena' only appears in his 2001 memoir (Võ Nguyên Giáp 2001: 326). Remembrance of the past is crucial to the construction of a strong national identity for the Socialist Republic of Vietnam, and only certain kinds of memories are emphasized. This selective use of memories to form a national narrative supporting the state ideology becomes easier as alternate memories fade and disappear along with the generation of people who experienced Điện Biên Phủ first-hand.

Commemorating the Vietnamese dead, wounded and missing in action

Until the 1990s internal travel within Vietnam was restricted by a travel permit system and poor transport conditions. A trip from the capital, Hanoi, to Điện Biên Phủ normally took five days. This meant that few Vietnamese could go to remember the battle or grieve for lost family members at the place itself. It remained necessary, therefore, for memories to be transmitted at a remove from the site through films, pictures, school textbooks, books, memoirs, storytelling, museum artefacts and commemoration ceremonies in Hanoi and other Vietnamese towns and cities. As on the French side, film-making played a major role. The levels of funding were, however, vastly less than in France and film's contribution to focusing popular attention on the battle was less dominant, given the attention paid to the state's ideological interpretation of events in the media, school curricula and museums.

Commemoration ceremonies marking the Điện Biên Phủ victory have been considered since 1954 as among the most important public events in Vietnam. Large victory ceremonies, organized every five years, became occasions for bringing together senior political leaders and heroes to remember martyrs, praise significant contributions and sacrifices to the national independence cause, and express determination to overcome remaining difficulties (Đài truyền hình Trung Ương 2004). Activities to commemorate the Điện Biên Phủ victory are organized in schools, state-led institutions and mass organizations, and have taken on various forms, including parades, public performances, exhibitions, storytelling competitions and school camps. When television arrived in Vietnam, again tightly controlled by the political authorities, such events were staple fare.

In 1954 General Giáp's initial instinct had been to not keep the physical evidence of the war; instead he thought the soldiers' 'new task' was to return the plain to the local people for cultivation purposes (Võ Nguyên Giáp 2001: 386). Gradually, however, as transport links with Điện Biên Phủ improved, an increasing focus was placed on commemoration and celebrations at the battle site itself and its significance as national heritage has been formally recognized. The Ministry of Culture recognized the Điện Biên Phủ battle site as a national historical and heritage site in 1962 and extended the registration in 1981.

Conserving the war relics

According to a major provincial report dealing with investment, conservation, repair and interpretation of the battlefield (Lai Châu People's Committee 2002), at least six plans and associated projects were devised between 1959 and 1999 to conserve the vestiges marking the Điện Biên Phủ victory (Lai Châu People's Committee 2002: 2, 18–21). The first work aimed at commemorating the Điện Biên Phủ victory was undertaken in 1959 – the construction of a statue, called the Victory Stele, on the summit of the A1 hill. In 1984 a Điện Biên Phủ Victory Gallery House was opened; it was later turned into the current Điện Biên Phủ Museum, with its popular battle dioramas and artefact displays. Some of the most important physical remains were restored using authentic materials, including General Giáp's command headquarters at Mường Phăng 40 kilometres away, the vault used as de Castries' headquarters and the A1 hill.

However, since funding was limited, they had little lasting effect and early restoration work quickly deteriorated due to adverse climatic and management factors. As a consequence, in 1989 the Ministry of Culture and Information decided to restore again the most important vestiges, this time using durable materials such as reinforced concrete and cement shaped and patterned to emulate the original form and materials of the trenches and tunnels, bamboo huts and the sandbag walls of de Castries' vault (ibid.: 60). In 1999 VND2.3 billion (US$180,000) was spent for further urgent repairs to the four sets of remains considered to be the most important – Mường Phăng, de Castries' vault, A1 hill and the museum (ibid.: 32–3). However, for the fiftieth and fifty-fifth anniversaries of the Điện Biên Phủ victory in 2004 and 2009, an even greater conservation programme costing VND300 billion (US$23.5 million) was approved that included the construction of the new victory monuments and a new Điện Biên Phủ museum and the restoration of all vestiges again using durable materials (ibid.: 86).

There seems to be a belief that the physical remains of the battle are too simple to express the traumatic impact of war and the quasi-sacred value that the place has for veterans and the nation-state (ibid.: Appendix: Opinions of the Army's leaders). Instead commemoration ceremonies and educational activities are seen to play the major role in maintaining the battle's values as national heritage. Even so, the fear on the part of political leaders that revolutionary values are being eroded in contemporary Vietnam appears to be driving the recent emphasis on physical conservation of the battlefield. Whether the approach being taken will be successful in keeping Điện Biên Phủ alive in public memory and in regenerating the revolutionary spirit is yet to be seen. A concern is already being expressed that the recently restored vestiges do not satisfactorily convey the sacred feeling generally felt for the battle. One Điện Biên Phủ veteran visiting the historic battlefield is quoted as saying that he was 'sad, because the historic battle had left nothing, vestiges were roughly and carelessly restored … [so] how could our descendants when seeing [these vestiges] understand the historic battle' (Đào Thanh Huyền *et al.* 2009: 201).

The physical remains of any battle are never sufficient to reflect the complex meaning of the historic events that produced them, or the hardships, deaths, courage and trauma of people on both sides of a war. Their survival rate is also low. Heavy rainfall can quickly erase earthen structures such as trenches. Often stone and timber materials are removed, sometimes to aid in the reconstruction of surrounding settlements. At Điện Biên Phủ, the Cột Cờ stronghold on C1 hill ranked high in the memories of many Việt Minh soldiers. It was a point of intense and bloody combat between the Vietnamese and the French over a period of more than four weeks (ibid.: 216–31). Yet, just two days after the end of the battle for C1, General Giáp visited the site and could find no sign of the Cột Cờ (Võ Nguyên Giáp 2001: 381).

In the case of vestiges remaining today, especially those now engulfed by the town of Điện Biên Phủ, the basic spatial conditions and facilities for memorialization in ways appropriate to Vietnamese culture do not exist. In Vietnamese tradition, which reflects a Taoist and Confucian legacy from the centuries under Chinese political control and cultural influence, a sacred place is usually marked by a temple or a shrine housing an altar where people can burn incense and pray to their gods, heroes and ancestors. Most of the heritage places in Điện Biên Phủ disregard this tradition. Moreover, while the spatial elements of the battle were interconnected in 1954, and should remain so since they reflect interwoven events and shared emotions, there is no attempt to link them physically in the current heritage planning process. Each heritage place is protected by a buffer zone in isolation from the others in a way that makes it difficult to comprehend the scale of the battle.

The only exception where more sensitive management successfully supports the high level of feeling befitting the status of the battle is the Điện Biên Phủ cemetery adjacent to A1 hill (Fig. 2.5). Here, notions of courage and sacrifice are reflected in the solemn lines of soldiers' graves. Their names, on the graves and on the memorial walls, tie the graves to the soldiers' descendants. In Điện Biên Phủ, this is a rare place separated from the daily life of the town, where people can detach themselves from the present, remember the past and communicate with fallen heroes through the burning of incense and the performance of traditional ceremonies. In many ways the design approach resembles that developed by the Commonwealth War Graves Commission after the First World War, although the point requires further exploration to ascertain sources of design inspiration. The gate, statuary and incense burners provide the local Vietnamese design touch.

Meeting the interests of the state

While Buddhist South East Asia may generally prefer to 'forgive and forget', the importance of Điện Biên Phủ in supporting the state ideology and in nation building is clearly too great for such communal amnesia in Vietnam. Even though remembering the dead is essentially an activity carried on at the family altar (Hữu Ngọc 2008: 961), the Vietnamese government has constructed hundreds of war cemeteries across the country. It has also focused considerable effort on maintaining the spirit and meaning of the Điện Biên Phủ battle as a special tool for affirming personal sacrifice made for the fatherland and encouraging continued national solidarity and support for the

Figure 2.5 Cemetery at Điện Biên Phủ.

Communist Party which had led the people to victory and independence. This is typified by General Giáp's recent paper in the *Vietnamese Historical Journal* where he summarized the symbolic meaning of the battle, highlighting the sacred values that contributed to the Vietnamese victory:

> The strength which made the Điện Biên Phủ victory is the strength of the mass of the national solidarity, the strength of all the people, the whole nation … The decisive factor which led to the victory … is the leadership of our Party led by the great President Hồ Chí Minh. (Võ Nguyên Giáp 2004: 8–10)

This propagandization of the Điện Biên Phủ spirit has led to an emphasis on building heroic monuments, invariably in the heavy socialist realist style. Of these, the most impressive is the Victory Monument built atop D1 hill as part of the 2002 conservation plan (Fig. 2.6). The largest monument ever constructed in Vietnam, it is 12.6 metres high, sits on a 3.6 metres high base and is made from 220 tonnes of copper. Hailed as a great artistic success when inaugurated on 30 April 2004 to mark the battle's fiftieth anniversary, the

Figure 2.6 The Victory Statue.

rushed construction meant that building standards were not met and within two months of the inauguration, a period of heavy rain, sections of the monument's retaining wall sank or fell apart. Soon, too, the copper statue itself began to deteriorate due to the low quality of the metal used and poor construction techniques (Hạnh Ngân 2007). That this could happen to the most sacred and important national icon and coming so soon after the large and widely publicized fiftieth anniversary celebrations evoked much public criticism. At least 20 people, including the former President and two former Vice Presidents of People's Committee of Điện Biên province, and the former Vice Minister of the Ministry of Culture and Information, have been punished for their roles in the fiasco (Công Minh 2008; Đào Minh Khoa 2008).

Two other gigantic sculptural works were completed, in 2009, in the Mường Phăng Park that has been developed around General Giáp's headquarters and in Ná Nhạn village (Nguyễn Thu Thủy 2009). But not all are convinced that the larger the monument the greater its artistic or symbolic value. The celebrated painter Nguyễn Quân (2009) criticizes the current 'wave of monument building' as the product of the old-style thinking of leaders which considers 'building monuments is the only method to create propaganda art'. In his opinion, such thinking has its origin in the practice of the former Soviet Union in the period 1930–80. He points out that the traditional Vietnamese custom of praying contrasts sharply with the new commemorative practice of using monuments. In his view, the making of such a great number of monuments wastes money that could be put to better use improving public services or supporting the families of war veterans.

Meanwhile remembrance celebrations continue and seem to grow in scale. There is, however, some suggestion that traditional religious practices are being incorporated. On 18 July 2009, for instance, the official Day of Wounded Soldiers and Martyrs, a Great Requiem was held at the Victory Monument organized by the Điện Biên authorities and the Quảng Ninh Buddhism Board. Thousands of local people and Buddhist monks were involved, as well as representatives of General Giáp's family. The Vietnamese News Agency hailed the occasion as one 'for everybody to solemnly pay respect in front of the souls of heroic martyrs, who unhesitatingly sacrificed themselves for national independence and freedom, and made glorious victory' (TTXVN 2009). But to have allowed the monks such a central role was a return to more traditional practices and reflected the growing recognition by Vietnamese officialdom of the important place of religion in contemporary Vietnamese society.

Shifting attitudes: reconciling histories and heritage

This chapter has outlined the significantly different ways in which the French and Vietnamese who died at Điện Biên Phủ are remembered and memorialized. Factors explaining these differences include the contrasting outcomes of the battle for the two sides, the contrasting cultural attitudes to personal suffering, death, remembrance and memorialization, and the contrasting ways in which the two states, the Socialist Republic of Vietnam and the Republic of France, have sought to exploit the battle as part of their peacetime nation-building strategies.

The Vietnamese government has always led the memorialization process, although individual survivors continue to remember the battle and families remember their dead in the privacy of their homes. The official war cemeteries built across the country have designs not essentially different from those established by France and its allies in Europe and South East Asia following the two world wars, although the associated statuary is in the socialist realist style and Christian symbolism is absent. By contrast the French government preferred to close the page on a traumatic and embarrassing defeat and was only drawn reluctantly into active engagement in memorialization by the actions of an individual soldier, Rolf Rodel, supported by veterans' associations. This is not unusual: the dedication of individuals and veteran groups played a similar role at Long Tan, the Australian memorial site in southern Vietnam, and at Kanchanaburi and the Hellfire Pass on the Thai–Burma railway in Thailand (see Joan Beaumont's chapter, pp.19–40).

As the events of 1954 become more distant so it has been possible for Vietnam and France to leave behind their antagonism. Trade ties have been important to both sides, while Vietnam has benefited enormously from the growth in French tourist numbers. Rather than rejecting the colonial past, there is now an interest in protecting at least some of the French colonial buildings (Howe and Logan 2003: 249). Vietnam thus demonstrates very clearly the way in which notions of 'heritage' move with time and shifts in ideology. This is not to say that war sites and museums are likely to disappear from the Vietnamese scene in the foreseeable future; they continue to play too important a part in the state's nation-building strategy for that to happen. But it does mean that their interpretation is being softened, moving from a focus on the French colonial brutality to the heroism of the Vietnamese (Logan 2009).

France has continued to shower foreign aid on Vietnam as part of a concerted global campaign to prop up its political, economic and cultural influence in its former imperial territories. In 1997 France hosted the Seventh Francophone Summit in Hanoi in 1997, at the same time doubling its investments in Vietnam, inaugurating educational institutions whose curricula were delivered in French, refurbishing the Hanoi opera house and the National Library and National Archives Centre No. 1 and contributing to the construction of the new Museum of Ethnology. The presidential and prime ministerial visits in the 1990s were part of this campaign. Thus, President Mitterand visited in 1993 to 'lock onto a significant share of the Vietnamese market', one Vietnamese diplomat is quoted as saying (Hiebert 1993a). There was no doubt some personal motivation, too, since Mitterand had been in the French cabinet in 1954 and is on record as having said he would go to Vietnam one day 'to do justice to history' (ibid.). 'I am here to close a chapter, and even more so, to open another', he is said to have told his 1993 hosts (Hiebert 1993b), although the quotation is elsewhere attributed to the Vietnamese President, Lê Đức Anh (Journoud and Tertrais 2004b: 380). Vietnam's Foreign Minister completed the new script when he informed the press that the visit marked 'a complete reconciliation' between France and its former colony (Hiebert 1993b).

Back in the metropole meanwhile French historians were beginning to look again at the battle of Điện Biên Phủ and to reassess its significance, including its status in comparison with the Algerian war in the dissolution of the French Empire (Tyre 2008: 15). This built up to a flourish of academic activity around the fiftieth anniversary of the battle, with a large colloquium organized by the University Paris 1 – Pantheon-Sorbonne and the Ministry of Defence Centre for Defence History Studies (CEHD) in November 2003. Held at the École Militaire in Paris, it was attended by 300 French academics and students, high-ranking veterans, relatives of soldiers killed and École Militaire officers. There were five papers and a few attendees from Vietnam. The colloquium led to two publications by Journoud and Tertrais (2004a, 2004b), the first an edited collection of papers exploring the disjuncture between history and memory, the second a book focusing on the testimonies of survivors. Further colloquia were organized by University Paris 1 in Hanoi and Beijing. These were followed by the 2005 book *Dien Bien Phu, mythes et réalités 1954–2004 cinquantes ans de passions françaises* in which the authors, Alain Ruscio and Serge Tignères, conclude that the fiftieth anniversary celebrations in France were something of a swansong: 'time having done its inexorable work, this May 2004 was probably the last occasion, for the survivors in any case, to evoke the celebrated battle' (2005: 391).

What is left on the ground today at Điện Biên Phủ, and how is it interpreted? Apart from the small memorial instigated by Rodel and the cement bunker imitating de Castries' headquarters, there is little to tell the French story. In this respect, Điện Biên Phủ demonstrates Ryan's point, at least for the French side of the conflict: the battlefield remains silent, French stories of suffering are absent from the landscape and remembrance and memorialization have had to occur back in France. Even for many Vietnamese, the sense of authenticity has been lost, not only due to insensitive conservation approaches and the distortion of stories to fit the regime's ideology and political agenda, but also because of the priority given in provincial planning to the expansion of Điện Biên Phủ City into the hills, the very sites of the combat. The contestation between the Ministry of Construction and the much weaker Ministry of Culture in the planning process has been discussed elsewhere (see Logan 2006a, 2006b). This bears on the question of when states can begin to reuse hallowed ground, showing some arms of government placing small value on heritage conservation and pushing ahead with proposals that lack the sensitivity needed to allow heritage and new development to sit comfortably side by side.

In terms of the reconciliation of old enmities, the editor of the journal *Military History of Vietnam*, Nguyen Manh Ha, offers a way forward in his concession that the battle of Điện Biên Phủ is a 'bridge linking the past to the present and future', as it contributes to the renewal of Franco-Vietnamese relations: the extent of the losses experienced on both sides and the resulting pain have united the two countries in a single community of suffering (quoted in Journoud 2003). In Vietnam, the best hope for providing an interpretation of the events of 1954 in which the sensitivities of both sides of the conflict are taken into account may be in the reconstruction of the Điện Biên Phủ museum, which was proposed for 2009 (although still delayed at the time of writing) and at an estimated cost of VND360 billion (US$28.2 million). The ideological usefulness of the battle story in Vietnamese nation building may get in the way of this, however, and it may be that Vietnamese museums will never reach a point of being able fully to reconcile viewpoints about its national independence battles. The experience of the Hỏa Lò and other museums suggests that there is now hope that at least parallel stories can be told (Logan 2009). An important step towards seeing Điện Biên Phủ as a shared heritage will be for both Vietnam and France to move from promotion of the nation to the promotion of peace, from commemoration to education – a shift that is already occurring as the generations who lived through Điện Biên Phủ in 1954 inevitably pass away.

References

Advocacy and Intelligence Index for Prisoners of War-Missing in Action (AII POW-MIA). Online: www.aiipowmia.com/reports/exam5.html (accessed October 2009).

Association Nationale des Combattants de Dien Bien Phu (ANC). Online: www.dienbienphu. org (accessed 14 October 2009).

Biles, A., Lloyd, K. and Logan W. S. (1999) 'Romancing Vietnam: The Formation and Function of Tourist Images of Vietnam', in J. Forshee (ed.), *Converging Interests: Traders, Travellers and Tourists in Southeast Asia*, Berkeley: University of California Press.

Cole, C. (2003) *The Grave at Thu Le*, Sydney: Pan Macmillan.

Cole, C. (2004) 'The Third and Fourth Countries', *Griffith Review Edition 6 – Our Global Face: Inside the Australian Diaspora*. Online: www.griffithreview.com/edition6/109-essay/402.html (accessed 12 December 2009).

Công Minh (2008) 'Khởi tố nguyên Phó Chủ tịch UBND tỉnh Điện Biên' [Proceedings against Former Vice President of Điện Biên People's Committee], *Tienphong Online* 29 August. Online: www.tienphong.vn/Tianyon/PrintView.aspx?ArticleID=135243&Channel ID=12 (accessed 3 August 2009).

Le Courrier du Vietnam (2004) 'L'esprit de Dien Bien Phu vivra à jamais' [The spirit of Điện Biên Phủ will Live Forever], 9 May.

Đài truyền hình Trung Ương [Vietnamese Central Television] (2004) *Lễ kỷ niệm 50 năm chiến thắng lịch sử Điện Biên Phủ* [Commemoration Ceremony the Fiftieth Year Anniversary of the Historic Victory at Điện Biên Phủ]. Hanoi (television programme, recorded on VCD).

Đào Minh Khoa (2008) 'Đề nghị truy tố nguyên Phó Chủ tịch tỉnh trong vụ "rút ruột" tượng đài' [Proposal to Charge Former Provincial Vice President in 'Plundered' Statue Case], *CAND online*, 14 October. Online: www.cand.com.vn/News/PrintView.aspx?ID=101469 (accessed 3 August 2009).

Đào Thanh Huyền *et al.* (2009) *Chuyện những người làm nên lịch sử – Hồi ức Điện Biên Phủ 1954-2009* [The Stories of People who Made History – Memories of Điện Biên Phủ 1954–2009], Hanoi: Nhà Xuất bản Chính trị Quốc gia [National Political Publishing House].

de Galard G. (1953, 2003) *Une femme à Dien Bien Phu: récit* [A Woman at Dien Bien Phu: An Account], Paris: J'ai lu.

Hạnh Ngân (2007) 'Tượng đài Điện Biên Phủ đúc bằng đồng phế liệu?' [Was the Điện Biên Phủ Monument Cast from Scrap Copper?], *Tienphong Online*, 19 June. Online: www.tienphong.vn/Tianyon/PrintView.aspx?ArticleID=88383&ChannelID=3 (accessed 3 August 2009).

Hiebert, M. (1993a) 'Gallic Charm: France Seeks to Improve Ties with Former Colonies', *Far Eastern Economic Review*, 11 February, 12.

Hiebert, M. (1993b) 'French Dressing', *Far Eastern Economic Review*, 25 February, 10–11.

Howe, R. and Logan, W. S. (2003) 'Protecting Asia's Urban Heritage: The Way Forward', in W. S. Logan (ed.), *The Disappearing 'Asian' City: Protecting Asia's Urban Heritage in a Globalizing World*, Hong Kong: Oxford University Press.

Hữu Ngọc (2008) *Wandering through Vietnamese Culture*, Hanoi: The Gioi Publishers.

Jackel, A. and Duverger, X. M. (1993) 'Far from Vietnam', *Sight and Sound*, 3 (April), 23.

Journoud, P. (2003) *Paris, Hanoi et Pékin: trois colloques pour revisiter Dien Bien Phu, Genève et les relations franco-vietnamiennes depuis 1954*, Institut Pierre Renouvin electronic newsletter, 20 July 2004. Online: http://ipr.univ-paris1.fr/spip.php?article200#nh78 (accessed 20 October 2009).

Journoud, P. and Tertrais, H. (eds) (2004a) *1954-2004: la bataille de Dien Bien Phu, entre histoire et mémoire* [1954-2004: The Battle of Dien Bien Phu, between History and Memory]. *Actes du colloque de Paris, novembre 2003*, Paris: SFHOM.

Journoud, P. and Tertrais, H. (2004b), *Paroles de Dien Bien Phu: Les survivants témoignent* [Speaking about Dien Bien Phu: The Survivors Bear Witness], Paris: Tallendier.

Lai Châu People's Committee (2002) *Dự án đầu tư bảo tồn tôn tạo và phát huy giá trị khu di tích chiến thắng Điện Biên Phủ – Lai Châu* [Investment, Conservation, Repair and Value-enhancement Project of the Điện Biên Phủ Battlefield Complex – Lai Châu].

Logan, W. S. (2006a) 'Dien Bien Phu, Vietnam: Managing a Battle Site, Metaphoric and Actual', *Outre-Mers: Revue d'histoire*, nos 350–1 (special issue: 'Sites et monuments de mémoire), 1er semester: 175–92.

Logan, W. S. (2006b) 'Dien Bien Phu: Development and Conservation in a Vietnamese Cultural Landscape', *Electronic Proceedings, 'Cultural Landscapes in the 21st Century', 10th Forum UNESCO University and Heritage International Seminar, University of Newcastle-upon-Tyne, 11–16 April 2005* (revised July 2006). Online: http://conferences.ncl.ac.uk/unescolandscapes/files/LOGANWilliam.pdf (accessed 25 August 2009).

Logan, W. (2009) 'Hoa Lo Museum, Hanoi: Changing Attitudes to a Vietnamese Place of Pain and Shame', in W. Logan and K. Reeves (eds), *Places of Pain and Shame: Dealing with 'Difficult' Heritage*, London: Routledge.

Mackenzie, J. (2004) 'Forgotten German Veterans of France's Vietnam War', posted 2 May 2004. Online: www.militaryphotos.net/forums/showthread.php?t=13469 (accessed 25 August 2008).

Ministry of Culture and Information (MOCI), Centre of Monument Design and Restoration (2000) 'Conservation, Repair, Embellishment and Improving the Value of the Heritage Complex of the Dien Bien Phu Lai Chau Victory: Investment Project. Preliminary Research. Report Summary', Hanoi, unpublished report (in English).

Nguyễn Quân (2009) 'Nên tạm dừng xây dựng tượng đài đến năm 2020' [Call to Stop Construction of Monument until 2020], *VietnamNet*, 17 August. Online: www.vietnamnet.vn/vanhoa/2009/08/863883 (accessed 26 August 2009).

Nguyễn Thu Thủy (2009) 'Chiến thắng Điện Biên Phủ qua nghệ thuật điêu khắc' [Điện Biên Phủ Victory through Sculptural Art], *Hà Nội Mới Điện Tử*, 10 May. Online: www.hanoimoi.com.vn/vn/print/206640 (accessed 3 August 2009).

Outlook (2004) April, 13.

Pacific Asia Travel Association (PATA) (1995) *Annual Statistical Report*, San Francisco: PATA.

Royer, L.-C. (1935) *Kham, la Laotienne*, Paris: Éditions de Paris; republished 1997 Paris: Éditions Kailash.

Ruscio, A. and Tignères, S. (2005) *Dien Bien Phu, mythes et réalités 1954–2004 cinquantes ans de passions françaises*, Paris: Les Indes Savantes.

Ryan, C. (ed.) (2007) *Battlefield Tourism: History, Place and Interpretation*, Oxford and Amsterdam: Elsevier.

Simpson, H. R. (1994) *Dien Bien Phu: The Epic Battle America Forgot*, Washington DC: Brassey's Inc.

Task Force Omega Inc. website. Online: www.taskforceomegainc.org/freedom.htm (accessed 13 October 2009).

Taylor, K. W. (1983) *The Birth of Vietnam*, Berkeley: University of California Press.

TTXVN (2009) 'Đại lễ cầu siêu các anh hùng liệt sĩ Điện Biên Phủ' [Great Requiem Ceremony for Điện Biên Phủ Heroes and Martyrs], *Dan Tri*, 19 July. Online: http://dantri.com.vn/Print-338091.htm (accessed 3 August 2009).

Tyre, S. (2008) 'The Memory of French Military Defeat at Dien Bien Phu', in J. Macleod (ed.), *Defeat and Memory: Cultural Histories of Military Defeat in the Modern Era*, Basingstoke: Palgrave Macmillan.

Violier, P. (1993) 'The French Leisure Tourism Market in Vietnam', Paper presented to the 'Tourism Industry in Vietnam: Opportunities for Investment, Development and Marketing' International Conference, Ho Chi Minh City, 25–27 April.

Võ Nguyên Giáp (2001) *Điện Biên Phủ, điểm hẹn lịch sử - hồi ức do Hữu Mai thể hiện* [Dien Bien Phu, the Rendezvous of History – a Memoir Edited by Hữu Mai], Hanoi: Nhà xuất bản Quân Đội Nhân Dân [People's Army Publishing House].

Võ Nguyên Giáp (2004) 'Tinh thần Điện Biên Phủ sống mãi trong sự nghiệp của chúng ta' [The Điện Biên Phủ Spirit Lives Forever in our Cause], *Nghiên cứu lịch sử* [Historical Research Journal] 3, 3–11.

Windrow, M. (2004) *The Last Valley: Dien Bien Phu and the French Defeat in Vietnam*, London: Weidenfeld & Nicolson.

Chapter 3

War monuments in East and West Berlin: Cold War symbols or different forms of memorial?

Martin Gegner

Introduction

Twenty years after the German unification process in 1989–90 many social scientists (e.g. Deutsches Nationalkomitee für Denkmalschutz 2009) refer to the Berlin Wall as the key reference point for postwar German history. The wall is not only a symbol and physical manifestation of German separation between 1949 and 1989, it is also a symbol for the Cold War that followed the break-up of the Anti-Hitler coalition shortly after its victory in 1945. Though the wall is the most striking symbol of the Cold War, other signs and symbols of it – especially in Berlin – offer deep insights into the continuing politics of remembering in Germany. This city – as the former and new German capital – was for 40 years confronted severely with Cold War politics. This chapter investigates the political aesthetics and today's user sociology of a series of Berlin's architectonic monuments that are commonly considered symbols of the Cold War: Kaiser-Wilhelm-Gedächtniskirche and the Soviet cenotaphs in the Tiergarten, Schönholz and Treptower Park.

At first it seems strange to compare a church and three cenotaphs.[1] Yet these sites serve to open new perspectives on the practice of codification and recodification of architectural objects over time. While these monuments all commemorated the Second World War, when the Cold War intensified and threatened to turn into a third 'hot' world war these monuments were recoded to serve Cold War politics. In this they expose the fact that the political aesthetics of monuments are not one-dimensional, and are liable to change through public discussion, PR action and propaganda. The different layers of meaning cannot be hidden and interpretation might be reversed, deconstructed and reconstructed. As such, new forms of interpretation and meaning develop over the course of time.

Today, twenty years after German unification, both types of monuments also have in common the fact that they are no longer the focus of public awareness for either Berliners or Berlin's visitors. Today there are new monuments and new museums dealing with the special history of the German capital during the Second World War and the Nazi regime. The Berlin Wall is still of the greatest interest for those who try to understand the Cold War. But the wall, except for some hidden remains, does not exist any more. Kaiser-Wilhelm-Gedächtniskirche and the Soviet cenotaphs/cemeteries remain, and though the tower of the former requires significant conservation, these monuments will certainly survive in the near future.

Therefore, these two sets of monuments are good research objects to help understand which material political forms were used in the Cold War. This chapter is less interested in the artistic aspects of the ensembles than in their political and social interpretations. As such this research is focused on questions relating to how an 'official' public (re)constructs images, symbols and the significance of architecture and how an 'unofficial' public uses and views these monuments. They not only evidence different forms of Second World War memorialization, but show how their meanings are contingent on the politics of their creation. Furthermore, they can also hint at the conditions under which the Soviet Union and the Western allies accepted German unification. Finally, these monuments are important when appreciating the changed global position of a unified Germany after the end of the Cold War.

As far as the author is aware, these two types of monuments have never been compared and, similarly, contemporary sociological research on these monuments remains underdeveloped. The chapter therefore breaks new ground by attempting a comparison based on a sociological research that was conducted between March and September 2009.[2]

The Soviet cenotaphs

The Tiergarten cenotaph

History and political aesthetics

The Soviet monument in the Tiergarten, Berlin's 'central park', is special for war commemoration in Berlin for several reasons. First of all, despite the fact that it is a Soviet monument, it is situated in the former British sector which was part of West Berlin. Second, it was the very first war memorial erected, constructed in the autumn of 1945, soon after the end of the war, when relations within the Anti-Hitler coalition were still quite good. While Soviet troops had already withdrawn from Berlin's Tiergarten district, the British and the American military administrations supported the construction of this memorial. A competition for the design of the memorial had commenced in the Soviet Union in 1943 when the war turned in its favour (see Manina 1996: 475), and in late May 1945, only days after the German capitulation, the first preparatory work for the monument took place.

The cenotaph is located in close proximity to the Brandenburg Gate, the Reichstag, the Siegessäule – the Victory Column erected in memory of the Prussian victories over the Danish (1864), the Austrians (1866) and the French

(1871), and a symbol for the first German unification in 1871 – and the Reich Chancellery complete with the so-called Führerbunker, where Hitler committed suicide on 30 April 1945. It is built on the top of the former Siegesallee ('Victory Avenue'), that in the plans of the chief Nazi architect Albert Speer for the rebuilding of Berlin as the new capital for the Third Reich under the name of 'Germania' would have turned into the monumental 'North-South-Axis' that was to cross the 'East-West-Axis'.

This particular cenotaph was clearly constructed as a victory monument, not only because of its close proximity to the symbols of the German nation in general and the Third Reich in particular, but also because of its design (Fig 3.1). Two tanks, believed to be the first to reach the city limits, and cannons are located in front of the six semicircular granite columns that Mikhail Gorvits constructed. Despite popular belief, there is no definite proof that the granite was taken from the demolished Reich Chancellery (Köpstein 2006: 37, 38).

A larger-than-life bronze statue of a Soviet soldier stands atop this monument. While bearing an assault rifle on his right shoulder, his outstretched left arm and open hand declaim honour. Beneath the statue is the Soviet crest with a Cyrillic inscription stating: 'Eternal glory to the heroes who fell in battle with the German fascist occupiers for the freedom and

Figure 3.1 Soviet cenotaph in the Berlin Tiergarten.

independence of the Soviet Union. 1941–1945'.[3] German and English translations are inscribed on the outer columns. Lew Kerbel, the designer of the statue, describes the meaning of the monument: 'War is over. The soldier says farewell to his killed comrades and returns home' (Kerbel in Köpstein 2006: 16). This interpretation refers to the cenotaph's function as a cemetery. Soviet sources speak of about 2,500 soldiers buried here (Köpstein 2006: 42), and 200 are mentioned by name in the inscriptions on the six columns. Sarcophagi and urns further indicate the cemetery function.

Aesthetically and symbolically, the monument corresponds with Berlin's key landmark, the Brandenburg Gate, situated only some hundred metres eastward, and at that time marking the border between the Russian and the British sectors. Both monuments use columns and a victory statue in reference to peace only from the perspective of the victor. The neoclassical Brandenburg Gate with the Greek goddess of victory, Nike, on top was erected in 1791 to celebrate the battle victories of Prussian King Frederic II ('the Great'); the Soviet monument declares peace on the basis of the Soviet victory over Germany.

The monument was inaugurated on 11 November 1945 in the presence of high representatives of all the allies. The speeches of Marshall Shukov and General Lieutenant Telegin, leaders of the Red Army in Germany, stressed that the Soviet peoples and their soldiers shouldered the greatest burden in the defeat of German fascism. The victory was declared a globally historic moment and the Soviet dead were proclaimed heroes who had earned eternal honour. This reflected official doctrine in the USSR: *all* peoples of the Soviet Union had suffered from German aggression, and *all* had defeated the aggressor. Whilst within the Soviet Union it was the Russian population which suffered the most during the war and benefited most from victory, the smaller nations were also mentioned. Therefore, the victory over Nazi Germany played a critical role in the construction of a Soviet identity.

Apart from serving internal integration within the Soviet Union the monument was also to demonstrate to a defeated Germany that the Soviet Union now ruled their capital. Though the Allied Control Council of the four powers (Great Britain, France, the USA and USSR) was established as a shared supreme executive and legislative power in Germany on 5 June 1945, the Soviet authorities wanted to make clear that it was the Soviet Union that had freed Berlin from fascism. This was an undeniable motivation in building this cenotaph in the very (political) centre of the German capital. The Western powers never questioned this approach. As such, the inauguration of the Tiergarten cenotaph was also a demonstration of Soviet power within the British sector.

Only three years later, the 1948 Soviet blockade of the Western sectors of Berlin demonstrated that the Cold War was a reality. The building of the wall by the East German authorities in 1961 (one year before the Cuban missile crisis) raised the conflict to a new level and perpetuated the physical separation of the two German states which had existed formally since 1949. The closing of the borders by the wall had the effect that Soviet guards had to 'cross the wall' to reach the Tiergarten cenotaph, now a Soviet enclave in the British sector. From then on the annual wreath-laying ceremonies were attended only by the Soviet military and officials of the West Berlin communist parties. The other former allies did not participate and the Western public ignored these ceremonies. Located on the very edge of West Berlin, the cenotaph became for many West Berliners a symbol merely of Soviet occupation rather than of liberation. A 1955 official guide to the Tiergarten district artistic monuments and buildings does not even mention this Soviet cenotaph (Rave 1955). Even today the Berlin authority for monuments lists the Soviet cenotaphs as cemeteries but not as artistic monuments. Officially, they are 'testimony for Germany's unconditional surrender' (SenStadt 2009).

The geographical, social and political marginality of the cenotaph increased further after an activist of the NPD (*Nationaldemokratische Partei Deutschlands*, a party of revisionist Nazi supporters that still exists today) shot a Soviet guard at the site in November 1970. The soldier survived but the event caused major diplomatic collateral damage. The attacker failed, however, in his political aim to thwart the rapprochement policy of West Germany's Social Democratic chancellor Willy Brandt towards the German Democratic Republic (GDR) and the Soviet Union. All of Brandt's proposed treaties were ratified in 1970 and 1971. The assault did have other consequences though, and the British military administration in West Berlin surrounded the monument with an iron fence. The avenue in front of the cenotaph (formerly Siegesallee and East-West-Axis, now Straße des 17 Juni in remembrance of the East German workers' insurrection against the Communist government in 1954) was closed for 400 metres up to the wall in front of the Brandenburg Gate. The monument now lay in a no-go area between East and West. Only the Soviet guardsmen, guarded themselves by British soldiers, had daily access to the cenotaph. Until the fall of the wall, the monument occupied a nowhere land physically, and indeed in both Eastern and Western consciousness.

Soon after 9 November 1989 the monument was opened to the public again. A German–Soviet treaty conceived one year later saw the Federal Republic of Germany commit itself to the 'care and maintenance of the Soviet war cemeteries' (BGBL 1991: 708). In December that same year Soviet troops withdrew officially from the monument. From this day on the city of Berlin was responsible for the care and the security of the monument. Today, two to four guardsmen of the state police are permanently present at the monument.

In 1994 the complete withdrawal of Soviet troops from Germany was marked by wreath ceremonies at both the Tiergarten and the Treptow monuments. As legal successor to the Soviet Union the Russian Federation continues to conduct wreath ceremonies on 8 May (capitulation of the German Army in 1945), 23 February (Day of the Defenders of the Fatherland, formerly

Day of the Red Army) and on 7 November (Day of the Russian Revolution 1917, celebrated officially until 2005). Former Soviet states like Ukraine and Belarus sometimes take part in these ceremonies depending on the political situation in these countries (especially in relation to the degree of hostility or friendship expressed towards Russia).

Actual use in daily life

Today the Soviet monument in the Tiergarten is at the very centre of the city again. It has new 'rivals' in this area where monuments referring to wars of different epochs and places related to the Nazi regime are very dense. For example, the Soviet monument is located only a thousand metres from the Memorial to the Murdered Jews of Europe which was inaugurated in 2005.

Since it was opened to the public again in 1990 the Soviet monument in the Tiergarten has received an increasing number of visitors, reflecting the general rise in tourist numbers in Berlin. The monument is just a few hundred metres away from two major points of interest for tourists: the Reichstag and the Brandenburg Gate. Field research showed that in 2009 during the daytime an average of 160 tourists per hour stopped at the monument for more than one minute. Only 70 of these entered the complex and spent more than five minutes there. Of these tourists half spoke Russian. There was an average of 62 per cent of foreign visitors and 38 per cent German speaking.[4] The age distribution was very mixed. Though there were some older men (18 per cent), most of them Russian or English speaking, the majority of the visitors were young people (56 per cent).

Whereas most of the old men and also most of the young Russian-speaking families entered by the rear and carefully read the information boards at the back of the monument, the young visitors, especially when in groups, stayed in the vicinity of the weapons displayed at the cenotaph's entrance. Many of these climbed onto the cannons and tanks and had photos taken.

Those who were obviously consciously remembering the war (because they stood silently and still for some seconds in front or to the side of the monument) were in the minority. On average there were only nine individuals like this each hour. Some Russian-speaking parents were observed carefully explaining to their children (sometimes quite small) the inscriptions and answering any questions that arose. While there are always ten to twenty buses parked at this part of the Straße des 17 Juni, only an average of two (mainly German) organized groups visited the memorial per hour.

The described phenomena suggest that most Germans, when passing, consider the cenotaph as a reminder of the Soviet occupation and the city's separation rather than an anti-war monument. The gesture of the soldier, the tanks and cannons are symbols of the Soviet victory – and the German defeat. The nearby Reichstag and Brandenburg Gate, the strip where the Berlin Wall stood and the Memorial to the Murdered Jews of Europe are clearly more important for

German visitors. The lack of interest in the Soviet monument might also be understood in terms of the other monuments' higher and longer-lasting significance to a (positive rendition of) German history. Compared with the Reichstag and the Brandenburg Gate, the Soviet cenotaph stands for a relatively short and disesteemed period: defeat, occupation and separation.

Even the Memorial to the Murdered Jews of Europe is more popular amongst visitors. Moreover many visitors to this memorial's 'stele field' behaved as if they were participating in an accessible interactive abstract monumental piece of art and not at a monument that commemorates the biggest genocide in human history. They rest on the steles, they play, hide and contemplate in the labyrinth; some even eat their picnics on the steles. The abstraction seems to allow this use and younger visitors often do not seem to understand the intention of the monument.[5] Against an abstraction open to such diffuse decoding by visitors, the figurative Soviet monument with its grim bronze soldier and weapons is a concrete warning, leaving few options for interpretation. It shows that for more than 45 years Germany was not a sovereign state but dependent on the victors of 1945. More than any other place in Germany, Berlin was affected by the separation. The Tiergarten cenotaph is a symbol for the most powerful player of this game: the Soviet Union, in popular interpretation 'the Russians'. Whether the intended warning – never to start a war again – today is understood or whether Germans interpret the monument merely as a symbol for an ongoing Russian threat against them, this monument remains a barb in the political geography of the German capital.

Schönholz cemetery

Schönholz cemetery was the last of the three big Soviet war cemeteries built in 1948–9 in Berlin. It lies on the city's periphery in the north-eastern borough of Pankow. As this cemetery has seldom been used for official purposes it is not very present in Berliners' public conscience. Though Schönholz is a mass grave with more than 13,000 bodies, only about 20 per cent of the names of the buried – those who could be identified – are displayed. This is why Schönholz, of all the Soviet cenotaphs in Berlin, most exhibits the characteristics of a cemetery – a place for individual remembrance of lost relatives. The politics of the 'proper' commemoration of the 'war heroes' is and has been mainly carried out in Treptow. While the aesthetics of Schönholz, the architecture and the artistic elements, are similar to those of Treptower Park, the proportions are much smaller and the complex – more than the other monuments – has the character of a cemetery. One former Soviet soldier declared that 'Treptow is for everything official, for parades. Our soldiers lie in Pankow' (Krasnobajev/Krawzow in Köpstein 2006: 159).

The predominance of Pankow's use as a cemetery is why this monument is not investigated more here. In order to understand political aesthetics and Cold War symbolism, the cenotaphs in Treptow and the Tiergarten offer more information.

The Treptower Park cenotaph

History and political aesthetics

In late 1945 the Soviet Military Administration in Germany, SMAD, decided to build a central war cemetery for Red Army soldiers who lost their lives in the battle of Berlin in Treptower Park, a park south-east of the city centre near the river Spree. The call for tenders was published in October 1946, and asked competitors 'to erect a monumental historical memorial that eternalizes the remembrance of the killed Soviet soldiers and reflects the significance of the international liberation mission of the Soviet Army' (Manina 1996: 477). The competition, drawing fifty applicants, was judged in June 1947 in favour of architect Yakov Belopolsky and sculptor Yevgeny Vuchetich.

There are five main elements of the vast complex of about 200,000 square metres. First, two entrance gates in the style of classical triumphal arches stand to the north and south of the complex. Here the Russian inscriptions declare 'liberation of the homeland' and 'liberation of humanity'. The gates lead the way to a sculpture of a kneeling and bowing female named 'motherland'. Opposite her to the east almost 500 metres away sits the main sculpture: a 12-metre-high Soviet soldier with a sword in one hand and a child in the other. He is stepping on a broken swastika. The monument is situated on a grassy hill in the form of a kurgan, a typical pre-Slavic tomb common in Siberia and the southern Russian lowlands in the Bronze Age. Between the two sculptures and about 130 metres from the 'motherland' is a portal of two triangular marble Soviet flags. In front of them are two soldiers kneeling and bowing and holding automatic rifles (Fig. 3.2).

The route to the main sculpture comprises a 200-metre long and 100-metre-wide square divided into five grass squares symbolizing graves. They flank a central bronze wreath of around ten metres in diameter. The pathways around these are decorated with white ornamentals in the form of laurel on a red ground. On both sides of this central section are sixteen stone sarcophagi, five metres long and 3.5 metres high, one for each of the Soviet republics. Vuchetich also used artistic elements which remember specific events in Russian history related to the defence of the motherland against invaders from the West: Alexander Nevski's fight against the knights of the Teutonic Order and the battle against Napoleon. The monument, therefore, acknowledges the importance of all sixteen Soviet republics but claims a leading role for the Russian people.[6]

Each sarcophagus has two reliefs on its longest side. The reliefs show episodes of the war like 'occupation and resistance', 'hero towns', 'unique hero deeds' and Stalin quotations, on one side in Russian, on the other side the same text in German. Five thousand Soviet soldiers are buried in this cemetery but neither in the sarcophagi nor beneath the five squares. The graves instead surround the monument. Only four of them are buried in an individual grave.

Figure 3.2 The Soviet cenotaph in Treptow.

All the other soldiers are buried anonymously, though their names are mentioned within 'the book of honour' that is placed in the small mausoleum in the rotunda beneath the main sculpture.

The cenotaph was inaugurated on 8 May 1949. In contrast to the Tiergarten cenotaph inauguration neither representatives from West Berlin nor the Western allies were present. At this time the Cold War had reached its first peak. The Federal Republic of Germany (West Germany) would be founded only two weeks later on 23 May. In his speech the Soviet city commander of Berlin, Major General Alexander Kotikov, stressed that 'in the centre of Europe, in Berlin this monument will remind the peoples of the world permanently when, by whom and for what price victory had been gained … This monument in the centre of Europe is a symbol of the fight of the peoples of the world for socialism and democracy against the fire raisers of a new war' (Kotikov in Köpstein 2006: 152). Kotikov's speech insists that it was foremost the Soviet troops who liberated the world from fascism. From this approach derives the Soviet claim to its unique importance for political decisions in the centre of Europe. Kotikov also raises the danger of a new war, which can only refer to the former Western allies, and it is this political heritage of the Second World War that is also symbolized in the art and architecture of the Treptower Park monument.

Therefore the monument is a symbol for the lasting Soviet presence in the heart of Europe. The monumental approach that Kotikov had transformed into a verbal language speaks out clearly: we suffered most, we fought for our and your lives, we saved the world, we came here, we will not withdraw and we will never let an attack on us happen again.[7]

Kotikov repeated this sentiment in harsh terms when he was confronted with reports of local resentment against the monument: 'The dead that rest in foreign soil did not want the war, they would have preferred to stay with their wives and children. The monument shall also admonish the living not to begin a new war' (Kotikov in Köpstein 2006: 156). In the hard years after the war, when most Berliners suffered from hunger and the cold, negative feeling against the cenotaph was common. People asked why there was such a big investment in a cemetery when living conditions were so poor. Part of such resentment was surely also a response to this monumental demonstration of Soviet power in the German capital. This helps to explain why East German officials supported the dissemination of a story that Köpstein (2006: 106) calls a 'legend': that the main monument (the Soviet soldier with the child) is inspired by an incident reputed to have occurred in the last days of the war, in which a Russian officer, Nikolai Massalov, saved a little German girl from enemy crossfire during a firefight near Potsdamer Brücke. This and other similar stories have in fact been verified at different locations, with different 'heroes', yet there is no evidence of a direct link with the Treptow monument.

According to Helga Köpstein, an expert on the monument and generally Soviet-friendly, the combination of these 'true' stories with the Treptow monument must be regarded as a PR campaign aimed at improving (East) German–Russian relations. In 1964 Junge Welt, the biggest GDR newspaper with a readership of more than one million, launched a campaign to identify the little girl they called 'the girl from Treptower Park' and Nikolai Massalov, the officer responsible for saving her. In an article, journalist Rudi Peschel wrote that this story inspired Vuchetich's monument (Junge Welt 1965: 8). Even though Vuchetich rejected the suggestion several times it has still reached the (East) German consciousness as an historic truth (Köpstein 2006: 160, 170, 247). Today this story is not only told by taxi-drivers but also published on the Wikipeda site on the Treptower Park monument (Wikipedia 2009). This is an example of the recodification of an architectural monument, as historical truth and fiction merged in an attempt by GDR officials to offer an interpretation that allowed Germans to regard the monument as 'theirs'.

The character of the Treptow memorial is rather different from that of the Tiergarten cenotaph. Whereas that latter is a distinct victory monument, the Treptow monument intends to show that Soviet soldiers not only protected their homeland but also freed other peoples, including Germans, from fascism. It is also a distinct example of Soviet monumental architecture in the Stalinist style. Among an anonymous mass of dead fighters only four soldiers are mentioned by name, and though there is no sculpture of Stalin, the sixteen Stalin quotations also make it a monument to his personal cult.

It is hard not to be overwhelmed by the complex when entering one of the gates, passing the 'motherland' sculpture and turning into the monumental axis in the direction of the soldier. The intended emotional reaction of the visitor, a mixture of reverence for the dead and respect for, if not fear of, Soviet power, is hard to avoid, especially when visiting the monument for the first time. This is why this monument had a central place in official GDR politics. High government officials led ceremonies on the Day of the Liberation from Hitler Fascism, the Day of the Soviet Army and the Day of the Russian Revolution, and during visits of high-ranked Soviet delegations a wreath ceremony in Treptow was mandatory.

Soviet delegations themselves were deeply impressed by the monumental power of the Treptower Park cenotaph. Khrushchev, after visiting the Treptow monument, ordered an equivalent monument to be built in the USSR (Köpstein 2006: 158). This was built between 1959 and 1967 on the Mamajev hills in Stalingrad. Until the erection of this monument – again by Belopolski and Vuchetich – there had been no war monument in the USSR comparable in size and artistic expression to the Treptower Park cenotaph. There are two reasons for this: first, Soviet leaders had to deal with extraordinary hardships among their people. But, second, it is also quite clear that to them it was absolutely necessary that the Berlin war monuments in Treptow and Tiergarten be constructed as impressive political symbols. They were symbols of the moral and physical victory after pain and endurance, a warning against Germany and the West, and a sign of Soviet (fighting) power. So it was important that first in Germany, the land of the besieged, a war monument using these specific artistic and architectonical expressions be erected, before a similar yet grander and greater in scale expression, the 'Cenotaph for the Heroes of the Battle of Stalingrad' be constructed on the Mamajev hills. Here, the statue of 'Mother Home' stands 52 metres high, the biggest statue in the world.

Because of its Cold War history, the Treptow monument especially became very controversial. After the fall of the wall Soviet war veterans feared that the remembrance of Soviet sacrifice would be endangered in a unified Germany. This fear strengthened when on 28 December 1989, only six weeks after the fall of the wall, Nazi and anti-Russian graffiti were sprayed on the sculptures in the complex, mainly on the sarcophagi. An anti-fascist demonstration of leftist parties against this violence demanded better security and decisive state action to protect the monuments. Officially the GDR still existed (until 3 October 1990) but state order was weak and the police barely acted against neo-Nazi activists. Official protective action came with an amendment to the earlier German–Russian treaty, in which the Federal Republic of Germany agreed to care for the Soviet monuments. Nevertheless restoration work at the Treptower Park cenotaph did not commence for a further eight years.

The official departure of the last Russian troops (by which time the Soviet Union had already disintegrated) from Germany, on 31 August 1994, was accompanied by a final major wreath ceremony at Treptow, in which 1,200 Russian and 600 German Bundeswehr soldiers paraded in front of German Chancellor Helmut Kohl and Russian President Boris Yeltsin. Provisional restoration work concealed the poor state of the monument's conservation. Meanwhile Soviet veterans, alarmed by the state of the monument, asked for the deconstruction of the complex and its restoration in Moscow. The Russian Duma appealed to the Bundestag in April 1998 to realize the responsibilities of the German–Russian treaty and to take care of the monuments. On 1 September the same year, German celebrities led by Green politician Renate Künast published an 'appeal for the maintenance of the Soviet cenotaphs'. Finally in late 1998 restoration started. In 2005 all the main elements at Treptow had been restored, and today it remains physically in a good conservation condition. A problem that is only vaguely under control is the use of the cemetery as an ordinary park by many Berliners and tourists.

Actual use in daily life

Official activity in the GDR alienated the German population – sceptical from the beginning – from the Treptow cenotaph. People from the neighbourhood used the vast park area but avoided the monument. Only the passage between the north and the south gate remained in constant use, often as a direct route from the riverside to the neighbourhood south of Puschkinallee. Others interpret the monument as part of the park and go there to have a picnic or to sunbathe (Fig. 3.3).

Police regularly patrol the monument twice a day, but are not present continuously. Officers report that there are always incidents of disrespectful behaviour like those mentioned above (Gegner 2009a). As no penalties are given even the presence of police does not prevent these incidents from occurring.

Whereas the local population uses the Treptower Park monument principally for leisure, a growing number of (young) Western tourists visit the site with an interest in Stalinist architecture. In their eyes this ensemble, the most significant Western example of Soviet monumentalism, is viewed as 'great' architecture, though in describing it as 'totalitarian' interviewees express the same unease that afflicts buildings from the Nazi era, such as the Olympic stadium or Tempelhof airport (Gegner 2009b). The cemetery function of the complex is also undermined by its monumental form, as visitors, German and Western foreigners, often do not recognize the site's commemorative meaning for former Soviet people as a place of burial and remembrance for their war dead. To be fair, this shows the difficulty that younger generations with no direct link to the Second World War have in decoding (anti-)war memorials. If there is no explicit mediation via script,

Figure 3.3 Reinterpreting a war memorial: picnic at the Soviet cenotaph at Treptow.

picture or multimedia such monuments probably present a too concrete (with respect to the physical presence of the monument) experience and are too abstract (with respect to the memorial function) to be understood in the time of the Internet generation. This can be observed by the fact that 'classic' and well-made exhibitions on the Second World War, such as the former Museum of the German Capitulation (now Deutsch-Russisches Museum) in Berlin-Karlshorst lack public attention.[8]

Kaiser-Wilhelm-Gedächtniskirche

History and political aesthetics

In contrast to the Soviet war memorials in Berlin, the Kaiser-Wilhelm-Gedächtniskirche (KWG) (Emperor Wilhelm Memorial Church) had a previous political and clerical history and significance before it was turned into an anti-war memorial in the aftermath of the war. The significance of the church (especially for West Berlin) cannot be understood without a knowledge of the history of the earlier, 'first' Kaiser-Wilhelm-Gedächtniskirche.

In the last decade of the nineteenth century when Berlin rose to become a metropolis of more than four million inhabitants, the Evangelical State Church built a series of new churches to provide the increasing number of Berliners with clergy services. The new Emperor, Wilhelm II, generously supported these efforts, and the construction of the Kaiser-Wilhelm-Gedächtniskirche was one of his highest concerns. Wilhelm II supported the idea of having a clerical memorial to his grandfather, Emperor Wilhelm I, that aimed to connect religion and the German state. The new Emperor wanted monumental architecture to ensure this church functioned as a national symbol. The architect, Franz Schwechten, used Romanesque Revival-style elements which best matched the Emperor's architectural taste. The church was planned and built on the former Auguste-Viktoria Platz, today Rudolf-Breitscheidt-Platz, the undisputed heart of West Berlin. In addition to the church's construction the surrounding streets were built with highly representative business and residential buildings in the Romanesque Revival style.[9] Like other Berlin churches from that era, the church was built on a traffic island, surrounded by the busy thoroughfares of Kurfürstendamm, Tauentzinstraße and Budapester Straße.

The interior of the church is unique: aside from the usual clerical equipment the entrance mosaics and reliefs not only show the (battle) story of the Hohenzollern, house of the Prussian kings and the Emperor's ancestors, but also important scenes of the Wilhelm II government. Never before and very seldom later had there been so many signs and symbols of profane power placed in a church, let alone images of a living ruler. The aim, of course, was to present Wilhelm II as an Emperor by divine right.

The church was inaugurated on 1 September 1891. On 22 January 1943 Allied bombs damaged the church badly. The nave was completely destroyed, but the bell tower, though much of it remained standing, was ruined.

After the war the KWG *Stiftung* (foundation) responsible for the church and the Berlin city authorities struggled with what to do with the church given its very prominent location. An entirely new church was one option. A reconstruction of the church in the old style was also seriously discussed. A poll by the Institut für Markt- und Verbrauchsforschung of Freie Universität Berlin on 14 May 1959 found 52 per cent of Berliners favoured a full restoration of the church. To some extent this reflected the views of conservative elements of civil society who did not want to erase one of the last remaining architectural symbols of the empire in Berlin (Siedler et al. 1964: 79).[10] On the other hand many contributors to the discussion like the later West German President Gustav Heinemann sought to maintain the ruined tower as a warning against war and a symbol of the desire for peace (Deutschlandradio 2008). Further, and more dramatically, planners in the Berlin authorities considered the church ruins as a traffic block and, in the spirit of 1950s modernism, wanted to use the square as a gigantic traffic interchange.[11] In Berlin, as in many cities, modernist planners destroyed old fabric that survived the damage caused by the war. This modernist planning spirit is represented by Berlin's city conservator Hinnerk Scheper, a Bauhaus scholar, who was proud of not submitting KWG to Berlin's conservation laws (Frowein-Zieroff 1982: 338).

In 1955 the city and the KWG *Stiftung* finally organized a competition with the aim to (re)build a church on the square. In this sense the church foundation gained a victory over the city. With the church remaining in the Breitscheidplatz the foundation wanted to show that 'the church is in the middle of the world, that it is a counterpoint of the leisure and business world around' (Baumann-Wilke 1988: 55). However, critics also warned the church foundation:

> the church stands 'in time' … it stands in the middle of today's city centre, and its future form will be a symbol for the spirit that rules the reconstruction of Berlin. The form it will take is not only a matter for the church community, it is a matter for the whole of Berlin and for each citizen, for everything that is built today will remain in the eyes of posterity. (Kulturkreis im Bundesverband der Deutschen Industrie in Baumann-Wilke 1988: 46)

In this mood the jury of the competition rejected the idea of Werner March, architect of the Berlin Olympic stadium, to build an imitation of the old church.

In 1956 the competition committee decided that all nine competitors in the first round, including Egon Eiermann, the later winner who submitted two proposals, did not match the goal to integrate the tower into a new ensemble. Eiermann was then asked to revise his plans. Even in this revision, as a convinced modernist, he planned to destroy the partially ruined tower. Meanwhile the wider public in West Berlin vigorously debated the future of this city space, and it was ultimately they who saved the ruins. The liberal newspaper *Tagesspiegel* launched a campaign to save the tower and, together with West Berlin's *Berliner Morgenpost* and *BZ*, claimed that in a (non-representative) poll on 24 March 1957 almost 90 per cent of Berliners wanted the tower retained.[12]

Whether representative or not, authorities and planners refused to disregard public sentiments so soon after formal democracy had been established in

(West) Germany. This part of the KWG's history is an example of the politics of buildings in the public interest and the extreme importance of this process when it concerns national symbols and urban images.

Eiermann was asked to revise his plans a second time. He finally, though not convinced, agreed to integrate the ruined tower into a new ensemble in acknowledgement of public opinion. Eiermann then decided to surround the surviving tower with an octagonal main building and a new tower (Fig. 3.4).

Figure 3.4 Integration of a ruin into modernist architecture: side view of Kaiser-Wilhelm-Gedächtniskirche.

This integration of the old ruin corresponds with the similar architectural solution chosen for the cathedral in Coventry (that had also been badly damaged) and the separate construction of cathedral and campanile in many northern Italian towns like Florence and Pisa. The KWG should, of course, also have its history compared to that of the Frauenkirche in Dresden (see Tony Joel's chapter, pp.197–218) that remained a ruin for decades.

The new KWG ensemble was inaugurated in December 1961, some months after the Berlin Wall had been erected by the GDR authorities. One year later, with the Cuban missile crisis, the Cold War reached its peak. The combination of old and new in the Kaiser-Wilhelm-Gedächtniskirche has to be judged in this context. At the laying of the cornerstone in 1959 Bishop Dibelius, in the presence of (Crown) Prince Louis Ferdinand of Hohenzollern, emphasized the historical continuity of the old tower ruin within the new Kaiser-Wilhelm-Gedächtniskirche.[13] During the inauguration he also referred to the current political situation: 'Our brothers and sisters in the East again have to suffer the loss of freedom. Will we in West Berlin also have to endure this?' (Dibelius in Baumann-Wilke 1988: 112). The architect referred to his work on the same occasion as 'the most Eastern and because of this location most important contemporary Christian building' (Eiermann in Baumann-Wilke 1988: 113). The KWG, as a symbol for historical continuity or restoration, had now turned into a symbol of resistance against communism. The combination of the old and the new seemed to represent the fragile contemporary political situation. But it is important to realize that this shift in meaning was not evoked from the architecture itself but from the contemporary discourse, from the speeches of the architect and the principal. For the next three decades anti-communist symbolism remained the dominant interpretation of this multi-layered architectural ensemble.

Kaiser-Wilhelm-Gedächtniskirche was always open to different interpretations. This shows the democratic character of the ensemble of old and new and the different historical layers. This 'openness' could also lead to the misdirection of blame and war guilt. Although in popular perception the tower ruin has always been interpreted as a peace monument, there were no distinct official signs and attributions, especially with respect to the guilt associated with the Second World War. From the 1950s to the late 1960s the war generation in Germany generally refused to admit any personal responsibility for supporting Hitler and the war. Collective guilt had been rejected in favour of blaming Hitler and high-ranked Nazis solely. This changed only in the aftermath of 1968 when many students accused their parents of being Nazi supporters or at least inactive in the resistance. But still it took almost twenty more years for the acknowledgement of blame to be integrated in the Kaiser-Wilhelm-Gedächtniskirche. This is no coincidence. It was only into the late 1980s that former radical left-wing students became integrated in the political system through the SPD (Social Democratic Party) or the new Green Party. It was the end of the 1980s when they first gained political power, and when an acceptance of German guilt was entering mainstream attitudes.

When the memorial hall at the bottom of the tower ruins opened in 1987 it reflected the ambivalence of public politics by the end of the 1980s. Glasnost and Perestroika were opening up ground for reconciliation with the Soviet Union; the Cold War was ending, and Willy Brandt's Entspannungspolitik (policy of détente) had become a reality. On the other hand the ruling conservative chancellor Helmut Kohl had proclaimed that German society needed a spiritual–moral turnaround (geistig-moralische Wende) which had been interpreted by some as a call for greater conservatism. In this context German historian Ernst Nolte (1987) published his revisionist book *Der europäische Bürgerkrieg 1917–1945. Nationalsozialismus und Bolschewismus* that accused Soviet communism of being a predecessor of Nazism and to a large extent its real cause. This book led not only to the Historikerstreit (historians' dispute), but is still influential in the discussion of the causes and the crimes during the displacement of Germans from territories that are now Polish, Russian and Czech (for example in the actual discussion of a Museum for the Displaced). This is the political context in which the opening of the memorial hall must be seen.

The memorial hall exposes the Emperor's reliefs and the Hohenzollern mosaics. In order to prevent the place from becoming a kitschy and comfortable remembrance space for reactionaries, two distinct peace signs were introduced: first, two crosses, one made from nails found in the ruins of Coventry Cathedral, the other an Orthodox cross from Volgograd (formerly Stalingrad); second, the church's new nave bears the so-called Madonna of Stalingrad, a picture that a German soldier drew on Christmas Day 1942 during the battle of Stalingrad. This picture – which has sometimes been interpreted by right-wing political groups as a unique symbol of German suffering – and the two crosses link Kaiser-Wilhelm-Gedächtniskirche with two other sites of wartime loss and destruction: the devastation of Coventry by German bombing, and the turning point of the war, the defeat of the Sixth German Army at Stalingrad.

Though these two sculptures are rather small in the dimensions of the memorial hall, their integration interrupts the possible enthusiasm for the golden Hohenzollern mosaics and the reliefs of the imperialist empire that led to the First World War and to a certain extent also to the Second World War. In particular the Coventry nail-cross makes clear that it was the Germans who attacked their neighbours and that when the war turned and drew its direction to Germany after the Stalingrad defeat in early 1943, Germans were only about to endure what their enemies had suffered in the first three years of the war: massive bombing of their cities and invasion of their countries along with all their horrible successors including rape, killing and looting.

All this demonstrates that Kaiser-Wilhelm-Gedächtniskirche was never a simple, one-dimensional anti-war memorial; it was always ambivalent. It could also be read as an accusation of the Western allies who had bombed this church, as well as civilian targets across Germany. Because of the danger of fomenting anti-Western sentiment, a vast majority of experts, competition contributors and official commentators in the 1950s were in favour of the destruction of the tower ruin.[14] They did not want the Western allies accused of war crimes. In the Cold War the Americans and the English were 'the good guys' for official West Germany. So from the 1950s to the 1980s official rhetoric saw KWG as an abstract symbol of Berlin's suffering, both during and after the war. Here it could stand as a 'symbol of the free Berlin' (Baumann-Wilke 1988: 64), or a 'platform of Western civilization against communist indoctrination' (Engert 1987: 76). The distinct and direct reading as an anti-war memorial was only made possible with the opening of the memorial hall in 1987 (the year of the city's 750th anniversary). With the late integration of the Orthodox cross from Volgograd and the Coventry nail-cross and the opening of the old foyer, West Berlin authorities now made a statement about who was responsible for the war itself.

Actual use in daily life

When the Kaiser-Wilhelm-Gedächtniskirche was founded it had been in the centre of the Western city (at that time the independent town of Charlottenburg, today a Berlin district). With the separation of Berlin after 1949, and especially with the construction of the wall in 1961, Rudolf-Breitscheidplatz on which KWG is situated became the very centre of the half city of West Berlin. Though always the rich residential and commercial district, West Berlin lacked historical buildings. Where the Mitte district, with the Unter den Linden boulevard and the Museumsinsel (museum island), was in the East, the church became a symbol of West Berlin.

Near the KWG on the famous Kurfürstendamm boulevard shop chains, luxury hotels, restaurants and cafés developed. The very square around the church became a meeting point for tourists, dropouts, homeless and societal outsiders. In the aftermath of 1968 the square had been used for demonstrations of all kinds. Often there were violent clashes between demonstrators and the police. Breitscheidplatz was the public space of the West Berliners and the must-see attraction for visitors of all kinds; KWG was its symbol.

Since reunification of the city this has changed. KWG has been marginalized in public consciousness: the key city symbols are located in the former East, and KWG has become a symbol of the old West Berlin. The Mitte district has resumed its place as the centre of business and shopping. Tourists first of all visit the Museumsinsel and the alternative scene has changed to the former Eastern districts such as Friedrichshain. Whenever TV stations show images of Berlin, it is now the Reichstag or the Brandenburg Gate, sometimes the Fernsehturm (Television tower, at Alexanderplatz) Berlin's highest building, but not the KWG.

Nevertheless, today KWG is still situated on a very vivid square, it is still the focus of the Western districts of the unified Berlin and each day about 6,000 people visit the church and the memorial hall, far more than visit the Soviet cenotaphs in the East (including the central Tiergarten monument). Yet KWG's particular meanings are not so easily read in its new political and geographical context. The church community – a small one in comparison to others in Berlin – exploits this continuing popularity by renting the church's surrounding spaces to publicity and marketing stalls of all kinds. Though the square has always been used by all kinds of groups this reveals a very 'unholy' atmosphere. On one side of the entrance to the memorial hall is an Asian snack shop, on the other side a lady sells fresh food from all over the world. For an entrance to an anti-war memorial hall this seems somehow disrespectful.

The hall itself is open daily from 9 am to 7 pm. It is fairly crowded at all times. There are guided tours and the foyer is noisy. Most tourists enter the hall in casual wear, they take photos and very often talk loudly. The main focus of interest is the golden, ancient-lookalike mosaics on the ceiling. The nail-cross and the orthodox icon cross at the side of the foyer in front of a window that looks out onto the busy Kurfürstendamm are not only at the edge of the room, they are also at the edge of most visitors' attention. Though some of them read the inscriptions, attention is also distracted by the view from the window (Fig. 3.5).

Figure 3.5 Inside the memorial hall of Kaiser-Wilhelm-Gedächtniskirche.

The placement in front of a window discourages any iconic remembrance of the crosses. The whole impression of the hall is that of a post-modern gathering of relics from different times and places that have nothing in common. There is also a differentiated interpretation of the various parts of the church. Whereas the old part is an anti-war memorial, the new parts have always been interpreted as a symbol of Berlin's reconstruction. The entire ensemble with the mixture of old and new offers a complexity of interpretations.

In the new church itself, this is different. The deep blue glass mosaics create a ceremonial atmosphere and because of their thickness they also protect the octagon from the noise outside. This atmosphere transforms the Madonna of Stalingrad into a reliquary. The picture is kept on a hidden side of the octagon in the form of a shrine. It is a remembrance of the suffering of German soldiers in Stalingrad. The contrast between the dignified remembrance inside the church's octagon and the somewhat unhappy presentation of the Coventry and the Volgograd crosses in the foyer are questionable. It is obvious that the usage of the KWG as an antiwar memorial had good intentions but has not been planned and put into action very thoughtfully. The use of the church's surroundings as a flea market is often criticized by the Berlin public. The church community nevertheless claims that due to a lack of support from the Landeskirche (regional church) and the city of Berlin they require this income in order to maintain the tower, which is in a poor structural condition. In fact state support decreased dramatically after 1990 while other restoration projects, for example that of the Museumsinsel, gained hundreds of millions of euros in federal money. The decay of the public image of KWG is a direct outcome of its political and cultural marginalization among Berlin's public. The end of the Cold War and Germany's unification put the popular antiwar attitude expressed through KWG behind official new monuments like the 2005 Memorial to the Murdered Jews of Europe and the 2010 'Topography of Terror' museum in the very centre. Today the question of how the unspecific antiwar character of KWG can be restored or even communicated more precisely remains open. The image of KWG today is that of an indifferent anti-war monument.

Conclusion

Cold War politics dictated strict binaries that shaped commemoration of the Second World War in Berlin. Both the Soviet cenotaphs and the Kaiser-Wilhelm-Gedächtniskirche at the same time present different forms of memorialization of the war and stand as symbols of the Cold War. Loaded as they are with unanswered questions of guilt, shame and blame relating both to the Second World War and to the Cold War that followed, they are not easy memorials to interpret. Those questions were embedded in these memorials from their inception. The Soviet monuments memorialize the war from the victor's perspective. They are a warning to the German people. Yet at the same time, these memorials existed as signs of Soviet repression during the Cold War, and have never been truly accepted by the German public they addressed. The KWG's multi-layered history also defies simple interpretation. Though the tower ruin stands as an unspecific antiwar memorial, a specific expression of German guilt has long been hidden. Even today the signs of reconciliation – the two crosses from Coventry and Volgograd – are in danger of being undermined by restorative and revanchist interpretations within the memorial hall. The remembrance of Wilhelm I as the 'good' old emperor and of Allied bombing as a war crime threatens to overlay this specific anti-war significance. Here again, from 1950 until the 1980s, the church was also reinterpreted as a symbol of a renaissance of Berlin and resistance against Soviet suppression.

What these memorials show clearly is that interpretation of the Second World War in Germany has been, and remains, subject to deep political struggle. But it seems that today, twenty years after the German unification this series of monuments, as symbols of global Cold War politics, is of rather marginal interest to historians, art historians and archaeologists intent on exploring the more specific German history of the Cold War, including the division of Germany, the Berlin Wall and the history of the GDR as a whole. These are the new 'brands' in the 'commemoration industries'. The breakdown of the Cold War's political binary after 1990 has opened the field to closer investigations of the experiences of German people themselves in the two states of divided Germany. Researchers no longer seem interested in the 'big narrative' of the Cold War represented by the Soviet cenotaphs and the Kaiser-Wilhelm-Gedächtniskirche, as new monuments and museums on war, holocaust, displacement and terror regimes absorb public awareness.

Certainly today GDR history, revisionist interpretations of the Second World War and its aftermath for the German population occupy the main arenas of the public discourse on contemporary history, and are heavily contested by different interest groups in post-unification Germany. Major research centres like the Forschungsverbund SED-Staat (Research Network SED-state) dominate the discussion on Germany's recent past, and their agenda is rather to blame German communists for crimes committed in the GDR than to analyse the structural logic of a (propaganda) confrontation in the Cold War, which is represented by Kaiser-Wilhelm-Gedächtniskirche and the Soviet cenotaphs. Yet we should not ignore the overarching conditions and contests in which these emerging histories and heritage forms are located. The architectonic ensembles examined here are outstanding examples of a contested history in Germany that continues to resonate and remake itself, and they expose the importance that political powers assign to the political-aesthetical coding and recoding of architectonic signs and symbols in a battle for the 'right' public interpretation.

Notes

1 The Soviet cenotaphs are considered as one type of monument to be compared with Kaiser-Wilhelm-Gedächtniskirche though one has to assume several distinctions between the three monuments.
2 Each monument was observed once a month for one hour. Quantitative and qualitative data was collected, for the latter mainly using the methods of Visual Sociology. Six expert interviews with policemen at the Treptower Park and Tiergarten monument and with two visitor service men at Kaiser-Wilhelm-Gedächtniskirche were conducted.
3 All translations from German or Russian to English have been made by the author.
4 These figures refer to those observed speaking. About 12 per cent of visitors observed, mostly those who visited alone, did not speak.
5 Fearing this effect, German parliamentarians decided to integrate a large Holocaust information centre within the memorial.
6 The sixteenth republic at that time was the Karelo-Finnish Republic. In 1956 the Karelo-Finnish SSR had been integrated as an autonomous SSR in the Russian Socialist Federative Republic.
7 This approach is still dominant in the official Russian evaluation of the war, also the 'less heroic' parts like the separation of Poland according to the Hitler–Stalin Pact (Putin 2009).
8 During public holidays, when no school classes are obliged to go there, the Museum sometimes hosts only ten visitors per day.
9 For instance, where today one will find the high-rise Europa-Center, an early shopping centre from the 1960s, before the war there was a Roman-style building in which the Romanisches Café was located, the meeting point of intellectuals in the 1920s. The Europa-Center today is also on Berlin's conservation list as being representative of 1960s modern architecture.
10 The ruins of the almost entirely destroyed Stadtschloss (city castle) in East Berlin had been demolished in 1950 and replaced in 1973 by the GDR's Palast der Republik (Palace of the Republic), that itself had been demolished from 2000 to 2008 by the authorities of the unified Berlin. By vote of the Bundestag, the German parliament, the Stadtschloss will now be rebuilt with its ancient façades. The discussion on this process is one of the main topics of the local Berlin public and will continue in the near future.
11 An assumption that recalls modernist attitudes in the 1920s. Sigfried Kracauer considered the Kaiser-Wilhelm-Gedächtniskirche 'in the daytime nothing more than a huge traffic block' (Kracauer 1930 in Frowein-Zieroff 1982: 336).
12 One could call this an early act of basic democracy or populist action. It shows the power a local newspaper still had at that time.
13 Dibelius also refused to change the name of the church, a proposal that had also been made by the church's community (Baumann-Wilke 1988: 34).
14 On the other hand GDR officials in the case of the Dresden Frauenkirche had no ideological problem with identifying the Anglo-American bombing as a war crime, an interpretation that is still very popular within nationalist, revanchist and Nazi groups (see Tony Joel's chapter, pp.197–218).

References

Baumann-Wilke, Sabine (1988) 'Die Kaiser-Wilhelm-Gedächtniskirche von Egon Eiermann in Westberlin', Diss.-Schrift Hochschule für Bildende Künste Braunschweig.
BGBL-Bundesgesetzblatt (1991) 'Vertrag über gute Nachbarschaft, Partnerschaft und Zusammenarbeit zwischen der Bundesrepublik Deutschland und der Union der Sozialistischen Sowjetrepubliken. Unterzeichnet am 9. November 1990 von Dr. Helmut Kohl und Michail Gorbatschow in Moskau', Bonn: Bundesanzeiger.

Deutsches Nationalkomitee für Denkmalschutz (ed.) (2009) 'Die Berliner Mauer. Vom Sperrwall zum Denkmal', Schriftenreihe des Deutsches Nationalkomitee für Denkmalschutz Bd. 76/1. Bonn.

Deutschlandradio (2008) 'Diskussionen um die Kaiser-Wilhelm-Gedächtniskirche in Berlin', Track 4 in *Geschichte zum Hören 1958. Weltausstellung, Ostermarsch und Nabokovs 'Lolita'*, Compact Disc ISBN/EAN/UPC 123456789012, Berlin: Audire.

Engert, J. (1987) 'Die Spaltung Berlins', in J. P. Kleihues (ed.), *750 Jahre Architektur und Städtebau in Berlin. Die internationale Bauausstellung im Kontext der Baugeschichte Berlins (Ausstellungskatalog)*, Stuttgart: Hatje.

Frowein-Zieroff, V. (1982) *Die Kaiser-Wilhelm-Gedächtniskirche. Entstehung und Bedeutung.* Beiheft 9 der Schriftenreihe Die Bauwerke und Kunstdenkmäler von Berlin, ed. Senator für Landesentwicklung und Umweltschutz, Landeskonservator, Berlin: Gebr. Mann Verlag.

Gegner, M. (2009a) 'Interview with two Policewomen at Treptower Park cenotaph', 16 June.

Gegner, M. (2009b) 'Participatory Observation and Interview of US-American Youth Visitor Group', 16 June.

Junge Welt (1965) 'Die mutige Tat des Nikolai Massalow', *Junge Welt* 8/9 May 1965, S. 7.

Köpstein, H. (2006) *Die sowjetischern Ehrenmale in Berlin*, Berlin: ROSSI.

Manina, A. (1996) 'Sowjetische Denkmäler für Moskau und Berlin', in I. Antonowa and J. Merkert, (eds), *Berlin-Moskau. 1990–1950*, Munich and New York: Prestel, 475–8.

Nolte, E. (1987) *Der europäische Bürgerkrieg 1917–1945. Nationalsozialismus und Bolschewismus*, Frankfurt am Main: Herbig.

Putin, V. (2009) 'München war der Sündenfall. Nicht erst der Hitler-Stalin-Pakt ebnete den Weg zum Krieg', Aus dem Brief des russischen Ministerpräsidenten Wladimir Putin an die Polen. Translated by Vlada Philipp. Frankfurter Allgemeine Sonntagzeitung, 6 September 2009, 9.

Rave, P. O. (ed.) (1955) *Die Bauwerke und Kunstdenkmäler von Berlin, ed.* Landeskonservator Hinnerk Schepper, Berlin: Verlag Gebr. Mann.

SenStadt – Senatsverwaltung für Stadtentwicklung (2009) 'Friedhöfe und Begräbnisstätten. Sowjetische Ehrenmale'. Online: www.stadtentwicklung.berlin.de/umwelt/stadtgruen/friedhoefe_begraebnisstaetten/de/sowjet_ehrenmale/index.shtml (accessed 1 September 2009).

Siedler, W. J., Niggemeyer, E. and Angreß, G. (1964) *Die gemordete Stadt: Abgesang auf Putte u. Straße, Platz u. Baum*, Berlin: Herbig.

Wikipedia (2009) 'Soviet War Memorial (Treptower Park)'. Online: http://en.wikipedia.org/wiki/Soviet_War_Memorial_(Treptower_Park) (accessed 13 September 2009).

Chapter 4

'Inevitable erosion of heroes and landmarks': an end to the politics of Allied war memorials in Tarawa?[1]

Judith A. Bennett

Sites of wartime death and commemoration are vulnerable to the machinations of governments because they are affective loci for people of the states who have lost their young citizens. The passing of years and veterans alters the emotional significance of memorials in foreign lands and they become less artefacts of their times than active texts of current political agendas. At Tarawa, an atoll in the Gilbert Islands of about 23 square kilometres, commemoration and strategic interests have remained deeply interlinked since the fighting that occurred there during the Second World War. This chapter traces the patterns of growing and receding interest in marking Tarawa as a site of war heritage, and the complex and not always complementary strands of commemoration practised by former allies and enemies. Tarawa, a British colonial microdot, became a site of memory, where new meanings were emplaced on the landscape, with little reference to the indigenous occupants who suffered not only multiple invasions but also destruction of their environment (Greider and Garkovich 1994). If commemoration at Tarawa remains politically and strategically significant, then there are also stronger forces that may see the erosion of all landmarks, including memorials to the war dead.

War comes to the Pacific

Isolated and unremarkable until the war, the Gilbert Islands had been a tiny British protectorate since 1892, but Tarawa first entered the United States' mental geography in late 1943, as the first but costly amphibious landing of a major fighting force on a coral atoll. Because the American public was unprepared for their heavy losses, this engagement made a deep impression on social memory as well as operational history and tactics. Graphic film footage and photographs of the carnage in newspapers and magazines were among the earliest that Americans saw of the Pacific conflict (Alexander 2008). The war also cost Islanders' lives while the battle left environmental scars, visible and invisible.

Tarawa's strategic significance derived from its occupation by Japanese forces as part of a series of fortified islands intended to defend Japan's rapidly and vastly expanded frontier after December 1941. After a first, brief invasion in December

1941, the Japanese returned as occupiers in September 1942 to resist Allied forces that were now counterattacking in the south-west and central Pacific. While most of the few European residents managed to get away, those who chose to remain, including seventeen New Zealand Coastwatchers, were taken to Betio, an islet on the western side of Tarawa. They did not remain long: following American air attacks on Betio on 15 October, the enraged Japanese shot two civilians and appear to have beheaded the New Zealand Coastwatchers, the British Government Dispenser and one Australian attached to the British Fijian military. Later, in 1943, they executed an Australian based at Butaritari. Their bodies were never found (McQuarrie 2000: 99–103; Tonkin-Covell 2000: 278). Meanwhile, the Japanese heavily fortified Betio and, though only 2.26 square kilometres in area, constructed an airfield on the dogleg-shaped atoll. This base stood across the path of the Americans who were planning to attack the Japanese in the Marshall Islands and then go on to the Mariana Islands in order to regain the Philippines.

On 20–21 November 1943, the Americans landed on Tarawa with the largest invasion force assembled until that time in Operation Galvanic: 17 aircraft carriers, 12 battleships, 8 heavy and 4 light cruisers, 66 destroyers and 36 transports. A number of errors made capturing Betio harder than the Americans thought, the worst of which were misreading the tides and the tight fortifications of the Japanese. In spite of advice offered by former long-time residents that the best day to attempt a landing would be 15 November, the commanders decided on 20-21 November, the time of a neap tide which was unpredictable and could be lower or higher than the normal high tide. It was lower, which left the Higgins boats carrying the landing force of Marines stranded at the edge of the apron reef 600–1,000 yards from their objective. Men had to wade ashore across the reef and lagoon, exposed to heavy fire. They captured Betio and the rest of Tarawa but at huge cost. Of the 5,000 Marines who landed on the first day, 1,000 died and 2,200 were wounded. Overall, 1,600 Americans were killed and, except for 17 prisoners, about 4,700 Japanese and Koreans also died (Bennett 2009: 19–20) (Figs 4.1, 4.2).

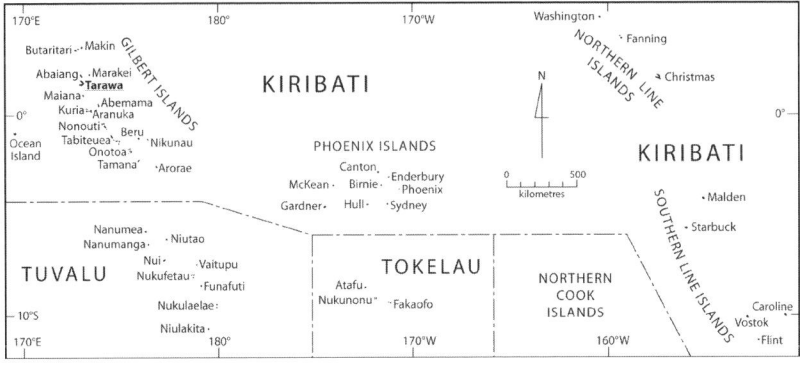

Figure 4.1 Map of Kiribati and Tuvalu, formerly Gilbert and Ellice Islands.

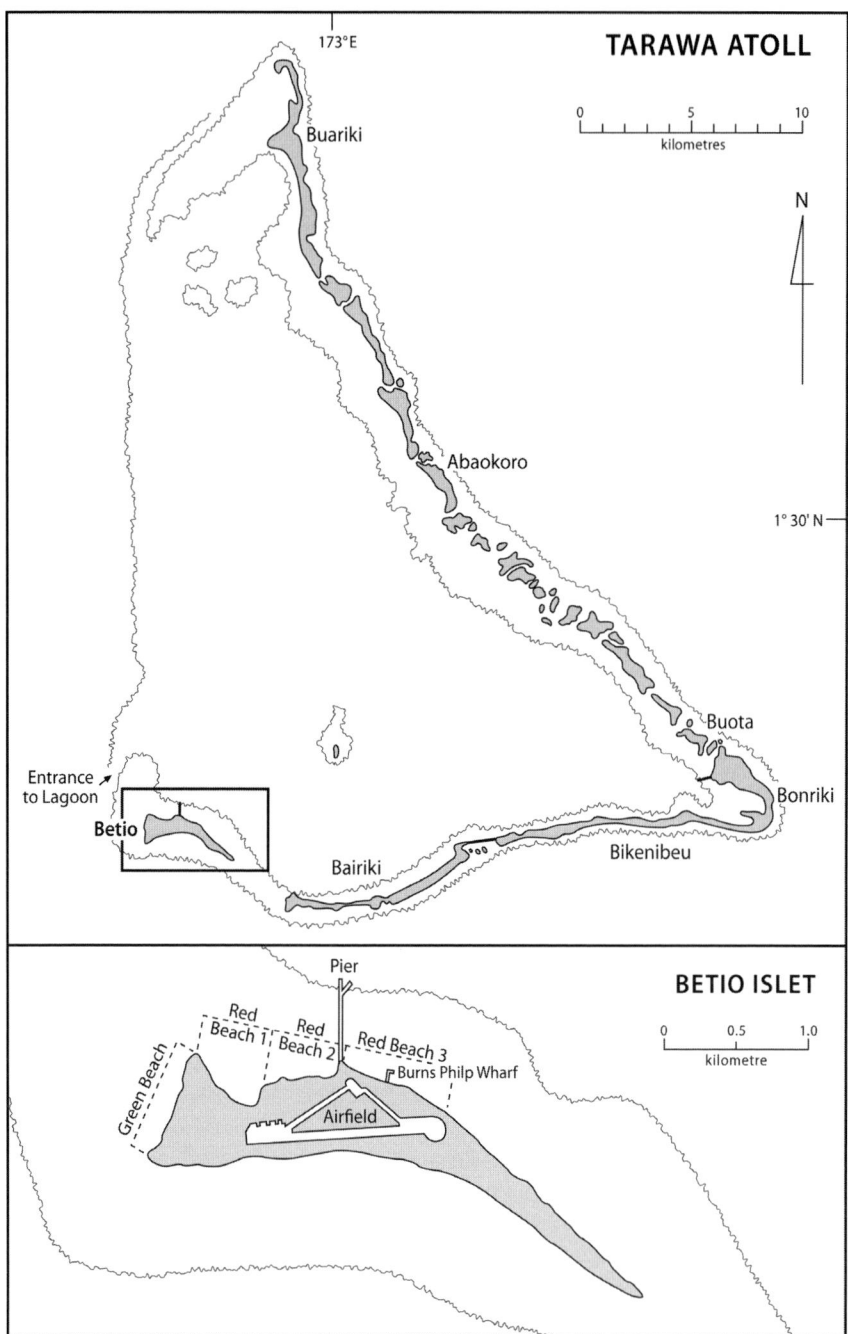

Figure 4.2 Map of Tarawa Atoll and Betio Islet in wartime.

Tarawa: whose significant place?

Ignorant of the realities of combat and the abilities of the Japanese as fighters, the American public were shocked at the scale of casualties and the explicit images of dead Marines (Alexander 2008). For them, a tiny Pacific islet suddenly became a focal point of the global conflict. This costly success had given the United States, 'a new name to stand beside those of Concord Bridge, the "Bonhomme Richard", the Alamo, the Little Big Horn, and Belleau Wood—the name Tarawa' (WPA 1968a). Tactically, Tarawa taught lessons to the military about amphibious assaults, Japanese fortifications and the need to heed local intelligence. Loaded with feelings of both loss and triumph, 'Tarawa' as a place assumed a near legendary status and meaning in US military history.

Immediately after the battle, Betio was covered in dead bodies. Journalist Robert Sherrod, who landed with the Second Marine Division, observed that 'no one can imagine the overwhelming, inhuman smell of five thousand dead who are piled and scattered in an area less than one square mile' (Sherrod 1944: vi). Burial was a necessity. The British District Officer who administered civilian matters organized a labour corps of more than 1,000 Gilbertese men, under the control of the New Zealand army officers, to work for the Americans who were now in command (McQuarrie 2000: 144–5; Bennett 2009: 142). They consigned the Japanese to a mass grave near the airfield. The living hurriedly buried the American dead close to where they fell in 43 small cemeteries or individual graves (Steere and Boardman 1957: 400). In late 1943 the Americans erected a memorial to the 22 executed British subjects with a cross made of coconut palm (Ellis 1946: frontispiece, 172, 187–8; *Pacific Islands Monthly*, December 1946: 42, September 1949: 74). A diplomatic gesture, it also had a political motive, smoothing the often-strained relations with the British administration.

After the front moved north, the Americans stationed at Betio tidied the several cemeteries, planted colourful shrubs, erected fences and marked the graves with inscribed crosses. By 1945, the Americans had attached several small memorials to the larger cemeteries where some of their dead from smaller plots had been 'consolidated', though often with loss of indicators of identification (Sherrod 1946: 20). Betio had assumed a double meaning in memory as a massed graveyard and a memorial to all the American dead, many hundreds of whom were not found. Other island battles, such as Peleliu and Iwo Jima, soon eclipsed Tarawa in American losses, which became just one among many battlefields of the Pacific War. For those who fought and survived the battle of Tarawa, as well as the families of all involved, however, its significance as a place loaded with intense emotions of grief, courage and pride would endure, even as its original intensity of meaning diminished in public.

The war in the Gilberts, particularly on Tarawa, also had significance for its own people. Oblivious to global politics pre-war, most derived a living from relatively sparse local resources: some sold copra dried from coconuts or earned cash as contract workers on the phosphate atolls of Nauru and Banaba. The uninvited war killed about 730 people at home as well as stranded workers on the islands. It also damaged in-shore fisheries and obliterated 2,000 of their *babai* pits, dug with great effort over the years from the coral stratum for the growing of the staple root crop, *babai* (*Cyrtosperma chamissonis*). The conflict also destroyed over 60,000 coconut palms as well as many pandanus trees, key providers of food and shelter (WPA 1947; McQuarrie 2000: 171–2; Jones 1951).

Less immediately obvious environmental damage was slowly mounting. The principle of overwhelming military strength depends on reserves, often in excess of actual need. Thousands of tons of this matériel and its embodied energy were wasted or 'surplus', left to litter land, lagoon and ocean floor (Bennett 2009: 179–97). And the people of the Gilbert Islands and the rest of the world had no idea the earth's atmosphere was warming, gradually causing sea levels to rise as a result of processes exemplified in the terrifying sample of industrialized conflict that invaded their beaches.[2]

Dealings in emotional landscape

Soon after the American landing, Tarawa's dual loading as a cemetery and a memorial with wider political implications became clear. Remembering the dead rapidly assumed overt political overtones for a series of interested parties. In December 1943, Lord Halifax, the British ambassador in Washington, had suggested that the King of England should present Tarawa to the United States 'as a tribute' to the dead and, in an area where Britain's own military forces were non-existent, to reinforce American commitment to regaining Britain's Pacific territories. Governor of Fiji, Phillip Mitchell, who as British High Commissioner for the Western Pacific was responsible for the administration of the Gilbert Islands, had already been on Betio on 5 December 1943. Seeing burials still going on, he decided that none of the 400 local residents should be allowed to return as 'it must become anyhow [a] war cemetery' (TNA 1942; TNA 1943a). Added to this was the physical devastation: 'Every palm tree has been destroyed or so badly damaged it will die. Every building is a heap of debris. So many are buried here that the superstitious natives would probably not return anyhow.' Mitchell supported handing over Betio, but not the entire island cluster of Tarawa. He noted that: 'We cannot give away two or three thousand British subjects, without their consent or obtain it without the most awkward publicity. And they might say no.' Mitchell developed a schedule of payments for the Betio landowners and planned to resettle them on Rabi Island in the Fiji group where the people from another of the Gilbert group, Banaba (Ocean Island), were to be resettled because of pre-war damage to their lands from British phosphate extraction. Mitchell neglected to seek the opinion of the Betio people, however. He enthused over the modified plan and even proposed an additional gift to the

Marines of six silver bugles made in London to sound the last post on Betio. Long an admirer of the Americans, he telegraphed the British Secretary of State indicating that the 'gift of Betio to be a national memorial to the United States forces in Pacific will give very great pleasure' (WPA 1943a).

The Australian and New Zealand governments were much less sanguine about the idea. They were preparing for a meeting about the future of the South Pacific in January 1944 in Canberra. On the agenda was their strong objection to any continuing US presence in the South Pacific (with the exception of American Samoa) following the peace. Australia and New Zealand aimed to maintain the South Pacific's pre-war status, as a 'British' lake (Wood 1958: 310–20; Kay 1972). Consequently, the Australian government replied that ceding Betio to the United States, 'might easily lead to embarrassment and misunderstanding, and could be used to prejudice both Australian and New Zealand interests' (TNA 1943b). The New Zealand government also thought that gifting Betio would be unwise:

> The admission of the principle of cession of British territory, whether it be inhabited by 3,000 or 30 natives, even for the most laudable reasons of sentiment, does open the door to similar action in the Pacific in the case of other Islands or points of strategic aviation or other economic interest. (WPA 1943b)[3]

Ironically, at Tarawa and Butaritari in mid-1944, the Islanders, impressed with American technology and generosity, had themselves asked for an exchange of control from Britain to the US, but when it came to high policy no one was listening to them and the movement soon dissipated. Whoever originated the idea, any decisive transfer of Allied territory was put on hold while the war continued (Macdonald 1982: 157–60).

The issue resurfaced as the Pacific War drew to a close in 1945. The balance of power in the South Pacific and, indeed, the world was shifting. The fall of British Singapore in February 1942 had shown Australia and New Zealand that Britain had been unable to protect them. The Canberra Pact of January 1944 wherein Australia and New Zealand declared their own Monroe doctrine for the South Pacific had not pleased the United States. But by mid-1945, the British Foreign Secretary opined that the Australians 'are feeling less alarmed as to American imperialism in the [South] Pacific than they were in January 1944', but believed that the Australian Minister for External Affairs, H. V. Evatt, would still not support the transfer of Tarawa to the United States (TNA 1945a). There had been calls in the American House of Representatives for this because for 'the cream of America's youth … Tarawa is their memorial'. The United States could exert some leverage beyond symbolism. With the end of the war, Britain lost the economic support of American lend-lease and instead was seeking a major loan from the United States. The US Secretary of State, James Byrnes, in discussion with the British Foreign Secretary on 3 May 1946, suggested:

the United Kingdom government should make an immediate announcement of their readiness to cede to the United States the Island of Tarawa ... the scene of one of the most glorious actions of the United States Marines during the war, and that its cession to the United States in memory of that action would make a deep impression on public opinion ... it ... should materially assist the proceedings in Congress on the Loan.

Knowing the earlier stance of Australia and New Zealand, the Foreign Secretary advised Byrnes that they would likely be unsupportive and that such proposals for cession 'ought only to be considered as part of a general scheme for common defence or in accordance with the security arrangements devised under the procedure of the United Nations' (TNA 1946a). Britain still got its loan, in July 1946.

By late 1945, Australia and New Zealand wished to maintain close ties with Britain but wanted another powerful friend in the Pacific and had even considered allowing one or two American bases to remain because they realized that alone they could not have defeated Japan (Firth 1999: 12; McKinnon 1993: 52). So when the Commonwealth prime ministers met in May 1946, Evatt's views had moderated. He stated that Australia was 'willing to set aside some area of the island for the United States to use as a memorial'. Since New Zealand had lost Coastwatchers there and already had a memorial, their representative Walter Nash added that, 'if part of the island was to be dedicated to the United States for a memorial he would like another part to be dedicated to New Zealand'. British Prime Minister, Clement Attlee saw major difficulties with any territorial transfer, since not only 'would the islanders' assent likely be needed, but also that of the British parliament, which was unlikely unless a wider strategic advantage were forthcoming' (TNA 1946b). On the other hand, the British High Commissioner of the Western Pacific, Alexander Grantham, with no concern for the Islanders, supported handing over Tarawa because it 'would cost us little either in money or inconvenience'. By late May, Australia and New Zealand seemed willing to consider negotiating transfer of Betio or even Tarawa if the United States assumed some clear obligation to defend the region (TNA 1946c).

The time for any such trade-off, however, had passed. The US government had begun to act to repatriate the American dead from the Southern Pacific Islands (TNA 1945b). In March 1946, the American dead on Tarawa were 'consolidated' at Lone Palm cemetery on Betio, prior to final exhumation late that year for removal to the United States, so reducing some of Betio's weight of meaning as a burial site (Steere and Boardman 1957: 408). More significant politically, the United States had gained the United Nations' trusteeship over Japan's former mandate of Micronesia, so the Americans 'were not interested in establishing any system of regional defense of the Southwest Pacific and their own defense interests lay further to the north' (TNA 1946c; Wood 1958: 343–5). Suggestions that Betio be ceded had attempted to capitalize politically on the poignant affect attached to a distant place where young Americans were buried. The politics of diplomacy and the politics of memory were deeply intertwined. Divergent pre- and post-war interests ultimately prevented any cession of territory: strategic realities coupled with the removal of the dead reduced American interest in commemoration at the site itself.

Battling for memorials

Though Tarawa's potential as a bargaining chip for great powers' diverse agendas was on the wane, varied modes of commemoration persisted. During a visit in December 1946 the British High Commissioner decided to erect a bronze Coastwatchers' memorial, which would require less maintenance than the existing painted structure (WPA 1946). Before that could be achieved, however, members of the New Zealand frigate *Taupo*, visiting the island in 1949, replaced the old one with a concrete structure, which 'merged harmoniously into the surroundings of coral and palms' (*Press*, 25 November 1949; *New Zealand Herald*, 1 November 1949; *Pacific Islands Monthly*, September 1949: 74). The following year saw more work by the High Commission on this memorial to 'victims of Jap sadism'. Because of a shortage of bronze in New Zealand grey granite was used instead and a wooden cross made, 'worked to resemble coconut wood', as the centrepiece of the memorial. A stand in front held an open book of granite bearing the names of the dead, and the inscription: 'Standing unarmed to their posts, they matched brutality with gallantry and met death with fortitude.' Raised on a plinth in 1950, it was set at the spot where the men were believed to have been killed, a part of the atoll landscape with its reef that had so hindered the American landing (WPA 1950).

The absence of memorials can speak almost as clearly as their presence. Although thousands of Japanese died on Tarawa there were no memorials to them. In the decade after the war, the Japanese did not seek to erect any, which was fortunate, as feelings towards them had changed little. A commentator on the upcoming 1950 anniversary, reflecting on why these islands still had more than an emotional significance to New Zealanders, noted:

> We have exchanged the Japanese menace for Red Asia, but whether we have gained anything thereby; and whether five years of enforced democracy has had much influence on the fundamental Japanese character is very open to doubt. (*Pacific Islands Monthly*, October 1950: 9 and cover)

Three years later in 1953 the colonial administration was reluctant even to allow a Japanese mission to collect the bones of their war dead. It was forced to moderate its views, however, because of the need for reciprocity in relation to respecting the Allied dead in Japan (WPA 1953; WPA 1954).

In spite of the human cost of taking Tarawa, no monument to the US Marines stood at Betio until 1968. The tenth anniversary in 1953 had passed with no British activity and no US request to commemorate the event on the island (*Annual Report* 1954). The American War Monuments Commission's policy on overseas memorials apart from cemeteries was unsupportive, leaving the costly practice of memorialization to civilians. It was only the reassertion of the region's global strategic importance during the Cold War – especially in terms of nuclear testing – that stimulated renewed official commemorative activity and closer relations between the US and Britain and its Dominions. The British in 1955 permitted the US to construct a weather observation station at Betio as well as aircraft access. In 1962 they allowed atmospheric nuclear testing by the US on Kiritimati in the Gilberts (Firth and von Strokirch 1997: 336–8; *Annual Report* 1955: 69; *Annual Report* 1957: 59; *Annual Report* 1963: 6, 88). These mutual concerns for global security help to explain Britain's initiation of an American memorial at Betio as the twenty-fifth anniversary of the battle approached. British officials applied to the newly formed Foundation for Peoples of the South Pacific in New York for funds to build a memorial library and museum. The Foundation, after requesting a range of other possible projects, decided to assist the construction of an expensive causeway from Betio to Bairiki Island. The British administration erected an eighteen-foot high obelisk at the end of the breakwater near the American landing site to function as Betio's guiding light (Harms 2004) (Fig. 4.3). An inscription acknowledged the role of the American forces while the Marines attached their own plaque. Another, dedicated to the Foundation's contribution to the planned Friendship Causeway, was mounted near the proposed site. The British Resident Commissioner neatly melded the two aspects of the guiding light at the unveiling on 23 November 1968. It would, he said

> stand [as] a monument to the sorrow, the gratitude and the hope of the people of these islands. It is not just a war memorial, it is also a guiding light for 'they that go down to the sea in ships and do business in great waters.'

The Commissioner went on to say, 'We promise to cherish it and maintain it' (Allen, 2001: 169; WPA 1968b; *Annual Report* 1969: 1, 5–6, photograph opposite p. 48, 56).

The dedication ceremony was a major event on this tiny atoll, with the USS *McMorris* anchored off the reef. For the first time, a generation after the events, significant American representatives were present at a milestone anniversary. Wartime military commander General Shoup was brought out of retirement to represent the American Marine Corps. High-ranking British and Gilbertese officials were also present, with the US vice-consul from Suva and a representative of New Zealand Air Force laying wreaths. Young Islanders, as

Figure 4.3 Guiding light and American memorial at Betio, November 1968, twenty-fifth anniversary of the American landing.

members of the scouting movement, took part. Along with a television team, several news correspondents attended, including Robert Sherrod and Robert Trumball who had both been at the US landings in 1943. Although originally expected well before the anniversary, the Japanese ship *Fuji Maru* arrived to inaugurate a new shipping service at the time of the ceremony. The captain and first mate were invited to the event with no recriminations (WPA 1968b; *Pacific Islands Monthly*, December 1968: 33).

Nevertheless, these Japanese were a reminder that others still held a commemorative stake on Tarawa, which was still sufficiently felt to motivate unofficial action. A year before, 'like wraiths in the night', so the *Pacific Islands Monthly* noted, a Japanese group covertly erected a 'post in the ground and wrote on it and left'. When translated the inscription read, 'Memorial for the Spirits of the Japanese who died fighting on the islands and atolls. Erected by the Association of the relations of the dead, July 22, 1967.' Local authorities seem to have removed it to the old Japanese gun turret, its fate unrecorded. Reluctantly, the colonial government now accepted in principle the memorialization by Japanese families of their dead. This would be formalized in official Japanese memorials, including a peace memorial in 1982, and ultimately memorial gardens dedicated in the 1990s, featuring both Shinto and Buddhist shrines (*Pacific Islands Monthly*, January 1969: 71; WPA 1968c).

New government, old considerations

Twenty years on in the 1980s, attitudes had moved even further. Much of the island Pacific had been decolonized. The British had departed in 1979 and the Gilbert and Ellice Islands were the two independent states of Kiribati and Tuvalu, not bound by the promises of colonial administrators. A small, resource-poor but proud nation, Kiribati, as with other island states, saw opportunities in the continuing Cold War. The Kiribati government's deal with the Soviets in 1985 over fishing rights and the potential for USSR 'spy ships' to visit the waters near Kwajalein in the Marshall Islands, where the US tested intercontinental missiles, resulted in a boost in US aid and an increase of their Peace Corps volunteers in the islands (Van Trease 1993: 60–4; Peace Corps Kiribati Programme 2009). Japan funded to completion the long-awaited causeway between Betio and Bairiki in 1987 'as a token of friendship and co-operation between Japan and Kiribati' with the possibility of Japan's tracking station on Kiritimati becoming a Japanese launching site for space rockets. Politically, Kiribati was willing to cooperate with all – the Soviets as well as the Western bloc – in its own interests while it, as its President Tabai stated in 1988, had 'no time for ideological debates' (*Pacific Islands Monthly*, August 1987: 40; July 1988: 27–8).

By the 1980s too, easier air travel brought more visitors (*Pacific Islands Monthly*, July 1980: 41; July 1981: 30). In 1985, journalist Tom Hennessy and photographer Leo Hetzel visited Tarawa, as they prepared articles for California's *Press-Telegram* about the former Pacific battlegrounds. What they found at Betio shocked them. In their eyes, the fate of the guiding light US monument offered the ultimate insult to their dead, the defilement of their sacred space: 'that weather-beaten pylon was about to be torn down to make way for a cold storage plant for fish'. Worse, 'the plant was to be built by a Japanese firm'. Hennessy met John Harms, a retired Marine in Kiribati on business who shared his concerns. Hennessy planned to erect a new monument. He tried unsuccessfully to persuade the Japanese consulate in Los Angeles to finance it so he, along with another Marine veteran, Roy Thaxton, campaigned among veterans to raise US$20,000. The American War Monuments Commission was still not interested. With the help of veterans in the quarry and monumental businesses as well as engineer 'Smoke' Powers, the money donated was able 'to buy a lot of monument' (Hennessy 2002: 20). When finished, flanked by a guard of honour, it went on display at Long Beach, California where many paid their respects. Harms then managed to gain the support of the US ambassador in Fiji, a World War Two veteran, as well as other contacts in the military and the Australian consulate in Tarawa and arranged to fly the nine-ton monument to Betio. It was erected with the help of US Peace Corps members on Tarawa, and the dedication took place on the forty-fifth anniversary of the landing, in 1988 (Hennessy 2002: 20; Harms 2005: 13–14.)

To be seen, to be heard

National political and strategic considerations do not always mesh well with emotional meanings attached to memorials. By the early 2000s some US veterans and their families were having second thoughts about the presence of the memorial in distant Tarawa. Many unable to make the trip wanted it back in Long Beach, California or the Marine base at Camp Lejeune, North Carolina, 'where a lot of people will see it'. There were also problems caused by rapid population growth. When the Pacific War broke out in 1941, the population of all the Gilbert Islands had been about 30,000. By the early 2000s, on south Tarawa alone including Betio, it was 40,300. Consequently, the American memorial is crowded in by settlement, provoking fears for its security and sanctity among interested Americans (Macdonald 1982: 165, 166, 174–5; Bennett 1987: 323; Barrie Macdonald, email to author, 7 February 2010; McQuarrie 2000: 35; Highland 2000; Sherborne 2009). The son of a veteran visiting Betio concluded: 'The island is used basically as a trash dump … There is graffiti all over the place. Bunkers are being used as pig sties. Some of the larger bunkers double as rest rooms' (Hennessy 2002: 21). To the north, Red Beach, as the Marines named their initial landing place, was being used as a rubbish dump (Field 1999; Sherborne 2009). There are parallels for separating the sacred from the profane in several indigenous Pacific epistemologies. Dead bodies and places of burial or death are loaded with dangerous spiritual power and are thus taboo (*tapu*); unclean things near them are anathema and even the everyday essentials such as eating and drinking are best left separate (Eliade 1959: 23–4).[4] To Islanders, however, the American memorial was not a sacred place.

Yet for all their disgust, some veterans understood the inherent contradictions of having their monuments in a foreign land. Unlike domestic memorials, there was little Islander involvement in the design and purpose of this structure dedicated to 'fellow Marines' and, after 60 years, few to keep the memory alive. Even though Americans had acknowledged the Islanders' contribution to the war effort on the memorial, it was very much an American artefact, designed elsewhere, to recall a battle long ago. Americans had never enquired as to the meanings in landscape of the landing areas to the Kiribati people, and seemed not to consider that there may have been an older and alternative epistemology.[5] The son of a veteran condensed the particularity of the memorial's meaning to his father's generation:

> I don't think anybody goes to Tarawa. And the natives are indifferent. That's understandable. [The battle] is like something that happened on the moon to them. They have their own problems. (David Dowdakin in Hennessy 2002: 21)

That reality was epitomized by the fact that the Kiribati government had originally hoped to locate the American and Japanese memorials together, a situation plainly unacceptable to surviving veterans (Evans 2004). Herein was the clash of the meaning of objects in landscape between the Marines and the Kiribati people. For the Islanders' expanding population, most of whom are under 16, the war was a distant event and the protagonists now as good or as bad as each other, since Japan at least gave development aid to the island (Field 1999). Although not wishing to antagonize, the accommodating Kiribati people viewed Japan and the United States as moral equivalents, since these were Cold War allies. Quite logically, they conflated wartime memorial structures into one category. Intense discussions by Association members with President Tabai saw more understanding of the delicacy of the situation but it took time to finalize the matter (Evans 2004). Still, population pressures continue to expose the limits of local engagement with these foreign memorials. In 2005, with little cognizance of national sensitivities, the Betio Town Council initiated moves to reclaim the land on which Japanese memorials stand, though the importance of continuing Japanese aid contributions seems to have prevailed and prevented the attempt (Brown 2005).

Resurrecting Tarawa

On the sixtieth anniversary of the Tarawa landings, in 2003, Betio witnessed an impressive ceremony around the American memorial. A former infantry major in the US Army reserve and Peace Corps member rallied other Peace Corps volunteers to organize the cleaning of the monument, gathering donations from diplomats and the Marines Association, involving local schools and government departments, as well as weaving floral wreaths, and, notably, beautifying the nearby Japanese garden and 'somehow' arranging the significant presence of the USS *Hopper*, a destroyer of the US Seventh Fleet, with a Marine colour guard and rifle detail. The ritual included the singing of 'Amazing Grace', the national anthems of both countries, laying of wreaths by official guests and 'many Kiribati people', the singing of a new song, 'Oh, Tarawa' by the Peace Corps, a 21-gun salute and the playing of taps and a short procession to Red Beach with 'America the Beautiful' sung and speeches by American officials (Hennessy 2003; Hill 2003). That the Peace Corps beautified the Japanese gardens speaks not only of a gentler memory of the

Figure 4.4 A Marine Corps colour guard renders honours during a joint ceremony with the Navy, commemorating the sixty-fifth anniversary of the battle of Tarawa. US Marines Memorial, Betio, November 2008.

past, but also an understanding that in preserving the former enemy's memorials, the presence of their conquerors, the Americans, is also validated (Fig. 4.4).

Despite such activity, underlying the wish of some veterans to have the US memorial back in the United States was the sad realization that, like the people of Tarawa, few of their younger compatriots remember the events at Betio. Whether the wider society in the US wanted to remember it or not, there was little to remind them specifically of Tarawa. It was listed as one of the several battles sites on the Marine Corps Memorial, Arlington, erected in 1954, and its name appears among many others on the national memorial to World War Two in Washington DC dedicated in 2004. Tarawa was simply one of an increasing array competing for significance in American social memory. Others were concerned that the US government was not paying sufficient attention to those who had died at Tarawa. In February 2009, former Naval ensign Leon Cooper, a veteran of the battle, went back to Tarawa after hearing that the landing beach was a garbage site. Cooper was shocked to find 'the desecration of hallowed ground' by waste, which he hoped to incinerate and at the same time provide power for the island's people. Cooper did not blame the cramped population but his own government for neglecting this 'sacred' ground and its responsibilities there. Cooper had also learned that bones of war dead often come to the surface and that the US government simply did not want to know about it – the standard reply being, 'We have accounted for our war dead' (Barber 2009). Accounted for, yet in 1946 only 49 per cent of the American dead were found and 800 of those could not be identified. At the time, however, the American people were not advised of this alarming statistic, revealed only in an obscure government publication in 1957 (Steere and Boardman 1957; Bennett 2009: 278).

Cooper's quest received much praise in the United States, after screening as a documentary on the Military Channel (Barber 2009). Via the mass media, this reminder of the 'last good war' and the inherent decency of a determined old warrior found a sympathetic hearing among present and former Marines but also gained a new audience familiar with more recent and less noble American wars (Nelan 1998). The American government remained aloof until a private organization headed and financed by Mark Noah produced an extensive report on the many missing remains (Nelson 2008). This report spurred into action Chicago Alderman and Marine veteran of Vietnam James Balcer, followed in mid-2009 by Congressman Dan Lipinski who championed the issue, resulting in US government agreement to send archaeological investigators to Tarawa to find and identify the dead (Lipinski 2009a, 2009b; Mark Noah email to author, 20 September 2009).[6] Most governments at war, as the US is, realize it is unwise to dishonour the dead of past wars if they wish to convince young citizens to offer for new conflicts overseas. Politics needs patriotism or governments fail.

Memorials: objects in the political landscape

In home places, memorial construction to war losses and participants is a subject of protracted community discussion, debate and effort. The community's children, husbands, lovers, brothers and fathers are being remembered, thanked and mourned with all those emotions eventually expressed in stone or bronze (Inglis 2001). As long as that community, its place and the memorial survive 'the reality of unpredictable nature', memories, even if transmuted with time, can endure (Pearson 2009: 165). Memorials to the dead in foreign places have a more precarious trajectory. Particularly when located away from designated war cemeteries, their existence depends on the commitment of the host state more than the desires of the veterans, families of the dead and the government that sent its sons to fight in 'some foreign field'.

Global strategic concerns have driven much state-sanctioned commemoration at Betio, which itself had once been offered as one large memorial to secure the United States in the Pacific. Even today, beyond the Cold War, it seems likely that the presence of an American warship and its personnel at the milestone 2003 anniversary of the landing was prompted by renewed strategic interest in Kiribati's future, following the installation of a Chinese tracking station on Tarawa (Windybank 2005, 2007; Field 2005). With New Zealand support, in 2002 the Australian government erected a 2.4-metre-high Coastwatchers' memorial of stainless steel on the south side of Betio. This arresting structure replaced the rotted cross of the old one. Continuing Australian aid to Kiribati makes the monument's survival more likely, though additional safeguards are its location in a small cemetery and significantly, for the first time, an acknowledgement of the Gilbert and Ellice peoples' 'bravery' under Japanese occupation (Vale 2002).

Government agencies such as those of the Australians and New Zealanders, and private individuals – whose impetus remains loyalty, pride and, still, grief, including Leon Cooper – are doing the work of 'impression management': constructing knowledge about a landscape to gain acceptance of their view of it (Greider and Gargovich 1994: 17–18). Assertion of interest in a place, even if couched as commemoration, is inherently political. The British and Americans have used their rituals and refurbished monuments to the Americans not only to remember the dead, but also as didactic texts for the people of Kiribati whose views on the memorials were not sought by Western media. In 1968, the British saw their monument to the Americans as a symbol of 'gratitude' which the Gilbertese were expected to have towards their liberators. In 1988, a statement inscribed on the new US monument more pointedly reminded the people:

> The political processes that took place on these islands, since the battle of Tarawa, would have been difficult to achieve without the gallantry and the blood of these most remarkable men of the United States Marines. Enjoy your independence and guard it well. (Allen 2001: 228)

It is hard to imagine that the Gilbertese in 1941 were in the slightest grateful for being thrust into a war that was not theirs, between two protagonists they scarcely knew. The Americans portrayed themselves as gallant liberators even though they, as well as the Japanese, did considerable damage to the island's environment, without recompense (Bennett 2009: 168–70).

Urged to guard their independence well, the people of Kiribati face an invader far stronger than Japan or mighty America: the obliteration of both their political independence and their home. Commemoration of Tarawa, whether practised as a reflection of global politics, regional development or private sentiment, has neglected the deeper resonances of war, industrialization and globalization in the twentieth century. No longer the passive recipients of 'liberation', or the pawns of global security concerns, these people were asking global and regional powers to assume responsibility for the interests they had pursued through war and diplomacy. In 2008 President Anote Tong asked New Zealand and other states to accept some of his people to establish a viable core to assist with remittances, but more importantly, to aid later migrants to adjust. He does not want his people to lose their dignity as climate 'refugees' but to start new lives elsewhere as settlers (*Pacific Islands Report* 2008; Marks 2008; Kiribati Climate Change 2009). They may well need another land because in a decade or so, along with most low atolls, Tarawa seems likely to become 'the new Atlantis', as global warming and the rising waters are already eroding several islands. In this respect, nature now appears more predictable, but whatever the outcome the still-increasing population is seeking a new home. If it erodes, tiny Tarawa will no longer be a battlefield for foreign armies, a weather station to facilitate foreigners' nuclear tests or a tracking station for foreigners' missiles. For those so full of remembrance for these Islanders inscribed on their war memorials, but who never thought to compensate them for waging a foreign war on their coral strands, it is time to consider some reparations for the erosion of land and landmarks that the industrialized nations' production of greenhouse gases are inflicting upon them. For heroes and for civilians caught in a global war there are finer memorials than those of stone and bronze.

Notes

1   Epigraph from Sherrod. I am grateful for comments on an earlier draft by Barrie Macdonald, Barbara Brookes, Mark Seymour, Tony Ballantyne, Takashi Shogimen, Tom Brooking and Rani Kerin as well as the editors of this volume. Any errors are mine.
2   There were early scientists who predicted this warming, but it took until the 1970s and 1980s for the scientific community to take this seriously, with governments lagging behind. See Flannery 2005.
3   For American ideas about Tarawa vis à vis Betio, see Sherrod (1944).
4   In some Polynesian societies such as Maori, the everyday, profane things are described as 'noa'. While 'tapu' in word and concept is in the Kiribati language, the word 'noa' is not.
5   The Kiribati people attached their own meanings to landscape, even in the face of modern alteration. See *Pacific Islands Monthly*, August 1987: 40.
6   In October 2010 an American team retrieved two sets of bones believed to be US servicemen (McAvoy 2010).

References

Alexander, J. H. (2008) 'An Enduring Legacy', *Naval History Magazine* 22(6). Online: www.usni.org/magazines/navalhistory/story.asp?STORY_ID=167 (accessed 1 February 2010).
Allen, D. K. (2001) *Tarawa—the Aftermath*, Ohio: Privately printed.
Annual Report, Gilbert and Ellice Islands Colony, 1952 and 1953 (1954) London: Her Majesty's Stationery Office.
Annual Report, Gilbert and Ellice Islands Colony, 1954 and 1955 (1955) London: Her Majesty's Stationery Office.
Annual Report, Gilbert and Ellice Islands Colony, 1956 and 1957 (1957) London: Her Majesty's Stationery Office.
Annual Report, Gilbert and Ellice Islands Colony, 1962 and 1963 (1963) London: Her Majesty's Stationery Office.
Annual Report, Gilbert and Ellice Islands Colony, 1968 (1969) London: Her Majesty's Stationery Office.
Barber, S. (director) (2009) *Return to Tarawa*, DVD, Create Space, ASIN: B002L6HAVI.

Bennett, J. A. (1987) *Wealth of the Solomons: A History of a Pacific Archipelago, 1800–1978*, Honolulu: University of Hawaii Press.

Bennett, J. A. (2009) *Natives and Exotics: World War II and Environment in the Southern Pacific*, Honolulu: University of Hawaii Press.

Brown, J. (2005) 'Report Betio, Tarawa', 6 June. Online: http://tarawatheaftermath.com/CurrentNews200506.html (accessed 8 September 2009).

Eliade, M. (1959) *The Sacred and the Profane*, New York: Harcourt, Brace and World.

Ellis, A. (1946) *Mid-Pacific Outposts*, Auckland: Brown and Stewart Ltd.

Evans, T. (2004) 'The Tarawa Monument', *Follow Me* 41(2), 22. Online: www.2marine.com/FollowPDFs/FollowMeMar-Apr2004.pdf (accessed 1 September 2009).

Field, M. (1999) 'Pacific Islands Report, 13 June 1999'. Online: http://archives.pireport.org/archive/search.htm (accessed 7 September 2009).

Field, M. (2005) 'Currency of Persuasion', *The Listener*, 198(3391). Online: www.listener.co.nz/issue/3391/features/3950/currency_of_persuasion.html (accessed 29 November 2009).

Firth, S. (1999) *Australia in International Politics: An Introduction to Australian Foreign Policy*, St Leonards: Allen and Unwin.

Firth, S. and von Strokirch, K. (1997) 'A Nuclear Pacific', in Donald Denoon, Stewart Firth, Jocelyn Linnekin, Malama Meleisea and Karen Nero (eds), *The Cambridge History of the Pacific Islanders*, Cambridge: Cambridge University Press, 324–58.

Flannery, T. (2005) *The Weather Makers: The History and Future Impact of Climate Change*, Melbourne: Text Publishing.

Greider, T. and Garkovich, L. (1994) 'Landscapes: The Social Construction of Nature and the Environment', *Rural Sociology* 59(1), 1–24.

Harms, J. (2004) Letter to Andrew Sharp, 8 June. Copy supplied to author.

Harms, J. (2005) 'In Harms' Way is Sometimes a Good Thing', *Follow Me* 42(1), 13–14. Online: www.2marine.com/FollowPDFs/FollowMeJan-Feb05.pdf (accessed 1 September 2009).

Hennessy, T. (2002) 'A Monumental Agreement,' *Follow Me* 39(1), 20–1. Online: www.2marine.com/FollowPDFs/Follow01_17-32.pdf - (accessed 1 September 2009).

Hennessy, T. (2003) '60th Anniversary Ceremony at Tarawa, 2003'. Online: http://tarawatheaftermath.com/TarawaStories14.html (accessed 21 September 2009).

Highland, S. (2000) 'World War Two in Kiribati', in Robert Borofsky (ed.), *Remembrance of Pacific Pasts: An Invitation to Remake History*, Honolulu: University of Hawaii.

Hill, T. (2003) 'USS Hopper Commemorates the Battle of Tarawa.' Online: www.navy.mil/search/display.asp?story_id=10830 (accessed 3 November 2009).

Inglis, K. S. (2001) *Sacred Places: War Memorials in the Australian Landscape*, Melbourne: Melbourne University Press.

Jones, K. Westcott (1951) 'Tarawa Atoll', *The Fortnightly* 175, 391–397.

Kay, R. (ed.) (1972) *The Australia–New Zealand Agreement* 1944, Wellington: Historical Publications Branch.

Kiribati Climate Change, 11 December 2009. Online: www.unmultimedia.org/tv/unifeed/d/14080.html (accessed 18 January 2010).

Lipinski, D. (2009a) 'Lipinski Presses Defense Department to Locate Remains of US Service Members in the Battle of Tarawa'. Online: http://disc.yourwebapps.com/discussion.cgi?disc=149620;article=12980;title=TarawaTalk (accessed 20 September 2009).

Lipinski, D. (2009b) 'Amendment No. 10 Offered by Mr. Kratovil', 25 June. Online: www.votesmart.org/speech_detail.php?sc_id=477252&keyword=&phrase=&contain= (accessed 29 November 2010).

McAvoy, A. (2010) 'Tarawa Shows Difficulties of Retrieving War Missing', 10 October. Online: www.mauinews.com/page/content.detail/id/541512/Tarawa-shows-difficulties-of-retrieving-war-missing.html (accessed 4 December 2010).

Macdonald, B. (1982) *Cinderellas of the Empire: Towards a History of Kiribati and Tuvalu*, Canberra: Australian National University Press.

McKinnon, M. (1993) *Independence and Foreign Policy: New Zealand in the World Since 1935*, Auckland: Auckland University Press.

McQuarrie, P. (2000) *Conflict in Kiribati: A History of the Second World War*, Christchurch: Macmillan Brown, University of Canterbury.

Marks, K. (2008) 'Paradise Lost: Climate Change' *The Independent*, 2 June. Online: www.globalpolicy.org/component/content/article/212/45369.html (accessed 21 September 2009).

Nelan, B. W. (1998) '1939–1948: The Last Good War', *Time*, 9 March. Online: www.time.com/time/magazine/article/0,9171,987924,00.html (accessed 21 September 2009).

Nelson, Melissa (2008) 'Researchers: 139 Marines found on Tarawa'. Online: www.marinecorpstimes.com/news/2008/11/marine_wwii_remains_112608w/ (accessed 21 September 2009).

New Zealand Herald (newspaper, Auckland, NZ), 1 November 1949.

Pacific Islands Monthly (Sydney, Australia), September 1949.

Pacific Islands Monthly (Sydney, Australia), October 1950.

Pacific Islands Monthly (Sydney, Australia), December 1968.

Pacific Islands Monthly (Sydney, Australia), January 1969.

Pacific Islands Monthly (Sydney, Australia), August 1987.

Pacific Islands Monthly (Sydney, Australia), July 1988.

Pacific Islands Report (2008). Online: http://archives.pireport.org/archive/2008/june/06%2D06%2D08.htm (accessed 18 January 2010).

Peace Corps Kiribati Programme Online: www.angelfire.com/co/dbrummel/pcv25.html (accessed 2 November 2009).

Pearson, C. (2009) 'Creating a Natural Fortress: Landscape, Resistance, and Memory in the Vercors, France', in Charles E. Closmann (ed.), *War and Environment: Military Destruction in the Modern Age*, College Station: Texas A&M University Press.

Press (newspaper, Christchurch, NZ), 25 November 1949.

Sherborne, C. (2009) 'Sinking Sandbanks', *The Monthly* 43, 16–19.

Sherrod, R. (1944) *Tarawa: The Story of a Battle*, New York: Duell, Sloan and Pearce.

Sherrod, R. (1946) 'Tarawa Today', *Life*, 5 August 20.

Steere, E. and Boardman, T. M. (1957) *Final Disposition of World War II Dead, 1945–1951*, U.S. Army, Quartermaster Corps, QMC Historical Studies, Series II, No. 4, Washington, DC: Historical Branch Office of the Quartermaster General.

TNA – The National Archives (UK) (1942) Dominions Office to Prime Minister, Australia, 26 December. CO 225/339/86563/1.

TNA – The National Archives (UK) (1943a) Halifax to Foreign Office, 15 December. DO 35/2124; P. Mitchell to Secretary of State, 9 December 1943, WO 106/5928.

TNA – The National Archives (UK) (1943b) Curtin to Dominions Office, 30 December. CO 225/339/8653/1.

TNA – The National Archives (UK) (1945a) Foreign Office to J. Balfour, 23 July. FO 115/4199.

TNA – The National Archives (UK) (1945b) Cosmo-Parkinson, Memo, 17 September, and enclosures. FO 371/44623.

TNA – The National Archives (UK) (1946a) Extract from conclusions of a meeting, 3 May. DO 35/2125.

TNA – The National Archives (UK) (1946b) Extract from meeting of Prime Ministers, 6 May. DO 35/2125.

TNA – The National Archives (UK) (1946c) Grantham to Secretary of State, 29 May; Secretary of State to Grantham, 23 May; Grantham to Secretary of State, 23 May. DO 35/2125.

Tonkin-Covell, J. (2000) 'The Collectors: Naval, Army and Air Intelligence in the New Zealand Armed Forces during the Second World War', PhD dissertation, University of Waikato, New Zealand.

Vale, D. (2002) 'Dedication of Memorial to those Killed on Tarawa', 11 November. Online: http://pandora.nla.gov.au/pan/38439/20040319-0000/minister.dva.gov.au/media_releases/2002/november/va142.htm (accessed 21 September 2009).

Van Trease, H. (ed.) (1993) *Atoll Politics: The Republic of Kiribati*, Christchurch: Macmillan Brown Centre and University of Canterbury.

Windybank, S. (2005) 'The China Syndrome', Centre for Independent Studies. Online: www.cis.org.au/policy/winter05/polwin05-5.htm (accessed 3 November 2009).

Windybank, S. (2007) 'Why China First Wooed then Jilted Kiribati'. Centre for Independent Studies. Online: www.cis.org.au/executive_highlights/eh2007/eh43307.html (accessed 2 November 2009).

Wood, F. L. W. (1958) *The New Zealand People at War: Political and External Affairs*, Wellington: War History Branch, Department of Internal Affairs.

WPA – Western Pacific Archives (1943a) P. Mitchell to Secretary of State, 20 December, and enclosures. WPHC SF 32/9. Western Pacific Archives (WPA), University of Auckland Library, New Zealand.

WPA – Western Pacific Archives (1943b) Dept. of External Affairs, NZ to High Commissioner, 31 December, enclosure. WPHC SF 32/9.

WPA – Western Pacific Archives (1946) Notes on visit of His Excellency, 17 December. WPHC 9, F32/68.

WPA – Western Pacific Archives (1947) Maude to High Commissioner, 3 March. WPHC SF 9/31/2, Vol. 1, WPA; Resident Commissioner to High Commissioner, 14 March. WPHC F 58/55, WPA.

WPA – Western Pacific Archives (1950) Attachment, Resident Commissioner to High Commissioner, 15 September. WPHC 9, F32/68.

WPA – Western Pacific Archives (1953) Secretary of State for Colonies to High Commissioner, 22 May and enclosures. WPHC 6/1, CF 32/33/3.

WPA – Western Pacific Archives (1954) Assistant High Commissioner to Resident Commissioner, 15 July 1954, and enclosures, WPHC 6/11, CF 184/9/1, Vol. 1.

WPA – Western Pacific Archives (1968a) *Time*, December 1943, cited in Assistant Resident Commissioner to High Commissioner, 12 July. WPHC 6/11, CF 184/9/1, Vol. 1.

WPA – Western Pacific Archives (1968b) Anderson to Davies, 25 November; Address by Resident Commissioner – Unveiling of Memorial Light; Address by Resident Commissioner – Laying of Foundation Stone, Friendship Causeway, 23 November. WPHC 30/11, F. 350/7/2.

WPA – Western Pacific Archives (1968c) Resident Commissioner to Secretary of State for Commonwealth Affairs, 20 September. WPHC 30/11, F. 350/7/2.

Chapter 5

Commemorating the American Civil War in National Park Service battlefields

Robert K. Sutton

In August 1998, superintendents from National Park Service (NPS) battlefields across the United States gathered for a week in Nashville, Tennessee, to discuss issues common to all of our parks. The meeting, called by the Regional Directors from the Northeast and National Capital regions of National Park Service, provided an opportunity for Civil War park superintendents to work together towards common goals. It was a critical moment in the management of Civil War parks, as discussion centred on the two key issues of how we manage the resources in and around our parks, and how we interpret the Civil War (1861–5) for our visitors. The impetus for the meeting came from two sources. A member of the United States House of Representatives, Jesse Jackson, Jr, had recently visited a number of National Park Service battlefields and was troubled to find that we interpreted the war by focusing on the battles – who shot whom, where and how – to the exclusion of almost everything else. Also, as the superintendent at Manassas National Battlefield Park (Bull Run) at the time, I was fighting my own 'civil war', trying to keep our local member of the House of Representatives from forcing the National Park Service to give up land to expand a highway intersection in the middle of our park. Thus, the short-term goals were to deliberate on immediate issues that affected Civil War battlefields, such as how public roads might impact on these parks, and long-term goals – how to manage these parks in the future. The latter goals were divided into two parts: the physical management of parks – preservation, environmental concerns; and the interpretation of our battlefields – how we could make them more relevant not only to contemporary citizens, but to future generations of Americans as well. This chapter examines the opportunities and conflicts flowing from the expanded interpretative framework that emerged from the meeting, suggesting that the process of renewal and challenging former orthodoxies has been as important as its products, as the United States prepares to mark the sesquicentenary of the Civil War between 2011 and 2015.

Americans are proud of their National Parks. Whereas much of our culture, ideas, games, place names, political models and cuisines have been borrowed from other places and other countries, one idea uniquely our own is the concept of 'national parks'. Over a century ago, we decided that the most beautiful scenery, the highest mountains, the tallest trees, the most important prehistoric and historic sites, the most significant battlefields, the most significant ecosystems, in short, the best of everything we have, should be set aside as national parks forever. Many Americans and much of the world associate National Parks with the grand parks in the West – Yellowstone, Yosemite and the Grand Canyon – but over 60 per cent of our parks are primarily cultural parks, including our Civil War battlefields. When Congress established the National Park Service in 1916, the mandate it gave us was 'to conserve the scenery and the natural and historic objects and the wildlife therein and to provide for the enjoyment of the same in such manner and by such means as will leave them unimpaired for the enjoyment of future generations'.[1]

By tackling the management issues of roads in parks, surrounding land development and the care of resources in battlefields, those who met at Nashville were taking steps to follow the mandate passed by Congress in 1916. The parks that make up the National Park System currently number 392 units, ranging from parks above the Arctic Circle in Alaska to the Virginia Islands in the Caribbean Sea, and from the Coast of Maine to Guam in the South Pacific. Each park is administered by a superintendent who has discretion in the interpretative stories told. For example, Marsh-Billings-Rockefeller National Historical Park in Woodstock, Vermont, is the first National Park designated for conservation history and the evolving nature of land stewardship in the United States. Yet, for the past six summers, the park has sponsored an enormously popular tour focusing on the Civil War home front in Woodstock. Of 284 Woodstock men who fought in the Union Army against the Confederacy, 39 died on battlefields. Two of the namesakes for the park – George Perkins Marsh and Frederick Billings – were strong supporters of the Union cause. So, although the actual battles took place hundreds of miles away, Woodstock played an important role in the war, and the park administration has the flexibility to tell this story.

Civil War battlefields themselves came to the National Park Service through a rather circuitous route. Starting in 1864, the Gettysburg Battlefield Memorial Association was founded, in part, for the purpose of acquiring land that was part of the battlefield. Although groups such as the Grand Army of the Republic (GAR) lobbied Congress to acquire the land, Gettysburg was not the first battlefield to come under federal ownership. That designation belonged to Chickamauga and Chattanooga in Georgia and Tennessee. Over time the interpretation, or reinterpretation, of the battle of Gettysburg, giving credit to the Confederacy for its valiant efforts, and allowing both sides to take ownership of the battle and erect monuments on its 'sacred ground', while at the same time avoiding any discussion of what they were fighting about, were key elements in both sides coalescing to create a federal park (Foote 2003: 128). Gettysburg, Chickamauga and Chattanooga and other battlefields were first managed by the United States War Department. The process of lobbying Congress to set these parks aside as federal parks was part of the reconciliation between North and South, similar to the efforts to create Gettysburg National Military Park. Later, in 1933, these military parks were transferred to the National Park Service by the Executive Order of President Franklin D. Roosevelt.

The gathering at Nashville concerned itself with tackling long-term management of all of the resources in our parks, cultural and natural. Here we confronted pressing conservation issues that had been emerging for several decades. Traffic issues were problems in many of our battlefields. Not surprisingly, many of the roads in and around our parks were constructed in the same rights-of-way as the roads that carried troops to battle during the Civil War. The fact that transportation agencies wanted to increase the capacity of these thoroughfares was symptomatic of the fact that our parks, established in many cases in rural settings, were now surrounded by suburbs and exurbs of larger cities. Bearing in mind our own jurisdiction within parks, and using the precept that National Parks were set aside for as long as there is a United States of America, the decisions relating to roads in parks were fairly easy. We concluded that 'modern roads and traffic shall not adversely affect the integrity of [our parks] and the quality of the visitor experience'. Further, we established the principle that 'the National Park Service will not cede land to expand existing road corridors or create new corridors through Civil War Battlefields it holds in trust for the American People' (National Park Service 1998: 6–7) (Fig. 5.1).

Other problems of long-term conservation were more difficult, concerning as they do the management and maintenance of heritage landscapes. As places of remembrance for veterans and civilians since the war itself, the battlefields have been marked in enduring ways. Almost as soon as the war ended, white women in the South organized Ladies Memorial Associations which retrieved the remains of Confederate dead and gave them dignified burials in dedicated

Figure 5.1 Intersection at Manassas National Battlefield Park, part of the catalyst for the meeting of superintendents at Nashville, Tennessee in 1998.

cemeteries, which now lie at the heart of numerous battlefield parks (Janney 2008). Soldiers from both sides also returned to erect monuments, marking out former battlefields in what Kenneth Foote describes as acts of sanctification or consecration. Here, a site is 'set apart from its surroundings and dedicated to the memory of an event, person, or group. Sanctification almost always involves the construction of a durable marker, either some sort of monument or memorial or a garden, park, or building that is intended to be maintained in perpetuity' (Foote 2003: 8).

Battlefield landscapes changed, first with the erection of monuments, later with the construction of visitor facilities and, finally, as nature took its course, forests replaced open fields. Conversely, some areas forested during the war were later cleared for farming. Fence lines disappeared. Temporary structures, such as earthwork fortifications, disappeared or eroded. So, the challenge for park managers was to balance the commemorative and visitor facilities of battlefields with the wartime landscapes on which blood was spilled.

For some managers, caring for the monuments is a challenge. Gettysburg National Military Park has over 1,400 monuments, markers and memorials to commemorate this pivotal battle. For other managers, restoring the battlefield landscape to its 1860s appearance was an issue. In parks such as Gettysburg and Manassas, several hundred acres of mature forest had replaced open fields. Cutting trees in a National Park is controversial (*Washington Post* 2008; Janiskee 2008; *Gettysburg Times* 2009; *Chicago Tribune* 2007). To most historians and park managers, it seems perfectly reasonable to restore battlefields to their historical appearance; to many conservationists, on the other hand, cutting trees in National Parks for any reason is wrong. Thus, park managers planned tree-removal projects, using good ecological science to ensure that stream banks were not eroded and wildlife habitats were not destroyed. For example, at Manassas, the park scientist demonstrated that removing trees created a meadow environment, actually improving the rapidly disappearing habitat for song birds in Northern Virginia (National Park Service 2005).

The discussion concerning development of land adjacent to our battlefields was more complex. In the United States, land that is inside the boundaries of National Parks is under federal government control and protection, but only in rare cases is any land outside these preserves protected as well. Land outside the boundaries of our Civil War battlefields is under the jurisdiction of local governing bodies. Antietam National Battlefield in Maryland, about 60 miles west of Washington DC, commemorates the site of over 23,000 casualties in one day of fighting in 1862. In 1991, the state government, along with several private entities, joined forces to purchase the development rights for approximately 2,500 acres of agricultural land surrounding the battlefield. The preservation of the area around the battlefield, as well as the potential for increased tourism, were the chief motivating factors for this effort. On the other hand, the area surrounding Manassas National Battlefield Park has been

Figure 5.2 Panorama of Manassas National Battlefield Park, showing maintenance of scene and vistas, much as they were in 1861–2.

developing rapidly in the past 30 years. Prince William County, Virginia, in which most of the park is located, has grown from 144,636 residents in 1980 to 364,734 in 2008. The population of Loudoun County, Virginia, adjacent to the park, has grown from 57,427 in 1980 to 289,995 in 2008 (United States Department of Commerce, United States Census Bureau, Population Division, updated 25 April 2009). The Commonwealth of Virginia and the local governing jurisdictions have not, historically, seen the value in protecting the land directly adjacent to the park. Thus, one of my primary responsibilities then as superintendent was to work with local jurisdictions to try to control development around the park so that tall buildings, cellular telephone towers and other structures did not obstruct the historical views of the battlefield (Fig 5.2).

Because the National Park Service does not have the authority to dictate how local governments should manage the areas adjacent to our battlefields, and because the priorities for land management for these areas vary from jurisdiction to jurisdiction, we concluded that our best approach should be first to become fully familiar with land-use issues, zoning and economic development objectives, as well as the decision-making processes for local jurisdictions surrounding battlefields. Second, battlefield park managers should work with local landowners and governing bodies to ensure that both can achieve their objectives, while at the same time protecting the integrity of the visitor experiences at battlefields. Park managers should involve local governments and citizens in any comprehensive park planning processes to ensure that they have a say in how the parks are developed and managed. Finally, the park managers should become promoters for the benefits the parks bring to the local community, such as touting how much visitors spend in the local economy (National Park Service 1998: 8–10).

The National Park Service's long-term stewardship and dedication to preserving national parks has, nevertheless, been accompanied by a certain ossification in interpretation of Civil War sites over the past century, a fact that also informed our Nashville meeting. When the first Civil War battlefield – Chickamauga and Chattanooga National Military Park – was set aside as a national preserve in 1890, at the urging of Civil War veterans from the North and the South, the stories of the battles, told by the participants, were powerful, and resonated with contemporaries. Their descriptions of Civil War battles, such as Chickamauga and Chattanooga, by the veterans who fought there were, no doubt, meaningful to those who visited in the 1890s. As these first-hand observers died, however, generations of battlefield park rangers, whom we fondly refer to as 'cannonball historians', although further and further removed from the experiences of the actual participants with each generation, continued to focus on the military outcomes with little discussion of the how and why these battles related to the social, political and economic evolution of the nation. In other words, the Civil War as presented in National Parks increasingly had little relevance to modern America.

The National Park Service has a responsibility to interpret the Civil War for Americans, which it takes seriously. In the National Park Service plan that we submitted to the United States Congress in 2008, *Holding the High Ground: A National Park Service Plan for the Sesquicentennial of the Civil War*, we recognized that we continue to use 'our battlefields to define the Nation's Civil War experience in largely military terms – through the eyes of the participants of battle'. Further, the National Park Service had 'failed to find ways to engage large segments of Americans in ways that demonstrate how the war is relevant to them'. Thus, by focusing on the battles, commanders, and military strategies, the greater context of the war was obscured and lost. This is no small matter: the legacies of the Civil War are critical to understanding and defining modern America. The NPS therefore has a crucial role to play, understanding that 'the cost of the war and the value of its lessons intertwine to create a cornerstone of our national identity. The National Park System embodies many of the sites that constitute that cornerstone.'

The Nashville meeting and subsequent *Holding the High Ground* service plan (2008) signified that recognition of the need to expand interpretation, and provided a forum for determining the scope and nature of that expansion. The war was and is an event experienced differently by different people. 'That this is so adds vivid texture to the examination and interpretation to one of the seminal events in the history of human and civil rights.' Most importantly, parks managers recognize that since historical scholarship is a continually evolving process, in which scholars often disagree in the interpretation of events, 'it is important for parks to recognize and tell our visitors that history is a subject of continual debate, rather than a set of fixed facts' (National Park Service 2008). This has been the effect of the reflexive process that has washed through the administration of NPS Civil War parks, and increasingly so as the sesquicentennial of the war approaches in 2011.

Of course the process of expanding our interpretation of the Civil War did not begin with our meeting in Nashville, nor will it end with the sesquicentennial. In 1992, Harpers Ferry National Historical Park in West Virginia opened a permanent museum, 'Black Voices of Harpers Ferry', which dispelled many of the stereotypes about African Americans on the eve of the Civil War, showing that 12 per cent of the town's population was black, of which half were free. These African Americans were not in the shadows, but integral parts of the town's early life. Our meeting in Nashville understood that we were doing our visitors a great disservice by not providing them with the fundamental meanings and contexts of the Civil War Era, such as the exhibit at Harpers Ferry was doing. The impetus to develop new interpretative themes was not driven by visitation – Civil War parks were (and are) as popular as ever – nor from complaints that the stories we told were irrelevant. Instead, we as Civil War park superintendents recognized that our parks provided the best public laboratories for Americans to understand why the Civil War was such a critical event in their history. Early on, in the development of National Parks, our managers recognized that for the parks to be relevant to our citizens, we needed to keep our stories fresh, based on the best information available at the time. The year 1998 was when many of our park superintendents recognized that the relevance of the Civil War extended well beyond who shot whom, where, when and how, and when new interpretative standards were established.

Developing our interpretative themes was like building a scaffold. To build the base of this scaffold, in 2000, we obtained a grant to sponsor a symposium, *Rally on the High Ground*, at Ford's Theater, in Washington DC, the site of Abraham Lincoln's assassination in 1865 and now an NPS managed site. We invited the leading scholars of the Civil War period to share their research – the cutting-edge work in the field – with our superintendents, interpreters and the general public. In large part, the symposium grew out of the desire of our park managers and park rangers to expand their interpretation of the Civil War. Many of the park superintendents are appointed to their positions as managers, rather than as experts in the fields interpreted in their parks. So, while some of our Civil War park managers are trained in graduate history programmes, others are landscape architects, biologists or law-enforcement professionals. The park rangers who support them are the backbone of the organization, but here too there were similar problems. Interpretative park rangers, as opposed to those rangers who enforce park regulations, greet the public, lead tours and give interpretative talks as part of their paid duties. Many of these park rangers are themselves the 'cannonball historians', referred to earlier, who have spent their careers talking about the military histories of their parks. Thus, *Rally on the High Ground* provided an opportunity for these park managers and staff to hear from leading experts the most current research in the field. For all in attendance, and for the park staff who were not able to attend, I edited and published the papers in a volume entitled *Rally on the High Ground*, which became a major source for building these expanded interpretative themes. Although the publication was intended for park staff, it became a popular title for the general public as well, and is currently in its third printing (Sutton 2001).

The *Rally on the High Ground* symposium provided a framework for expanding interpretation at our parks. Such wide-ranging goals as we set ourselves are not easily achieved, and certainly not without controversy and resistance. In practical terms, within the organization many of our park rangers wanted more in-depth training on how they could implement these concepts into their park programmes. So, for the second level of our scaffold, we invited 20 park interpretative rangers to a two-week intensive institute, in which we explored new interpretative topics and methods. We asked each participant to bring stories from their parks, not related to traditional military history, that would place their Civil War Era parks within the continuum of the period, focus on the social, economic, cultural and political issues that caused the war, illustrate the human experiences during the period or discuss the aftermath of the war. The overriding principle was that each story needed to establish the relevance of the Civil War to Americans today. We helped each participant develop his/her programme, and placed them on our National Park Service website, so that rangers from other parks could follow their examples and so that we could share these stories with the general public (National Park Service Civil War Institute n.d.).

Greater challenges emerge in the nature of interpretation. A series of issues have demanded the expansion of the interpretative framework in NPS parks. The impact of the war on families is one. Women, especially in slave-owning families in the South, assumed the responsibilities of managing slaves and plantations while their husbands were away at the war. Four out of every five men of military age in the South entered the military, compared to about one-half of Northern men. Further, a much higher percentage of Southern men died in the war – 18 per cent from the South as compared to 6 per cent from the North. Most Confederate women belonged to families who owned small farms or no land at all; they did the best they could to run farms and to feed their children without their men's labour. But as the war continued, Southern families suffered from hunger as food and other necessities were in short supply. In addition, many families in the South had to deal with the devastation of battles that were fought in their backyards. While families mourned the more than 620,000 men who did not come home, many more families welcomed home veterans missing limbs, sick with diseases they contracted during service and suffering from poorly understood psychological impediments, now known as post-traumatic shock (Faust 2001: 81–90; Escott 1985) (Fig. 5.3).

Addressing the varied motivations of the soldiers also allows for a greater understanding of the ideals in conflict in the Civil War. For African American soldiers, many of whom had been former slaves and whose numbers reached 200,000 in the Union Army by the end of the war, the motivation seems clear – to end the institution of slavery and stake a claim to citizenship through military service. For most Confederate soldiers the incentive was to preserve their rights and to gain independence from the United States government.

Figure 5.3 Young girl holding a photograph of her father who died in the Civil War.

The reasons Union soldiers fought were more complicated. Nearly all were fighting to preserve the Union. A few, early on, were fighting to end slavery, but as the war progressed and emancipation became a Northern war aim, more Federal soldiers became abolitionists. Nearly all of the soldiers from the North and the South had never shot at another human being before the war, yet most willingly accepted the role of killers of other men very quickly.

At Ford's Theater and at our institute we confronted the political, economic and social consequences of the Civil War, and, more particularly, recognized the institution of slavery at the root of all of them. Acknowledging that 'slavery was the principal cause of the Civil War' remains highly controversial in an America still sensitive to its history of slavery. The institution of slavery is the most difficult and troubling part of our past. Rather than experiencing a gradual demise after 1776, as many American revolutionary leaders thought would occur, slavery thrived in the United States as a key economic, social and political institution. On the eve of the Civil War, 4,000,000 people remained enslaved in the United States. The value of cotton, the principal export, had never been higher, the value of slaves as property had never been higher, and 60 per cent of the wealthiest families lived in slave-holding states, whereas only 30 per cent of the population of the United States lived in these states. Many Americans who either are descendants of Confederate soldiers or sympathize with the Confederate cause cite 'states' rights' as the principal cause of the war. As recently as April 2010, Virginia Governor Bob McDonnell issued a proclamation declaring April 'Confederate History Month'. In his proclamation, he talked about the sacrifices Virginia's Confederate soldiers made during the war and how they willingly rejoined the Union after the war, but he neglected to mention the institution of slavery. After a national furore, Governor McDonnell changed his proclamation, adding that 'it is important for all Virginians to understand that the institution of slavery led to this war and was an evil and inhumane practice that deprived people of their God-given inalienable rights' (Weigel 2010).

In the past ten years, we in the National Park Service have been keenly aware that talking about slavery is controversial, and the problem is reflected in our own ranks. Some believe we should not talk about slavery as a cause of the Civil War at all; others believe we should place a stronger emphasis on the issue, almost to the exclusion of anything else. What the 1998 Nashville conference showed, and the 2008 plan reaffirmed, was that the NPS must engage with the issue, with appropriate historical resources, if parks are to fulfil their mandate and address issues central to national self-perception. To Americans, freedom is one of the most important words in our vocabulary. It means different things to different people. To the American slaves, who with the Thirteenth Amendment to the United States Constitution achieved freedom from bondage, the concept of freedom was profound. With the Fourteenth and Fifteenth Amendments, they were granted equal protection of their rights, and for all males, the right to vote. Though the American nation resiled from its commitment to freedom and denied many of the blessings of liberty in the years after the war, the Civil War still represented and promised, as Abraham Lincoln said in his Gettysburg Address, a 'new birth of freedom' (Foner 2001: 91–102). The National Parks Service has a role to play in interrogating that concept, not least of all through addressing the issue of slavery.

Engaging with the issue of slavery is also difficult because it challenges one of the key myths of the war. The American Civil War is unusual in that for generations the vanquished – the Confederate Army – captured the popular memory of the war, rather than the victors. When Confederate General Robert E. Lee delivered his farewell message to his troops after the surrender in April

1865, he initiated what has since become known as the myth of the 'lost cause' of the Civil War. 'After four years of arduous service marked by unsurpassed courage and fortitude,' he declared, 'the Army of Northern Virginia has been compelled to yield to overwhelming numbers and resources.' The 'lost cause' perpetuated the view, especially among Confederate veterans and their supporters, that the Confederacy was engaged in a noble war, fought by honourable men, to defend the cause of states' rights. The South lost, not because the cause was wrong, nor because the officers and soldiers were inferior, but because they faced insurmountable odds of manpower and industrial might.

Lee's Farewell Address and a body of literature, beginning with Edward Pollard's 1865 book *The Lost Cause: A New Southern History of the War of the Confederates*, followed by a second volume in 1866, *The Lost Cause Regained*, engrained the 'lost cause' in the Southern and later Northern psyche. Pollard and others – most notably the United Daughters of the Confederacy and the Sons of Confederate Veterans – influenced the content of textbooks, and, by adopting an activist approach to curriculum planning, these Confederate sympathizers were able to perpetuate the 'lost cause' for generations beyond the end of the Civil War (McPherson 2007: 93ff; Cox 2003). Historians' explanations of the defeat, however, run counter to the 'lost cause' mythology, as they propose multiple social, economic, political and military factors that contributed to the Southern loss and the Northern victory. Nevertheless, the 'lost cause' mythology remains potent and popular: in 2010 Governor McDonnell still insisted that Virginians, as part of the Confederate Army, lost the war because they were 'ultimately overwhelmed by the insurmountable numbers and resources of the Union Army'.

Given its persistence, this interpretation has also had considerable purchase among park managers, and by focusing on strategy and tactics for generations, our park interpreters have managed to deftly avoid discussions of why the North won and the South lost. There are also structural reasons why attention to the greater issues surrounding and central to the war has been circumscribed among parks service managers and interpreters. Many of our military parks, starting with Chickamauga and Chattanooga, were set aside with specific legislation that directed the War Department, which was the first manager of this park, to commemorate the battles fought there, the brave soldiers who gave their lives on this sacred ground, and for the parks to serve as laboratories to study the military actions that took place there. Thus, when this and other military parks were transferred to the National Park Service, park interpreters avoided the issue of why the North won, and a great deal of controversy, by focusing on site-specific military history.

Some academic historians have consequently criticized us for telling 'symbolic history' or 'institutional' history, rather than wrestling with more substantive issues. In 1988, the journal *The Public Historian* published a round-table discussion, 'Government Sponsored Research: A Sanitized Past?'

Here, a panel of public historians within and outside the National Park Service discussed historian John Bodnar's criticism that histories published by federal agencies tended to '[erase] any record of social tensions or individual struggles'. The discussion that followed, for the most part, defended Park Service histories, based on the context of their purposes, but one scholar suggested that sometimes these studies 'are not placed within the proper context and thus their usefulness is diminished' (Thelen *et al*. 1988).

Historians in the academy and the Park Service do present their work to different audiences and for different purposes, and yet the two are not necessarily entirely antagonistic. In 1995, the National Park Service signed an agreement with the Organization of American Historians (OAH), the leading academic association that focuses on American history, to work collaboratively on park projects. Since that time, many leading American historians have visited National Parks to advise park managers on the ways in which history is presented in their parks. In many cases, these visits have facilitated new interpretative approaches, and, in one instance, Gettysburg National Military Park based its new multimillion-dollar museum on the historical themes the visiting historians recommended. Conversely, the OAH has benefited from collaboration in that park employees have sponsored sessions at annual meetings, and students from the member colleges and universities in OAH have been hired or received internships from parks. The principal benefit from the collaboration, however, has been that park service employees have benefited from the newest interpretations of American history, and academic historians have developed an appreciation of presenting their findings to an audience beyond the academy.

Of course, the National Park Service has not jettisoned its dedication to formal military history and to site-specific battle analysis. For a long time, however, we have focused a great deal of attention on the experiences of military commanders. On one hand, their example can bring us inside the Civil War experience. The fate of three commanders at the battle of Chickamauga is instructive. Union General William Rosecrans, who failed to cover the Union line and almost lost the battle, saw his career enter a downward spiral; Confederate General James Longstreet's fortuitous exploitation of Rosecrans' error made him a hero, albeit a flawed one, as he ultimately failed to capture the Union Army. Finally, the story of General George Thomas, who saved the situation for the Union Army, also allows us not only to delve into military strategy and drama, but to examine key aspects of identity, attitudes and experiences surrounding the war as a whole. Thomas was one of the few United States Army officers from Virginia who opted to stay with the Union Army. By deciding to stay in the Union, however, his family disowned him, turned his pictures to the wall and refused assistance from Thomas before his death in 1870, and from his friends later. Thomas' family, which owned more than 20 slaves, was among the elite of Southern slave-holding families. Yet, after the war, Thomas became a strong advocate for African Americans, having observed, first-hand, the fighting prowess of black soldiers under his command (Einolf 2007; Cleaves 1986).

While Thomas and other commanders will always be an important part of our battlefield interpretation, to serve our more than 11,000,000 annual battlefield visitors it is important to keep current with the evolving military historiography. Thus, we also need to talk about the participants on the ground – the common soldiers – who were far more concerned about killing or being killed in the battle, than whether or not their commanders were effective. Again at the battle of Chickamauga, Ambrose Bierce, one of America's most important post-Civil War literary figures, provides a different, more immediate insight into the experience of the Civil War. A Union officer, Bierce's fictional short story, 'Chickamauga', describes in graphic detail the horrors of battle, with no reference to those in command. Much later, in 1898, after Chickamauga became a military park, Bierce's reflections on the battle were even-handed and sensitive to both sides: '[O]n that historic ground occurred the fiercest and bloodiest of all the great conflicts of modern times – a conflict in which skill, valor, accident and fate played each its important parts; the result a tactical victory for one side, a strategic one for the other' (cited in Blume 2004: 141–2).

With the symposium at Ford's Theater, the two-week institute that followed, and the dialogue that began between interpreters, managers and scholars, we built a scaffold for expanding our interpretation of the Civil War Era. This work is, to be sure, part of a long tradition of interpreting our stories and resources for our visitors in National Parks. For generations, our interpreters have magically transported visitors back in time to the events that took place in our historic parks, and have inspired awe in the beauty of our natural parks. We have set high standards for interpreting history and the environment. Starting with Freeman Tilden's *Interpreting Our Heritage* (1957), in which the author set forth six principles for effective interpretation, by suggesting such concepts as 'interpretation is not instruction, but provocation', to the more recent publication, *Meaningful Interpretation* (Larsen 2003), which focuses, in a very practical way and through the experiences of park rangers, on techniques by which interpreters can transcend simply presenting facts to their visitors to guiding them to find meaning in their park visits, our goal has been to link tangible places and objects to intangible ideas to help our visitors discover their own meanings in our parks through a variety of interpretive media.

Following in that tradition, in the late 1990s and early 2000s at Manassas National Battlefield Park we had the opportunity to develop new interpretative media. In part, what we were able to do at Manassas inspired me to encourage other Civil War battlefield parks to expand their interpretation as well, and to find the necessary funds to sponsor the symposium and institute mentioned above. We developed a new visitor-centre film to introduce themes so that our visitors could connect with the artefacts in our permanent exhibit and to the actual places on the battlefield where these events took place. The film focused on a Union artillery officer, Captain James Ricketts, who was wounded at the First Battle of Manassas, on 21 July 1861. He thought he would not survive his wounds, and directed one of his officers to give his sash and sword to his wife, who was living in Washington DC, about 25 miles away. Believing he was still alive, Fanny Ricketts managed to make her way through Union and Confederate lines to find her husband in a makeshift hospital on the battlefield. Her graphic descriptions of her journey and the horrors of the wartime hospital, recorded in her diary, are depicted in our film. To connect visitors to the objects shown in the film, Ricketts' sword and sash are on exhibit in the visitor centre, as well as the red bowl Fanny used to wash her husband's wounds. About 200 yards from the visitor centre, visitors can also see the spot where Ricketts was wounded.

Through these various forms of media, we wanted to show the horrors of battle, the effect of the war on families and the ingenuity of one woman who would not be deterred from reaching her husband. Through the film, we were also able to tell another story that did not lend itself to any other form of interpretative media. One of the Union doctors attending the wounded described Fanny Ricketts' arrival in a coach driven by a free black man. After she entered the hospital to tend to her husband, the doctor saw Confederate soldiers take the man away, and observed that he was not seen again, and presumed sold into slavery.

Reaching towards a more complex and contemporary interpretation of the Civil War past is not an exercise in providing a new master narrative, but given the persistence of the war's traditional mythologies and the political currency of its issues, the process has resulted in significant debate, disquiet and even outrage among stakeholders. Especially in dealing with slavery as the principal cause of the Civil War, we have been subject to scrutiny and accusation. In a review of our symposium publication, *Rally on the High Ground*, one critic wrote, 'this book is, quite honestly, the guidebook of politically correct, government-approved erroneous "history" that the National Park Service is expected to accept, and perpetuate'. He goes on to say that 'these prominant [sic], learned "historians" [who participated in the symposium] continue to assert that slavery was not only a factor in secession and war, but THE cause of secession and war'. (Amazon.com 2008). When one Civil War park superintendent gave a speech in which he mentioned that slavery 'might' have been a cause of the Civil War, within a few weeks the Southern Heritage Coalition had sent 1,100 cards and letters to the Secretary of the Interior demanding that he either resign or be fired. Another superintendent reported that a modern pro-Confederate group, which at one time had owned the park he managed, was raising money to bring a lawsuit to regain ownership of the park from the 'corrupt and anti-Confederate National Park Service'.

We are then cognizant that not everyone agrees with the expansion of our interpretation of Civil War battlefields, but the NPS cannot resile from its more open and engaged approach to interpretation of the Civil War past in its parks. Among the nearly 300,000,000 owners of our parks – the American people – there are also defenders of the new approach: 'it's not surprising', wrote one online reviewer, 'that the Park Service's "Rally on the High Ground" effort has rattled some cages among people with an investment in older patterns of interpretation at Civil War battlefields – it was, in fact, explicitly designed to rethink and to change those older patterns, but to do so in a considered way that draws on the best of current scholarship about the war. This collection gives a good overview of historical thinking on the subject among this generation of historians, and challenges us to see these battlefield sites in a much broader perspective than has traditionally been done' (Amazon.com 2008).

In the decade since our symposium at Ford's Theater, the demographics of our visitors appear not to have changed significantly, though interest in our parks has expanded as interpretation has changed. While our observations are anecdotal rather than scientific, we have found that the American public is generally positive about our expanded interpretation. This observation will be tested in the immediate short-term. Starting in 2011, the United States will begin its sesquicentennial commemoration of the Civil War. Visitation to our National Park Service battlefields likely will increase. Many Americans will reflect on this pivotal event in our history. Numerous re-enactments of the battles near our parks will draw thousands of spectators, and hundreds of speeches will talk about the valour of the men who fought. And, no doubt, numerous books will be published to add to the nearly 56,000 books currently available on the Civil War.

As this occurs, the National Park Service remains committed to using our battlefields as laboratories for Americans to explore the importance of this era in our history. To that end, as noted earlier in this chapter, we have prepared a blueprint for the sesquicentennial, *Holding the High Ground*. In this document, we recognize that 'the approaching Sesquicentennial of the American Civil War offers the current generation its most important opportunity to know, discuss, and commemorate America's greatest national crisis while at the same time exploring its enduring relevance to America at the beginning of the 21st Century' (National Park Service 2008). Thus, we will continue to explore and share the broad themes of the Civil War Era with which we started more than a decade ago, and will pay particular attention to the newest research on subjects such as women in the war, the war in the West and the history of the commemoration of the war.

When Albert Henry Woolson died on 2 August 1956, as the last undisputed Civil War veteran, the first-hand stories of the war died with him. For years, the paradigm of National Park Service Civil War battlefields has been to tell the stories of the battles in the tradition of the veterans of the war. These veterans saw the war through the lens of their own battlefield experiences, and for years we have tried to replicate those stories. As we have embarked on a new century, we have charted a course from which we do not plan to deviate. We will continue to tell those battlefield stories even as we add other voices and other stories to our narratives of the American Civil War. Into the sesquicentennial of the Civil War and beyond, we will continue to wrestle with complicated issues such as the causes and meanings of the war. Only by honouring the complexity of history and the many people affected by the war can the National Park Service help our visitors contemplate and better understand who we are as a people.

Notes

1   16 USC 1–4; August 25, 1916, chapter 408, 39 Stat. 535. Laws in the United States are listed as 'USC' (United States Code). The preceding number, in this case 16, is the section of the code in which it is listed.

References

Amazon.com (2008) Customer Reviews. Online: www.amazon.com/Rally-High-Ground-National-Symposium/product-reviews/1888213728/ref=cm_cr_dp_all_recent?ie=UTF8&showViewpoints=1&sortBy=bySubmissionDateDescending (accessed 30 November 2010).

Blume, D. T. (2004) *Ambrose Bierce's Civilians and Soldiers in Context: A Critical Study*, Kent, OH: Kent State University Press.

Chicago Tribune (2007) 'It's War Again Around Gettysburg: This Time it Isn't a Civil War Face-off but a Clash with Nature to Restore the Historic Site to its 1863 Appearance', 3 September.

Cleaves, F. (1986) *Rock of Chickamauga: The Life of George H. Thomas*, Norman: University of Oklahoma Press.

Cox, K. L. (2003) *Dixie's Daughters: The United Daughters of the Confederacy and the Preservation of Confederate Culture*, Gainesville: University Press of Florida.

Einolf, C. J. (2007) *George Thomas: Virginian for the Union*, Norman: University of Oklahoma Press.

Escott, P. D. (1985) *Many Excellent People: Power and Privilege in North Carolina, 1850–1900*, Chapel Hill: University of North Carolina Press.

Faust, D. G. (2001) 'The Civil War Homefront', in Robert K. Sutton (ed.), *Rally on the High Ground*, Fort Washington, PA: Eastern National, 81–90. Online: www.nps.gov/history/history/online_books/rthg/chap6.htm (accessed 30 November 2010).

Foner, E. (2001) 'The Civil War and a New Birth of Freedom', in Robert K. Sutton (ed.), *Rally on the High Ground*, Fort Washington, PA: Eastern National, 91–102. Online: www.nps.gov/history/history/online_books/rthg/chap7.htm (accessed 30 November 2010).

Foote, K. E. (2003) *Shadowed Ground: America's Landscapes of Violence and Tragedy*, revised edition, Austin: University of Texas Press.

Gettysburg Times (2009) 'Tree Cutting Resumes at Spangler Springs', 10 July.

Janiskee, B. (2008) 'National Park Service Struggles to Restore and Protect Historic Sightlines at Manassas National Battlefield Park', *The National Parks Traveler*, 21 July. Online: www.nationalparkstraveler.com/2008/07/national-park-service-struggles-restore-and-protect-historic-sightlines-manassas-national-ba (accessed 30 November 2010).

Janney, C. E. (2008) *Burying the Dead but Not the Past: Ladies Memorial Associations and the Lost Cause*, Chapel Hill: University of North Carolina Press.

Larson, D. L. (ed.) (2003) *Meaningful Interpretation: How to Connect Hearts and Minds to Places, Objects, and Other Resources*, Fort Washington, PA: Eastern National.

McPherson, J. M. (2007) *This Mighty Scourge: Perspectives on the Civil War*, New York: Oxford University Press.

National Park Service Civil War Institute (n.d.) *Stories of the Civil War*. Online: www.civilwar. nps.gov/cwss/manassas/index.htm (accessed 30 November 2010).

National Park Service (1998) *Holding the High Ground: Principles and Strategies for Managing and Interpreting Civil War Battlefield Landscapes. Proceedings of a Conference of Battlefield Managers, Nashville, Tennessee (1998)*, 24–27 August. Online: www.nps.gov/history/history/categrs/ mili2/high_ground_1998.pdf (accessed 30 November 2010).

National Park Service (2005) 'Environmental Assessment: Brawner Farm-Deep Cut Vista Enhancement, Manassas National Battlefield Park, Virginia', United States Department of the Interior.

National Park Service (2008) *Holding the High Ground: A National Park Service Plan for the Sesquicentennial of the Civil War*, Washington DC: National Park Service.

Sutton, R. K. (ed.) (2001) *Rally on the High Ground: The National Park Service Symposium on the Civil War*, Fort Washington, PA: Eastern National. Online: www.cr.nps.gov/history/online_ books/rthg/index.htm.

Thelen, D., Kasten Nelson, A., Bodnar, J., Warren-Findley, J., Mazuzan, G. T. and Pitcaithley, D. T. (1988) 'Government Sponsored Research: A Sanitized Past?', *The Public Historian* 10, 31–58.

Tilden, F. (1977) *Interpreting Our Heritage*, third edition, Chapel Hill: University of North Carolina Press.

Washington Post (2008) 'Trees Lose on Manassas Battlefield', 18 August.

Weigel, D. (2010) 'Bob McDonnell Surrenders, Signs Peace Treaty', *Washington Post*, 7 April. Online: http://voices.washingtonpost.com/right-now/2010/04/bob_mcdonnell_surrenders_ signs.html (accessed 30 November 2010).

Part II

Identities

Chapter 6

'Our ancestors the Incas': Andean warring over the conquering pasts

O. Hugo Benavides

The Incas provide one of the richest sources of historical representations in the Andes. As the main historical conquering polity in South America there is no community in the region that has not had to deal with the cultural aftermath of the Inca legacy. At their imperial height the Incas controlled most of the Andean highlands from what today is Colombia, in the north, to the disputed territory between Chile and Argentina, in the south. Like all empires the Incas' occupation and control of the land was a violent one, not only in its initial conquering of its enemies but above all in its more supposedly 'peaceful' mechanisms of subjugation for integrating the conquered communities to the empire.

As coincidence would have it the Spanish conquest of the Americas occurred at the highest point of Inca territorial and political expansion, as well as in the middle of a bloody war for succession between the rivalling factions of Huascar and Atahualpa. In a way, both characteristics would prove influential in the rapid demise of the Incas at the hands of the new European invaders. In the first case the Incas' rapid ascent to imperial power made many Native American communities either actively hostile to the empire or, at the very least, wary of the Incas' expanding territorial control. It would be these same hostile subjugated communities that proved eager to support another invading force, the Spanish, which was willing and ultimately capable of stopping the Incas' violent imperial surge.

Little did anybody know, Spaniards included, that in less than two centuries little would be left of the mighty Inca Empire. What outright warfare and violence did not accomplish, the ravaging European epidemics and the ethnocidal colonial policies would. The Spaniards would ultimately prove more brutal and foreign to the established ways of Andean life and culture, furthering the imperial extraction of resources and the implementation of forced labour and tribute, reifying racial hierarchies and annihilating autonomous forms of cultural development (Murra 1989).

These different historical developments make the Incas quite an ambiguous symbol throughout the Andes. On the one hand there remain (almost five centuries later) territorial place names for battle sites between Incas and other

Indian communities which highlight the empire's brutal political domination. Not unrelated to these hostile communal memories was the presence of the Incas' own governing social policies. Some policies imposed mandatory labour as tribute to the Inca state while others instituted the forced removal of whole populations throughout the empire. Hostile communities were obligated out of their homelands and brought to live closer to Cuzco, the imperial capital, while faithful communities were sent out to live in the outlying parts of the empire as a form of political proselytizing (this uprooting was referred to as *mitas* in the native Quechua culture).

On the other hand, however, even these painful communal memories cannot erase the enormous defeat that Incas would suffer at the hands of the Spanish. The European invasion destroyed almost every single Inca accomplishment, from the decimation of sophisticated urban centres filled with richly decorated temples and palaces, to the loss of an official writing and recording system (quipus) which is still not fully understood today (Urton 2003). It is this particular destruction of Inca livelihood that marks the ambiguous manner in which many national groups, both Indigenous communities and not, relate to the once invading Inca forces.

This particular historical ambiguity is particularly salient in the central Andean nation-states of Peru and Ecuador, which in many ways were the territorial heartland of the Inca Empire. These two countries have also, and not by pure chance, been at odds with each other since their national foundations in the 1830s, when both claimed independence from Spanish control. One could argue that this hostile relationship between Peru and Ecuador is part of an Inca legacy, marked by the pronounced division between the northern and southern parts of the empire (de Diez Canseco 1983). This argument is further supported by the fact that it was this very geographical division which marked the fight between two brothers: Atahualpa representing the northern region of Tomebamba (today's Ecuadorian city of Cuenca), and Huascar the southern one of Cuzco (in what is today Peru).

Rather than construct a particular historical continuity of warfare and hostility among Andean communities, however, I would argue that it is more instructive to assess the particular manners in which this history has been produced and represented over the past five centuries. The very ambiguity of the Incas' legacy as both an invading empire and as a representative of Indigenous victimization points to a productive and complex process of historical hermeneutics that is far from straightforward. It is precisely because of the very nature of historical production that the past always looks to represent itself as smooth, continuous and unbroken (Alonso 1988).

And the relationship between the different Andean nation-states could be described as anything but smooth and continuous. The conflict between Peru and Ecuador reflects these long-term tensions and historical disagreements. Most particularly, war and other forms of violence have been used extensively as a means to defend (and protect) national histories. But the very fact that most in the continent have an intimation that the past five centuries have seen more things go wrong than right is what makes violence such an attractive, and even logical, choice. It is this initial conquering violence, used by Incas and Spaniards alike, that is very much one of the founding elements of all Andean nation-states, and yet an organic assessment of the violent heritage shared by Ecuador and Peru might contribute to our ceasing to think of violence as a valid tool of political development.

Therefore, the main objective of this chapter is to examine some of these historical incongruencies by looking specifically at the manner in which the Inca legacy has been reworked within the Ecuadorian landscape. There is no doubt that the benefits reaped from the oppression of an Indian past has come back to haunt the Ecuadorian nation, and enabled a strong Indian movement to reclaim their ostracized past. To assess these varying political processes I will examine three particular contexts in which the Inca play an ambiguous role in the production of an Indian past that legitimized Ecuadorian national identity and that continue to fuel the historical conflict with its southern neighbour, Peru.

The first context examined is Cochasquí, the largest pre-Inca archaeological site located in the northern highlands of Ecuador. Cochasquí expresses a vital discourse of pride in a founding Indian heritage for the nation in which the Inca conquest is intertwined in the historical narrative in an ambivalent manner. The second narrative examined is that of the official Ecuadorian high-school history textbooks which offer a romanticized version of an imaginary Indian past in order to legitimize Ecuadorian national identity. The final history analysed is the recent one put forward by the Indian movement in Ecuador, the CONAIE (Confederación de Nacionalidades Indígenas del Ecuador). In the CONAIE's history the Inca past plays a vital role in a pan-Andean production of Indian identity.

Cochasquí: the Incas and their/'our' heritage

The site of Cochasquí is just 56 kilometres north of Ecuador's capital Quito (Fig. 6.1), conveniently located at an hour-and-a-half drive from the city. The site is also very close to a cluster of small landholders who make up the *comuna* of Cochasquí (made up of five small 'neighbourhoods'). In total, the present configuration of the site exhibits fifteen pyramids, nine of which have access ramps and six which do not, and five to six mounds, although over 30 round mounds have been defined at the site (Wurster 1989; Benavides 1986).

The site expresses an ambiguous relationship with the Incas and territorial sovereignty. One of the main elements of the guided tours is the need to establish Cochasquí as a pre-Inca site. The fact that these pyramids are pre-Inca is constantly emphasized, as is the fact that the Incas, like the Spaniards consequently, were invaders in the territory, and that, as such, subjugated and enslaved the local population:

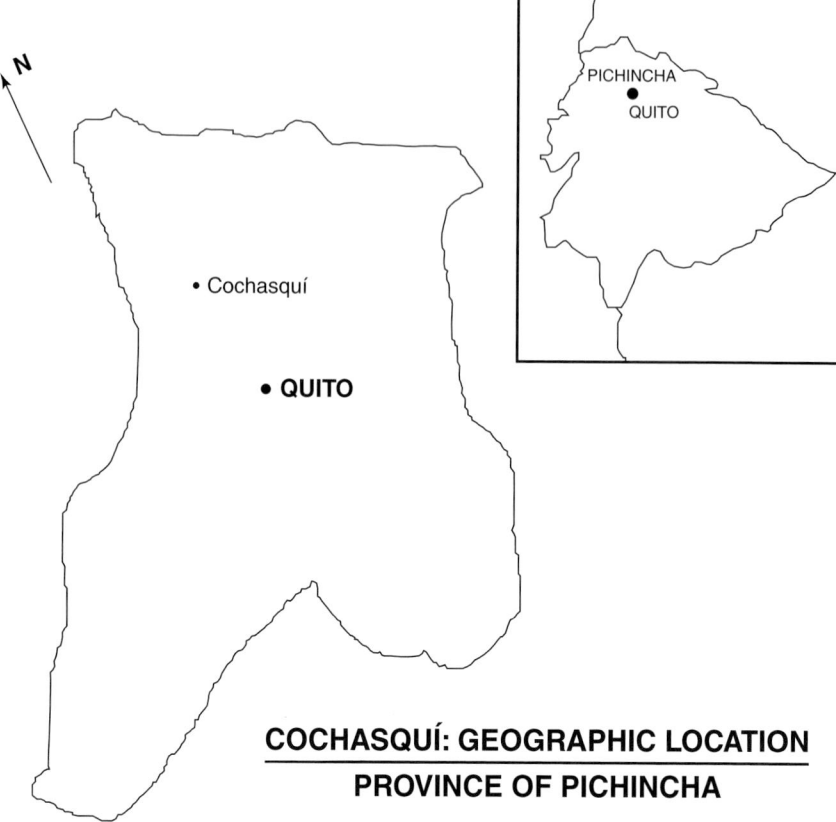

Figure 6.1 Map of Cochasquí: Province of Pichincha.

Well, this people or this culture to which we legally belong as Ecuadorians corresponds to the Quitu-Cara culture, which we know to be pre-Inca, that is, before the conquest of the Incas, a people who supported a harsh struggle against the Incas. They have calculated that this struggle lasted 17 to 20 years and that they did not allow themselves to be easily dominated. Even though we know they were peaceful people. (Pullas de la Cruz 1997: 11)

Great emphasis is also placed on the long resistance that the entire area presented against the southern invaders, which united its forces under the leadership of a female leader, *la Princesa/Reina Quilago*, who kept the Inca forces at bay for almost two decades. It was only through her marriage with their ruler, Huaina Capac, that the Incas were able to conquer and subjugate her people:

It is said that the Inca conquest was precisely possible because of treason, with the matrimony of Tupac Yupanqui [read Huaina Capac] with a female chief of the area. It was through this marriage that the conquest of the Inca became possible, since during all this time they could not conquer the area. (Interview with Wacho, 15 February 1997)

In this particular version of a national narrative the Incas are not part of the Ecuadorian heritage, but rather representative of the foreign invaders that throughout history have taken over the Ecuadorian territory and left it reduced to one-third of what it originally was in 1829 (Efrén Reyes 1950; Villacrés Moscoso 1967). This national myth of territorial loss has been ever present in modern Ecuadorian history, being part of the constant border hostility with Peru. The worst episode occurred in 1941 when Ecuador lost over half of its Amazonian territory, and the most recent one in 1995, which gave way to the recent diplomatic peace talks with Peru (Espinosa 1995). In this interpretation it is no coincidence that the Incas had their main capital in the present-day territory of Peru.

The Incas' comparison (or equation) with Peru makes it possible to see Cochasquí as Ecuador, as 'our own culture'. At Cochasquí, the local communities, 'our' ancestors, defended themselves against the Inca (read Peruvian) invasion, which makes it plausible to see contemporary conflicts with Peru as having occurred since ancient times. This is also clear in the following incident volunteered by one of the guides. According to him a group of Peruvian tourists abandoned the tour because they were angered by the guide's explanation of the site's resistance to the Inca conquest. For him, their reaction expressed their difficulty and inability to accept their historical legacy of conquest and oppression towards Ecuadorians. In his analysis, they were unwilling to accept the truth. But although saddened, he had no remorse; 'it was not my fault, that is just how history is' (Interview with Juanito, 15 February 1997).

But the Incas are portrayed not only as the enemy. In many instances they are Ecuadorian or, rather, Ecuadorians are their descendants. This is an ongoing theme within the nation's discourse of claiming Inca sites such as Inga Pirca and Tomebamba or Inca figures like Atahualpa and Rumiñahui, as 'ours', as eminently Ecuadorian:

With the victory in Quipaipán, Atahualpa not only maintained control of the Kingdom of Quito, but also became the only ruler of the Inca kingdom; because of this reason he took command over the Inca imperial capital [in Peru] of Cuzco, where he officially proclaimed himself the emperor of the Tahuantinsuyo [original Quechua name for the Incas]. In this manner, the two fractions in which the Inca kingdom had been divided with Huayna Capac's death became whole again, under the sovereign government of the Quiteño Atahualpa. (García González 1997: 177)

This favourable presentation of the Incas is also present at Cochasquí, which makes it possible for Ecuadorians to be equated with the Incas, and to make their history an Ecuadorian one.

The main instance when this reversal occurs at Cochasquí is when the Spanish conquest comes into play. At this moment, it is the Spaniards who become Ecuador's enemies, and the Incas who saw their end at the hands of the Spaniards are equated to Ecuador and its destruction. It might be true that the Incas are the enemies, but ultimately they are our 'own', almost family, with the Spanish the ultimate foes in this history:

> because this was a very advanced culture, very intelligent, that unfortunately, tragically was destroyed because of this problem of the Spanish conquest and [religious] conversion in the area. (Interview with Juanito, 15 February 1997)

Another way that the Incas are subtly identified with Ecuador is through the celebration of the *Inti Raymi* (summer solstice). In the display of autochthonous elements, such as costumes, language, music, food and *chicha* (maize beer), there is an implicit acceptance of the celebration of the *Inti Raymi*, an Inca festivity of the summer solstice, as a celebration of Cochasquí's heritage and, therefore, Ecuador's. The Incas are also implicitly equated to the original constructors of the mounds in two other instances.

The first is in the official site museum, where Inca pottery, specifically *aríbalos* (traditional Inca jars/pots), is displayed. This is not done with either pre-ceramic or colonial artefacts, which are also present in the area. Although no direct attention is placed on the *aríbalos* per se, they are presented as belonging to 'other' cultures, and appear at the site as a product of regional trade. It is quite telling that with rare exceptions (one or two guides), in all the tours I observed the Inca origin of the *aríbalos* was not mentioned.

The second instance is when the royal Inca road, which connected Otavalo to Quito and passed by Cochasquí, is referred to. In this instance the Incas are no longer the conquering enemy but another of the ancestral communities of the site. The Incas' accomplishments are here intertwined with those of the local inhabitants of Cochasquí. Since this road figures prominently in the Spanish *cronista*'s description of the site, once again in the shadow of the Spaniards' conquest, the Incas are more easily integrated into Cochasquí's own history.

One can sense an urgency to tell the truth about Cochasquí's ('our', 'Ecuador's') history. The visit to the site is supposed to right Ecuador's historical wrongs or inadequacies. This is effective as long as tourists themselves are willing to go through this 'ordeal of truth', which is evident in the guide Juanito's appreciation of the Peruvian tourists. But the truth is far from straightforward or self-evident. What initially starts out as a quest to put the Incas in their rightful place as enemies of the nation is overturned within the narrative itself, and they end up being 'us', or we become 'them', their descendants. The historical discourse at Cochasquí has an internal logic of its own, at least one independent of the guides' initial logical intentions, and the site stands as a testimony to that ambiguous rendition of identity.

National textbook history: the 'Quitus' and the Incas

The same narratives are played out not just at physical heritage sites, but in the nation's school texts. For the textbooks and Ecuador's official history there is no doubt that: 'we can never do without – either to historicize Ecuador or to understand America – his [Juan de Velasco's] "History of the Kingdom of Quito"' (LNS n.d.: 68). As highlighted in this statement, Velasco's history is considered of utmost importance for Ecuador's political leaders. For them every Ecuadorian student must read Juan de Velasco's history (originally written in the late eighteenth century), and know that in it they will find pleasure, inspiration and patriotic pride, because beyond question Velasco is one of the spiritual founders of the country (Vistazo 1997). In such statements it becomes clear that if the Quito nation resisted and outwitted the onset of the Inca conquest, it can also survive the 'treacherous attack of modern historiography'.

The textbook's description of the Inca invasion of the Quiteño territory is transfixed with a national imagery: Tupac Yupanqui is presented as the first Inca to penetrate the realm of the Kingdom of Quito, colonizing the region and founding the Inca city of Tomebamba to rival the traditional Inca capital of Cuzco in its splendour. It is also in Tomebamba where supposedly the next Inca, Tupac Yupanqui's son, Huayna Capac is born. These men again occupy the difficult space as both usurpers of traditional culture, and victims of Spanish conquest.

Tupac Yupanqui's next battle is against the *Schyri* (leader) himself, Hualcopo Duchicela, and his chief general, Eplicachima. The presence of generals within the Quiteño force is central to Velasco's narrative of resistance. To the names of the two previous leaders mentioned many others such as Nazacota Puento, Pintag and Quisquis should be added. All of these generals symbolize the enormous valour and courage in defending the national territory against the foreign invaders. Their courage was recognized even by the Inca himself who asked for drums to be made of the skin of a couple of these generals to honour their valiant spirit (García González 1997; Pareja Diezcanseco 1990).

At this point, the Inca once again offers the possibility of surrender to the *Schyri*, who again vehemently rejected the offer stating 'with a profound sentiment and love for the territory of his ancestors that only death would make him lose his Kingdom and freedom' (García González 1997: 169). Tupac Yupanqui makes his final offensive and captures the capital of Quito, while Hualcopo and what is left of his army flee to the region of Atuntaqui. Afterwards there is a general respite since Tupac Yupanqui returned to Cuzco to take care of other empire affairs.

Later, it is Huayna Capac who has to reconquer many of the groups and the territory over which his father had already gained control. He does this easily using his birth city of Tomebamba as his imperial centre. He also finally ends the last Quiteño resistance to the Inca Empire by killing the *Schyri* Cacha in the battle of Atuntaqui and marrying his daughter Princess Pacha who had been proclaimed as the new *Schyri*. Out of this marriage is born Atahualpa, who Velasco claims to be the last ruling Inca, born both of Inca and *Schyri* blood in the capital of Quito (García González 1997; Pareja Diezcanseco 1990).

At his death Huayna Capac divided the *Tahuantinsuyu* into two equal parts. The south or *Collasuyu* was left to Huascar, Huayna Capac's first born, while the north, the ancient Kingdom of Quito or *Chichasuyu* was left to Atahualpa, the Inca's son with the *Ñusta* Pacha. However, after an initial attack from the 'effeminate' Huascar (Navas Jimenez 1994: 85), Atahualpa and his generals Quisquis and Calicuchima kill Huascar and all the members of his lineage and ransack the capital of Cuzco. This enables Atahualpa to proclaim himself sole ruler of the *Tahuantinsuyu* and the Kingdom of Quito. Ironically enough, fratricide is one of the reasons, along with adultery and promiscuity, that the Spaniards would use to condemn Atahualpa to death in Cajamarca (García González 1997; Andrade Reimers 1995; Pareja Diezcanseco 1990).

The enormous inconsistencies in Juan de Velasco's account of the ancient Kingdom of Quito are so readily apparent that not even the textbooks can ignore the huge controversy that this history has produced in the past two centuries. Most of the critics of Velasco's history question its empirical validity because of the fact that there is no independent evidence to support it. In the wake of the emergence of an archaeological discipline in the country (in the late nineteenth century) it became clear that there were no archaeological remains to prove the existence of an ancient Quito nation. Not only did most of the protagonists appear to be made up or non-existent, but the polity itself seemed to have been 'invented' since there were no material cultural remains to support its existence (Jijón y Caamaño 1918; see also Salazar 1993–4: 4).

At the same time claims by Velasco's supporters that the Inca and Spanish invasions had ravished the Kingdom of Quito's material remains seemed unreasonable in the light of the enormous amount of pre-Columbian evidence of other groups being uncovered by these early archaeologists. All of this led this first generation of archaeologists in the late nineteenth and early twentieth centuries to feel that Velasco's history was:

> A conspiracy inspired by giving the much loved country, from which he was exiled, a grand aura in its past history that the nostalgic Jesuit did not want to be any less than the one of the empire of the Incas. (LNS n.d.: 66–7)

The history of the Kingdom of Quito was also questioned on many other counts. Not only is there no archaeological evidence to support it but any other ethnohistoric or linguistic evidence to ground Velasco's narrative empirically is also lacking. It seemed to have been purely based on oral traditions recounted to Velasco while living in the colonial *Real Audiencia de Quito*. Furthermore, he actually wrote his history decades later while in exile in Italy and without any aid other than his memory. Finally, many of the structural elements within Velasco's narrative closely resembled the ethnohistoric description of the Inca Empire itself and of the Spanish monarchy system of the period (Navas Jimenez 1994: 54).

But, perhaps not surprisingly, there have been many Ecuadorian scholars in the past two centuries (LNS n.d.) who have come to the rescue of Velasco's narrative of a Quito nation. They argued that Velasco had not written the history from memory and that he actually had documents to help elucidate his narrative. They argued that the interest of the 'Peruvianphile' critics in decentring the importance of the history of the ancient Kingdom of Quito was responsible for casting doubt on Velasco's history. For the official history any doubt about its Indian past threatens the mythical national identity, and at the same time exposes the unjust manner in which Indians have been treated throughout Ecuador's history.

The CONAIE: reclaiming the past to write an Indian history

Most recently, the Indian struggle has allowed the Indian to gain a new understanding of the pre-Hispanic past that the Ecuadorian nation-state claims as its own. The Indians no longer see themselves outside history but rather as full historical figures which, although silenced, have been able to regain their full conscious participation in history (Macas 1991; CDDH 1996). This knowledge is what allows the CONAIE (the Confederación de Nacionalideades Indígenas del Ecuador) to write and narrate the pre-Hispanic past from a first-hand position. It is no longer 'them', or even their ancestors, but 'we', 'ourselves', 'our' communities that participated in the indigenous social process of the Americas and that have been decimated by the Spanish and colonial encounter:

> In the territory that corresponds to the current Ecuador, *we were* living as multiple societies that had different degrees of socio-economic and political complexity [*behetrías*, chiefdoms, etc.]. *We were* not isolated communities, *we were* related in terms of commercial, cultural and kin exchange, etc. *We maintained* contact between the highland, coast and Amazon and in other cases with others so far away like communities in Mexico, to the north and Chile to the south. (CONAIE 1989: 19. Emphasis mine)

But this is far from an easy task. For the CONAIE this Indian history has been silenced for over five centuries (CEDEP 1986), being erased, changed and mutilated in every way possible to alter the elements of the discourse and present the Indian in a negative light. As the Indian movement continuously states, this mutilating task was first carried out by the white Spaniards and later by the white/*mestizo* Ecuadorians (Yupanki 1992), and history has been so distorted that even important Indian figures, such as Rumiñahui and Atahualpa, have been mobilized in state narratives to support and represent the hegemonic Ecuadorian nation:

> the dominant classes have even appropriated or expropriated the history of our peoples, such as the case of Rumiñahui, recognized by the state and its ideology as the father of the Ecuadorian nation. (Maldonado 1992: 153)

In this view the ransacking of history not only detracts from a genuine Indian past but has the audacity to use these same stolen Indian elements to legitimize the racist ideology of the nation-state. It is this same racist ideology that fuels official historical narratives, like that of Juan de Velasco (see above), where Indian figures are used to further national pride but not any kind of Native American heritage, and to hide these communities' destruction at the hand of the white/*mestizo* racial majority.

As the CONAIE expresses, through its struggle this historical genocide is what has forced Indians' reformulation of the past in their own terms: to 'straighten' history's distortions by proposing an alternative and more realistic historical picture in which Indians may speak and act for themselves (Pakari 1994). This new reformulation has two essential parts. Its first part is to reclaim all those Indian elements that have been usurped by the Ecuadorian nation-state and reinterpret them within the new native, Indian discourse (Bulnes 1994; Macas 1991). The second part demands the unearthing of the Indian past that has been buried by the European and Ecuadorian elite to justify their political domination over other Ecuadorians. This demands learning about events and revolts that have been traditionally silenced and recognizing previously unknown figures' historical contributions (Tamba 1993).

These historical tasks are carried out by both individuals and organizations, although it is the CONAIE (1988, 1989) which has taken upon itself the task of representing the alternative history to the widest possible audience. At the local level there are conscious efforts to retell history in the simplest way possible for those (Indian and none) who have been stripped of their past and identity. In this sense there are small educational pamphlets which through cartoon-like drawings present an alternative picture of the past. In these simple narratives the Spaniards and the dominant white/*mestizo* society are unequivocally presented as the evil elements of 'our' society, bringing torture, pain, havoc and ultimately death to the Indians. The pamphlets also make it clear that the Indians have suffered not only physical injury but a cultural one, that the dominant groups have not only victimized them but then told their story in their own terms and blamed the Indian for their own wrongdoing, shortcomings and cruelty. The pamphlets' task is not only to narrate history truthfully according to the Indian representatives but also to rescue or regain that sense of self that has been stripped away through the robbery of history (Perugachi 1994; Campaña Continental 1990; CEDIME 1987).

The CONAIE's history of the Indian organizations presents a generalized first-person account of the Indian communities and Inca presence in the ancient territory that is now recognized as Ecuador. This history is mainly transmitted to the Indian community in terms of educational pamphlets and magazines, as well as to the large national community in scholarly and political papers in journals and conferences. The main characteristics of the ancient Indian polities are that their organizations were based on the family, that there were no social classes or differentiation and that reciprocal relations were the most essential organizing element for these societies.

In the same vein, the Incas' presence in their territory is seen in a very positive light. According to CONAIE, the Incas established a redistributory system that made sure that all the members (including the poor, widows and orphans) were fed and taken care of. And even though the Incas used physical coercion to establish their own socio-economic organizations upon the existing polities, these are not seen as being completely foreign to the Indian Andean reality. That reality did, however, change drastically with the Spanish conquest and the exploitative relations established during the colonial period in Ecuador (CONAIE 1989: 20–2).

The Indians, through these narratives, are able to present a different vision of themselves that is more benevolent, caring and understanding of their own situation and plight. At the same time it allows them not only to see themselves in a different light but also to understand the exploitative and oppressive condition in which they have been immersed most of their lives:

> In that manner they took away from us the Inca Atahualpa, the Quipuc, the wise ones, the warriors, all whom governed with the Inca. All that we had was taken away by the ones of nice eyes but of a black heart like the devil. They still have not tired of killing us, abusing us, but even like that, we still continue to live, we still exist. (Chela 1992: 49)

It is the CONAIE and their national leaders who are actually the most instrumental in putting forward a new Indian history. They are the most concerned about dispelling 'ancient myths' and replacing them with an 'authentic history': 'It hurts in the community, they don't know history ... that the *Caras*, the *Quitus*, but the people don't know, it is painful' (Pakari 1994: 58).

It is this renewed Indian consciousness of their struggle, their national political participation and the narrating of the past in their own words that offer an alternative understanding of Ecuadorian history. The CONAIE has presented the most radical critique of the Ecuadorian nation-state to date. Essential to its contesting practice is a retelling of the national history in its own terms. These are terms which incorporate an Indian past which has been traditionally integrated into national readings, mainly the Jesuit priest Juan de Velasco's account of the Kingdom of Quito, that have served to nullify its revolutionary potential.

However, the CONAIE itself seems to be incapable of releasing itself from the hegemonic tendencies that are slowly erasing and homogenizing important Indian differences and identities. In other words, it is in great danger of promoting an alternative version, not to, but of a national hegemonic discourse. It is ironic that even in its transnational pan-Indianism the Indian movement is still very much caught within the national hegemonic stronghold.

In this complex reality, the Indian movement's financial support and identity exist in a very fragile global context. As the economic and cultural processes of globalization link Ecuador and the world, the potential for such revolutionary change as the CONAIE has promoted diminishes. It is limited in pursuing wider goals by a global order and global institutions—such as the IMF, World Bank and first world NGOs—which are not prepared to sponsor radical social and political change through their development funds. Under these conditions, the Indian movement may have to face its own hegemonic reordering, not as the promoter of a transnational Indian identity, but as a political alternative only within the confines of the Ecuadorian nation as it currently exists. Although the CONAIE consistently expresses itself as a tool of greater democratization for itself and the nation, current unequal global conditions are more likely to see CONAIE co-opted into a hegemonic enterprise before the Ecuadorian state experiences any kind of democratic dissolution.

These racialized conditions only deepen the hegemonic co-option of the movement's ideals and cultural programme. CONAIE is increasingly likely to conduct its future politics and cultural programmes within the confines of Ecuadorian nationalist narratives and a social order that render its original aims of fostering pan-Indian identity and agency less and less achievable. Muratorio (1998) has singularly expressed how the CONAIE is beginning to constitute itself as a hegemonic community along Western notions of gender, language, ethnicity and class. It is not surprising to realize as Muratorio points out that the head positions of the movement are mostly occupied by academically educated Indian men with membership in the larger Quechua/Spanish-speaking ethnic communities. It seems ironic that the movement's options would be limited on both sides: on the one hand a more democratic reordering of the global order would signify its demise, and on the other hand its national success would secure its own form of political/gender domination and that of other racialized groups.

Conclusion

The analysis of these three different historical Ecuadorian narratives assesses the role of cultural heritage in the underlying conflicts between Ecuador and Peru. The Inca legacy, I argue, highlights several of the problematic characteristics that contemporary Andean nations must contend with, but also the problematic nature of cultural heritage in the production of modern identities. More specifically, these same identities are heavily invested in utilizing a pre-Hispanic past to be able to recreate their new local identification in ways that are translatable or legitimized in contemporary terms. All three cases show the subtle, and at times jarring, relationship between the past and the (vanishing) present (see Spivak 1999), as well as between the local and transnational ideological constructs of the world today.

The cultural heritage enterprise highlights the conflict between the construction of a world defined by the local constitution of difference and the supposed global homogeneity of culture. This is what allows native populations to be hailed as central historical figures by a transglobal heritage discourse while these same communities are vilified within their own national realm, as the CONAIE is in Ecuador. What constitutes Ecuador as such an example is an Indian past (not a present) sustained by an archaeological practice that responds to a Western global ideal of culture.

A localized effect of this cultural heritage enterprise challenges us to come to terms with an Indian (as well as an African) heritage that has been made subservient to the European (and North American) desires which pervade all the official political, religious and economic settings of the continent. On the other side, however, there is also a post-modernist turn that looks to recuperate Indigenous/native identities all over the world, and that no longer turns a blind eye to their historical suffering. In many ways, this new form of exoticization of 'the other' also serves to shame the nation's historical repression of its own Indigenous population and the manner in which this ethnocide has further legitimated the interests of the wealthy white/*mestizo* elite.

In this manner, there is a double problem within the historical legacy of the Andes. The first is coming to terms with the historical origin of violence as a social tool of transformation, one that is even earlier in origins than that of the European conquest. However, the European conquest itself brought in a second, and equally, if not more, problematic dimension, and that is the coupling of that violence to a historical understanding of the present. As Foucault (1998) outlines, our age, more than any other, has reified historical understanding to new ethnological heights and made it seem natural that periods are linked in chronological fashion when they are not necessarily so.

It is this particular discursive violence that further serves to legitimize warfare as a successful tool of political transformation. However, more importantly it is this same discursive violence that ignores the travails of history, and the manner in which social genealogy, history itself, is an uneven palimpsest of records intersected by contesting notions of power and ideology. Again, as Foucault states (1998: 369):

> Genealogy is gray, meticulous, and patiently documentary. It operates on a field of entangled and confused parchments, on documents that have been scratched over and recopied many times.

And the better we are able to excavate and express this historical palimpsest for what it is the closer we will be to disarticulate the normative hold that this discursive violence and historical analysis have in today's global politics. In the Andes, this means recognizing the complexity of an Indian past and an Inca legacy that has been reused and rewritten many times over to legitimize contrasting political and economic interests. The lesson that this complex picture presents, I hope, is not to continue to build harrowing rooms of 'authentic' histories but rather realize how these conflicting interpretations contribute to who 'we' are today, and, more meaningfully, will always be essential tools to question who 'we' are to become.

References

Alonso, Ana Maria (1988) 'The Effects of Truth: Re-Presentation of the past and the Imagining of a Community', *Journal of Historical Sociology* 1(1): 58–89.

Andrade Reimers, Luis (1995) *Biografía de Atahualpa*, Quito: Fundación Ecuatoriana de Desarrollo.

Benavides Solis, Jorge (1986) *La Arquitectura y el Urbanismo de Cochasquí*, Quito: FUNSABER.

Bulnes, Martha (ed.) (1994) *Me Levanto y Digo: Testimonios de tres Mujeres Quichuas*, Quito: Editorial El Conejo.

Campaña Continental (500 Años de Resistencia Indígena y Popular) (1990) *Queremos que nos Escuchen*, Quito: Campaña Continental 500 Años de Resistencia Indígena y Popular.

CDDH (Comisión por la Defensa de los Derechos Humanos) (1996) *El Levantamiento Indígena y La Cuestión Nacional*, Quito: Abya-Yala and CDDH.

CEDEP (Centro de Educación Popular) (1986) *Primer Concurso de Testimonio: La Historia de mi Organización*, Quito: Escuela de Formación Popular 'Fernando Velasco', and CEDEP.

CEDIME (Centro de Documentación e Información de los Movimientos Sociales del Ecuador) (1987) *Derechos de la Mujer Indígena*, Quito: CEDIME.

Chela, Tránsito (1992) 'Somos Hijos de Pachacamac: Entrevista a los Mayores de su Comunidad', in *Indios, Tierra y Utopía*, Quito: Centro de Estudios Y Difusión Social (CEDIS).

CONAIE (Confederación de Nacionalidades Indígenas del Ecuador) (1988) *Primer Encuentro de Derechos Humanos CONAIE-ECUARUNARI*, Quito: CONAIE.

CONAIE (Confederación de Nacionalidades Indígenas del Ecuador) (1989) *Las Nacionalidades Indígenas en el Ecuador: Nuestro Proceso Organizativo*, Quito: TINCUI-CONAIE and Abya-Yala.

de Diez Canseco (1983) *Estructuras Andinas del Poder: Ideología Religiosa y Política*, Lima: Instituto De Estudios Peruanos.

Efrén Reyes, Oscar (1967) *Breve Historia General del Ecuador*, 3 vols, Quito: Talleres Graficos Nacionales.

Espinosa, Simon (1995) 'Hacia un Nuevo Ecuador', in *Tiwintsa*, Quito: Editorial El Conejo.

Foucault, Michel (1998) 'Nietzsche, Genealogy and History', in J. Faubion, (ed.), *Aesthetics, Method and Epistemology/Essential Works of Foucault, 2*), New York: The New Press.

García González, Luis (1997) *Resúmen de Geografía, Historia y Cívica, Primer Curso, Ciclo Básico*, Quito: Editora Andina.

Jijón y Caamaño, Jacinto (1918) 'Examen Crítico de la Veracidad de la Historia del Reino de Quito del P. Juan de Velasco de la Compañía de Jesús', *Boletín de la Sociedad Ecuatoriana de Estudios Históricos Americanos* 1, 1-3.

LNS (Librería Nacional Salesiana) (n.d.) *Historia del Ecuador: Primera Parte*, Cuenca: Editorial Don Bosco.

Macas, Luis (1991) *El Levantamiento Indígena Visto por sus Protagonistas*, Quito: Instituto Científico de Culturas Indígenas, and Amauta Runacunapac Yachai.

Maldonado, Luis E. (1992) 'El Movimiento Indígena y la Propuesta Multinacional', in E. Ayala Mora (ed.), *Pueblos Indios, Estado y Derecho*, Quito: Corporación Editora Nacional.

Muratorio, Bianca (1998) 'Indigenous Women's Identities and the Politics of Cultural Reproduction in the Ecuadorian Amazon', *American Anthropologist* 100(2), 409–20.

Murra, John (1989) *La Organización Económica del Estado Inca*, Mexico: Siglo XXI, Instituto de Estudios Peruanos.

Navas Jimenez, Mario (1994) *Historia, Geografía y Cívica*, Quito: Grafica Mediavilla Hnos.

Pakari, Nina (1994) 'Nina Pakari', in M. Bulnes (ed.), *Me Levanto y Digo: Testimonios de tres Mujeres Quichuas*, Quito: Editorial El Conejo.

Pareja Diezcanseco, Alfredo (1990) *Breve Historia del Ecuador*, Quito: Libresa.

Perugachi, Rafael (UNORCAC) (1994) *Rafael Perugachi: Un Dirigente Muerto a Puntapies*, Quito Union de Organizaciones Campesinas de Cotacachi (UNORCAC) and Centro de Estudios y Difusión Social (CEDIS).

Pullas de la Cruz, Virgilio (1997) *Historia Hecha en Cangahua: Guía del Centro Monumental Arqueológico y Vida Socio-Cultural de Cochasquí*, Quito: Ediciones Abya-Yala.

Salazar, Ernesto (1993–4) 'La Arqueología Contemporánea del Ecuador (1970–1993)', *Procesos: Revista Ecuatoriana de Historia*, 5: I and II Semester.

Spivak, Gayatri (1999) *A Critique of Postcolonial Reason*, London: Routledge.

Tamba, Floresmilo (1993) 'El Movimiento Indígena en la Provincia de Pichincha', in Federación Indígena Pichincha Runacunapac Riccharimui, *Historia de la Organización Indígena en Pichincha*, Quito: Abya-Yala.

Urton, Gary (2003) *Signs of the Inka Khipu: Binary Coding in the Andean Knotted-String Records*, Austin: University of Texas Press.

Velasco, P. Juan de (1841 [1790]) *Historia del Reino de Quito en la América Meridional, (Tres Partes I–III)*, Quito.

Villacrés Moscoso, Jorge (1967) *Historia Diplomática de la República del Ecuador*, Guayaquil: Imprenta de la Universidad de Guayaquil.

Vistazo (1997) 'Padre Velasco', *Vistazo* 723, 2 October.

Wurster, W. (1989) 'Ruinas Existentes', in U. Oberem and W. Wurster, (eds), *Excavaciones Arqueológicas en Cochasquí, Ecuador*, Germany: Verlag P. von Zaben.

Yupanki, Atik Kurikamak (1992) 'Comentario', in E. Ayala Mora (ed.), *Pueblos Indios, Estado y Derecho*, Quito: Corporación Editora Nacional.

Chapter 7

'We are talking about Gallipoli after all': contested narratives, contested ownership and the Gallipoli Peninsula

Bart Ziino

The 1915 Gallipoli/Çanakkale campaign, on one hand an unsuccessful Allied attempt to invade Turkey, on the other a successful defence, has been a wellspring of nationalist mythologies and identities for Turkey, Australia and New Zealand. Each has developed public rhetoric and rituals that enshrine the Gallipoli experience as critical to their understanding of the character of their nations. For Turkey the Çanakkale war holds an important place in the foundation story of the modern republic, in large part because of the emergence there of Mustapha Kemal, later first president of the republic. Kemal's success here is celebrated as a forerunner to his role in asserting Turkish independence and the integrity of the Turkish homeland, as well as his fundamental reforms of Turkish society itself. For Australia and New Zealand, Gallipoli produced the Anzac legend, which proclaimed the emergence of the former British colonies on the world stage, and insisted on the unique traits of these men from the new world. In Britain, too, Gallipoli produced its own romantic mythology, though without the nation-building focus it had elsewhere (Macleod 2004). The battlefields and cemeteries of that campaign have a history of negotiated, sometimes enforced, management and interpretation that goes back to the beginning of the conflict. While a narrative of conciliation between former enemies has long dominated the peninsula, the extraordinary increase in tourism in the past two decades, Australian overtures towards listing part of the site on its own National Heritage List and a series of controversial roadworks, have made contestation between Turkish and Australian conceptions of the site and its significance much clearer. The Gallipoli landscape and its management are, in other words, informed by the mythologies attached to the landscape, and they are not necessarily complementary. This chapter traces a history at the site of dispute and resolution, contest and accommodation, and the potential not only for conciliation, but for further contest between national mythologies and identities that are not consistent, but intersecting, at a place where both claim significant foundational moments in their national past.

As a heritage site, the Gallipoli landscape bears much of the weight of authenticating the national identities attached to it. The presence of the dead of 1915 is a literal investment in the soil. Some 8,700 Australians and 2,701 New Zealanders number among the more than 28,000 Allied deaths at Gallipoli, though these pale against an estimated 86,000 Turkish deaths, most of whom remain individually anonymous and unmarked. Among Australian travellers to Gallipoli, Bruce Scates has found that the 'site loaned immediacy to once distant events' and that at 'one level, this had much to do with asserting a sense of national identity' (Scates 2006: 199). Such travellers are hardly the first to express such sentiments: the rhetoric of Anzac was well entrenched even as the war continued. Shortly before Anzac Day in 1937, the Melbourne *Argus* venerated the men of Anzac and their legacy, cautioning that: 'We cannot allow them to fade into the limbo of forgotten things. They are part of our heritage. The story of Anzac is a memory which Australia will treasure, for it tells of a supreme test of valour and endurance.' Anzac, it continued, was central to vindicating Australian character, for 'A nation which could not in emergencies produce its own heroes would be bankrupt in the highest moral qualities' (*Argus* 24 April 1937). Despite the extremes of the rhetoric, the site itself retained the potential to validate the legend. When Peter Weir, who would later direct the 1981 film *Gallipoli*, visited the peninsula in 1976, he expressed his sense of discovery, though only in that the place confirmed what he already understood of the Anzac legend: '*it did happen, they did die, we do have a past*' (Gammage and Williamson 1981: 5. Italics in original). Thus, does the site continue to serve as an anchor point for confirming and renewing the basis of the national mythology and the identity founded upon it.

Gallipoli/Çanakkale's place in Turkish national identity took shape in the context of the declaration and consolidation of the Turkish republic after 1923, and, in particular, in the image, words and actions of the key figure in that process, Mustapha Kemal, later to be Atatürk (father of the Turks). The Çanakkale war was unique among the Ottoman Empire's campaigns of the war for more than one reason. First, it was the only unquestionable victory of the war; second, it featured the perhaps decisive presence of Mustapha Kemal as military leader. It was also the only campaign of the war fought in direct defence of the Anatolian homeland. This latter point ties Çanakkale nicely to the very real defence of the Turkish heartland that Kemal conducted in the subsequent War of Independence. The emergence of the modern Turkish republic can thus draw a lineage through what was otherwise a defence of the Ottoman Empire in 1915, and state narratives of the Turkish past do just this. As Işıl Cerem Cenker and Lucienne Thys-Şenocak observe, 'the official history emphasizes a clear break between the late Ottoman period and the republican era and rejects any continuity. Defining oneself in opposition to the Ottoman empire became an essential part of the process of becoming a new Turkish citizen' (Cenker and Thys-Şenocak 2008: 73–4). At a more popular level, journalist Fazile Zahir, writing in Istanbul's conservative *Zaman* newspaper, explains the 'heroic epic' of Çanakkale in terms of a 'matchless victory combined with the appearance of a great leader and future founder of the republic, Mustafa Kemal Atatürk. This land of the martyred, Çanakkale, will always stand as a symbol of our beloved country's independence' (*Zaman* 28 April 2008).

The first right to shaping the symbolic environment of Gallipoli fell to the victorious Turks at the end of 1915. The departing Allies had already marked the landscape with the bodies of their dead, and more than one message was left imploring the victors to 'take special care of their last resting place' (*Argus* 10 February 1916: 7). Despite later accusations, for the most part the victors respected those requests. The Turks raised some few memorials to their own dead: at Lone Pine and the Nek, Turkish monuments marked the heavy fighting and losses of the Allied offensive in August 1915 (Bean 1948: 343). Another Turkish monument that celebrated the Allied defeat was, however, destroyed by the newly victorious Australians as they returned to the peninsula in 1918 (Scates 2006: 138). Such erasure was not conducted wholesale, but it does point to the fact that, after 1918, the Allies intended to mark the Gallipoli landscape permanently, and on their own terms. For Australians, at least, part of the intent lay not just in their own mythologizing of the Gallipoli Peninsula, but in meeting anxieties about the non-Christian soil in which their dead lay (Ziino 2007: 59–81). Attempts to secure an 'Anzac estate' on Gallipoli, whereby the entire battlefield would become Australian, or at least British, had been popular since 1916. The idea gained a momentum, which to some extent it still carries, when Australia's Official Historian of the war, Charles Bean, advocated the preservation of the battlefields in their entirety as a memorial in themselves. Bean pointed out that:

> The site contains, besides the graves, the most wonderful Battlefield in the world, and also a vast store of relics, from life-boats and gun-carriages to innumerable shell fragments, from which local land proprietors will make profits unless the Australian Government anticipates them.

He recommended, therefore, that the peace terms then being decided at Versailles 'ensure that the complete Anzac site, including the Turkish trenches on the reverse slope adjoining' be vested in the Imperial War Graves Commission, on which Australia and New Zealand were already represented (Bean 1919).

In effect, Bean was suggesting that the Turks simply be alleviated of their sovereignty. The idea of the so-called 'Anzac Estate' got no support from the British authorities, though it did not lose its popular attraction. When Turkish nationalists repudiated the Treaty of Sèvres, and Mustapha Kemal's forces seemed set to march on the peninsula in September 1922, the idea emerged again. An English engineer suggested that a shipping canal be cut from the Gulf of Saros to the Dardanelles, so isolating the peninsula entirely. 'The so formed island of Gallipoli', Melbourne's *Age* reported, 'could then be

Figure 7.1 Beach cemetery, Gallipoli, under construction in 1923.

placed in the hands of an Anzac commission' (*Age* 28 September 1922: 7). The idea of claiming the entire peninsula, in whichever manner, was never likely to be accepted by either side, and while Australians and others wrung their hands in anxiety over the protection of their commemorative space, British officials at Gallipoli were also aware of Turkish sensitivities, as they detected a deep conviction that the cemeteries were 'a cloak for ulterior and sinister designs' (Neville Henderson to Sir Fabian Ware, 11 February 1924. National Archives of Australia [NAA]: A458, P337/7). Nevertheless, by 1925, the Imperial War Graves Commission had completed more than 30 cemeteries at Gallipoli, as well as three major memorials, which both marked their ultimate victory and named the dead whose bodies could not be located or identified. At Lone Pine was erected the Australian memorial; the New Zealanders were commemorated on the heights – held so briefly by them – of Chunuk Bair; the British memorial dominated the visual approach to the Dardanelles further to the south at Cape Helles. The French, less obtrusively, marked their losses at Morto Bay (Fig. 7.1).

The 1923 Treaty of Lausanne brought the certainty desired in terms of the permanency of Allied memorials and cemeteries on the peninsula, as it provided for cession of the land enclosed by those cemeteries. Reading the meaning of the treaty, however, remains difficult today, and there are still those who insist that Article 129 'grants the whole ANZAC area to the then British Empire' (Sellars 2005). This reading of the treaty is a comfortable retreat for those intent on claiming the Gallipoli landscape as peculiarly Australian. It ignores, or at least attempts to subsume, a powerful Turkish mythology of the Gallipoli campaign, which is reflected in the fact that the battlefields today are populated as much by Turkish commemorative fixtures as they are by the memorializing work of the Allies in the decade after 1918. That memorial response took time to develop, as did the foundational narratives of the Turkish republic. It was Mustapha Kemal himself, who in the 1930s set a conciliatory tone for the Turkish commemorative presence on the peninsula. This was almost certainly a corollary of his reorienting of Turkish society towards the secular West. At its heart is his famous and moving entreaty to the bereaved mothers of the Allied dead to 'wipe away your tears', as their sons had 'become our sons as well'. A narrative of forgiveness and friendship worked well to support those aims, and remains central to the dominant conception of the campaign today. There is some evidence over the succeeding decades from those who visited the peninsula of a confidence, or at least lack of anxiety, about the treatment of the dead. After visiting Gallipoli in 1963, Australian veteran Jim Keast reflected on the 'profound personal respect' between Australians and Turks, though he measured this by the absence of any Turkish presence around the Anzac battlefields (Keast 1974: 16). Two years later, accompanying a fiftieth anniversary pilgrimage to Gallipoli, Ken Inglis noted that Turkish officials spoke 'as if the two armies had been not enemies but participants in a common ordeal, sacrificial victims offered to the god of war' (Inglis 1998).

Despite Jim Keast's approving observation that the former (Anzac) battlefields lacked a Turkish presence in 1963, the urge towards a more permanent Turkish marking of the Gallipoli landscape had begun to reassert itself after Atatürk's death in 1938. In 1939 the Turkish government sponsored a monument overlooking the southern part of the peninsula, inscribed with a quote from Atatürk. In 1941 and 1943 further memorials marked particular parts of the battlefield, while in 1948 the government erected a memorial to the dead of the successful Krithia battles (Holt and Holt 2000: 69, 72, 127). With a much more expansive view, in 1944, an architectural competition opened to determine the design for a major memorial on the southernmost tip of the peninsula. Though construction did not commence until 1954, and limitations on government finances caused delays, a popular fundraising campaign through the press both exposed Turks to the project and reflected their willingness to contribute. Construction was completed in 1960, though the monument's details were not finished for some time. The bas-reliefs that were eventually installed recalled Atatürk's narrative of conciliation, as they feature Turkish soldiers shaking hands with their enemies, and tending to their wounded. That narrative is strong and persistent: a 1967 speech by Australia's Governor-General Richard Casey, himself a veteran, relating a story of a Turkish soldier delivering a wounded enemy back to his comrades, was enough to inspire its larger than life realization in bronze some years later. Still, if the Çanakkale Martyrs' Memorial was intended to reflect Turkish pride in their humanitarian behaviour, it was also intended to assert their pride in victory. Comprising four enormous columns, capped by a 25-metre-

Figure 7.2 Relief on Çanakkale Martyrs' Memorial (1960), depicting a battlefield meeting between erstwhile enemies.

square concrete slab, the memorial stands more than 40 metres in height, and so dominates the entrance to the Dardanelles (Fig. 7.2). At the same time it challenges the British memorial at Cape Helles, until then the most visible monument on the peninsula to shipping entering the straits.

Further memorial activity continued through private agencies in the early 1960s, as the 'Society to Assist the Memorials of the Çanakkale Martyrs' erected monuments to mark significant sites of resistance to the Allied naval attack in March 1915 and the landings of 25 April (Holt and Holt 2000: 65, 104). The process continued intermittently: in 1970 a national competition resulted in a new memorial at Chunuk Bair, dedicated to the Turkish soldiers who died there in August 1915. Australians had not forgotten either, though at such a distance they sought to recall and connect to the Gallipoli landscape within their own territory. In 1974, the Gallipoli Legion of Anzacs in Western Australia successfully lobbied to have the cliffs below the state war memorial in King's Park named 'Anzac Bluff' on account of its apparent similarity to Ari Burnu, where the Australians had landed in 1915 (*West Australian* 20

April 1974). In Brisbane in 1978, fourteen years after a Gallipoli veteran conceived the idea, several pebbles from the beach at Anzac Cove were installed in a memorial fountain. Much moved by Atatürk's famous words, Alan J. Campbell had them inscribed on the memorial as a sign of Australians' admiration of the 'Great Turk' and the hope that relations between the two countries would continue to be more than amicable (İğdemir 1978: 33–67). With a plan also to plant a garden from seeds from the battlefields, Campbell was continuing in a long tradition of transplanting objects from Gallipoli in lieu of visiting the site itself (Ziino 2007: 156–7).

By the 1980s, the Turkish and Australian governments were again paying significant attention to the marking of the Gallipoli battlefields. This reflected the renewed interest in Gallipoli/Çanakkale that was emerging on both sides of the conflict, as veterans of the campaign grew fewer and fewer. In 1984 the Australian and Turkish governments came to direct discussions regarding the battlefields, when the Australian government took up a veteran organization's suggestion that the site of the Anzac landing be formally named 'Anzac Cove'. The proposal quickly received support from the Turks, and the site was ceremonially named on Anzac Day in 1985. Turkish authorities also raised a series of monoliths, including one at Anzac Cove, bearing Atatürk's image and words. On the same day, three sites in Australia and another in New Zealand were renamed in honour of Atatürk. Reflecting Atatürk's place at the heart of Turkey's Gallipoli narrative, the Kemal Atatürk Memorial in Canberra's Anzac parade again speaks to the conciliatory narrative that he himself espoused, while at the same time elevating this individual as a symbol of victory and renewal in Turkey.

The seventy-fifth anniversary commemorations of 1990 confirmed popular reconnection with Anzac in Australia, and in Turkey too a week-long programme of events marked the victory. We might observe here the popular consolidation of the idea that the Gallipoli story was one shared between former enemies. At Anzac Cove, veterans met again and embraced; Australian Prime Minister Bob Hawke praised the Turks for the respect shown to their enemy, before he claimed that Anzac Cove was indeed 'a little piece of Australia'. With the publication of Hatice and Vecihi Başarın's history of Turks in Australia in 1993, the prime ministers of both countries referred to the events of 1915 as the point at which ideals of mutual respect and admiration that characterize relations were founded (Başarın and Başarın 1993: viii–ix). Such ideals did not mean the production of a common identity, but were accompanied by renewed insistence on mythologies underpinning national identities. Along with veneration of Mustapha Kemal/Atatürk came a more democratic acknowledgement of the ordinary Turkish soldier, or 'Mehmetcik', whose valour had secured victory. In 1992, a cemetery was established in the grounds of the Çanakkale Martyrs' Memorial, commemorating 600 Turkish soldiers. In the same year, a series of statues of Turkish soldiers appeared in the landscape, some simply giving form to the

'Mehmetcik', and others highlighting elements of Çanakkale mythology, such as the 'man with the shell', recalling the story of an artilleryman's superhuman efforts to lift shells and feed the guns that repelled the Allied naval attack. In the Anzac sector, also in 1992, a cemetery was established to mark the deaths of men of the Turkish 57th Regiment, whom Atatürk had famously 'ordered to die' as they resisted the Allied landings. Here, however, there are no bodies beneath the slabs set in the ground, though they bear individual names and places of origin from all across Turkey. Within the same precinct is a statue of the last, elderly, Turkish veteran of the conflict, Hüseyin Kaçmaz (who died in 1994), holding a child's hand. It is a reminder that the same urges that saw state funerals for Australia's last Gallipoli veterans were also alive in Turkey.

As Australians and New Zealanders marked Anzac Day annually, so in the past decade has the Turkish government formalized annual commemorations that concentrate attention on such new memorial sites. In 2002, 18 March was officially designated 'Martyrs' Day', and 19 September 'War Veterans' Day', so joining Republic Day (29 October) as a time to contemplate the meaning of the events of 1915 and 1923. As one high-ranking military officer put it on Martyrs' Day in 2009, 'The battle at Çanakkale is the foreword to the Turkish War of Independence. The sacrifices made by the martyrs there gave shape to our nation's future' (*Zaman* 18 March 2009). More than anywhere else, it is at the heights of Chunuk Bair/Conkbayiri that we see that those similarities in commemorative trends are in contest, rather than convergence. In 1925, the Imperial War Graves Commission unveiled its memorial to the New Zealanders on the site. As Turks developed a more assertive attitude towards commemoration, they initiated a direct response to that memorial, on ground that spoke at once of momentary Allied success and the definitive defeat of the offensive. Here, in 1993, directly adjacent to the New Zealand memorial, they raised a bronze statue of Mustapha Kemal, who had directed the successful counterattacks on Chunuk Bair in August 1915, thus ensuring the failure of the Allied attempt to break out of the Anzac sector. On this spot, the memorial proclaims Kemal 'The hero of Chunuk Bair and the Suvla Bay area'. The two memorials today stand in an uneasy relationship, both claiming the same territory, and the right to attach their story to it, though it is the Turks who now mark Victory of Anafartalar Day each year on 9 August (Fig. 7.3). John McQuilton has already made the point simply, that Gallipoli is 'contested commemorative space' (McQuilton 2004: 153–4).

This remaking of the Gallipoli landscape, especially since 1990, was accompanied by dramatic increases in the number of visitors, Turkish and international, to the battlefields. A large area of the former battlefields had been protected with the declaration of the Gallipoli Peninsula National Historic Park in 1973. Visitors to the battlefields had been consistent, but those numbers began a steady upwards trajectory from the late 1980s. As numbers grew, plans for opening further campsites and providing facilities for expected increases in tourism began to give way to deeper concerns about the

Figure 7.3 New Zealand and Turkish memorials facing each other at Chunuk Bair/ Conkbayiri.

appropriate marking and preservation of sites within and outside the bounds of the park. Studies of a series of 1916 Turkish military maps also revealed the extent of significant wartime sites on the peninsula that remained outside the National Historic Park. This precipitated the creation of the Gallipoli Peninsula Peace Park in 1996, a remarkable expansion in which the park's area multiplied to more than five times its original size, to 33,000 hectares.

That expansion involved not just additional survey work, in which significant sites were recorded and described, but an attempt to reinterpret the area in terms of a longer history than that which commenced in 1915. Atatürk's conciliatory attitude still firmly underpinned the developing ideas of the Peace Park, but in 1997 the 'Gallipoli Peace Park International Ideas and Design Competition' sought to conceive the entire area in terms of 'a setting where alternatives to war can be imagined and encouraged'. Those behind the competition were not being trite: they insisted that the events of 1915 – 'all mythologised by national sensitivities' – had so defined the landscape that it overshadowed all other heritage values. They sought not to disavow the experience of the war, but to understand it less in terms of the powerful national mythologies it engendered than in a more mature and international perspective. 'Fine-tuning is not simply enough,' they declared, 'the Park needs a supra-identity which transcends and transforms. Peace is the proposed supra-identity for the Park' (Gallipoli Peace Park 1997). Complementing the competition were two solid volumes, providing analyses of each significant military site, as well as of the natural values relating to geology, flora, fauna and waterways. These volumes, produced under Professor Raci Bademli, an urban planner at Middle East Technical University Ankara, provided a comprehensive background for entrants to the competition, as well as reinforcing the fundamental reconception of the park from the highest levels. The winning design came from a Norwegian architectural team, who sought to limit vehicle access to the park, while producing a series of unobtrusive pathways linking the key sites. Bademli was pleased with the subtlety of the design, and its lack of imposition on the landscape. One of the judges felt that the design 'recovered the history of the site, restored the overwhelming presence and sacred peacefulness of Gallipoli, and enabled young Anzacs to experience the landscape as their forebears had done' (McMullin 2005; also Gough 2000). In 1998, it seemed the institution of the Gallipoli Peninsula Peace Park was set to provide a new and sustainable management and interpretative regime for the site.

None of this has yet come to fruition. Indeed, much has occurred that is antithetical to the ideals of the competition and the winning design. The failure to implement the design, and to fulfil the aims of the Peace Park competition, has several causes. Within Turkey, funding was affected by changes in political leadership, while the winning architects found the Turkish bureaucracy difficult to work with. Professor Bademli himself was distracted by other necessities, before his untimely death in 2003 further slowed any momentum that remained. On the other hand, the Australian and New Zealand governments, who had been regarded as interested stakeholders in the process, had not shown a particular commitment to the strategic framework, especially as the number of their own citizens visiting Gallipoli and attending commemorative services on Anzac Day increased. Towards the end of the decade the numbers had increased so much that the Australian authorities sought to move the service from the small Ari Burnu Cemetery to a new site. They were concerned about damage to the cemetery; they were also concerned about providing amenities for visitors as they pushed for a new 'Anzac Commemorative Site' to be approved and constructed before the 2000 service. Eighteen months of negotiations preceded construction, which Australian authorities insist made the site consistent with the Peace Park's principles. It was nevertheless an intervention in the landscape, quite outside the Norwegian design, and the first such site to be constructed outside the concessions detailed in the 1923 Treaty of Lausanne.

The number of Australian visitors, and the conviction that this was a place of profound sentimental importance that accompanied them, no doubt gave Australian authorities the confidence to assert the need to cater to their interests and comfort. The Director of the Office of Australian War Graves, Gary Beck, while pleased with the new site, continued to insist on enhanced services following the 15,000 travellers who attended the inauguration in 2000. He was concerned too about traffic arrangements for delivering people, who had otherwise been obliged to walk up to five kilometres to attend. Numbers increased to almost 20,000 in 2002, and Beck reported that while organizing the services was rewarding,

> it remains a frustrating experience, knowing that we will receive complaints from some about the lack of adequate amenities and services. We continue to introduce improvements as we are able, given that the Peninsula is a Peace Park where development has long been suspended in order to preserve the culture and heritage of the area. But there is an urgent need for Turkish authorities to recognise that growth in services and facilities is far outstripped by the growing number of visitors all year round. (Beck 2004: iii–iv).

The Turkish authorities were at least aware of Beck's wishes: when in 2004 he sought to reshape and increase the area of the commemorative site, a preservation and historical committee at Çanakkale three times refused permission to do so. Frustrated, but undeterred, Beck persisted.

Such informal insistence that Anzac Cove was in one way or another Australian came from popular as well as official channels, as it had for decades. Though most travellers would not be so extreme, in 2005 columnist Nick Richardson made his way to Gallipoli, a pilgrim 'on the way to this mythic cornerstone of the Australian identity, a place that we assumed to be our own, even though it was a foreign field' (*Herald-Sun* 22 April 2005: 20). Intentionally or not, this was the kind of attitude that Australian Prime Minister John Howard invoked in December 2003 when he nominated Anzac Cove as the first potential listing for Australia's new National Heritage List. This list strengthened legal capacities to ensure protection of Australian heritage sites, but it also opened the possibility of negotiating with foreign governments to list sites of significance outside Australian sovereign territory. Now, referring to the 'most defining event in Australia's history', Howard insisted that 'although it's not on Australian territory, anyone who has visited the place will know that once you go there you feel it is as Australian as the piece of land on which your home is built' (Howard 2003). Howard cited the approval of his New Zealand counterpart for the heritage listing, but not that of Turkey, though he had 'no doubt the Turkish Government will give permission'. In Australia, the *Age* labelled the idea of declaring a site in another country's sovereign territory a part of Australia's national heritage 'arrogant and insensitive' (*Age* 3 January 2004: 18). There had indeed been some twelve meetings between representatives of the two governments before Howard's announcement, and, for their part, the Turkish authorities continued to contemplate the implications of such a listing, but offered no immediate resolution.

Howard's nomination of the site to the Australian Heritage List began to show that the histories and identities attached to the Gallipoli Peninsula were not one and the same, or simply shared, and that they have their contemporary politics. That point became even clearer just over a year later, as a series of roadworks around the Anzac sector developed into an international controversy. Initial reports of the roadworks in March 2005 focused on the alleged disturbing of Australian remains by earthmoving equipment, while soil was also being dumped on the beach at Anzac Cove. The *Daily Telegraph*'s headline 'GRAVE DIGGERS' drew pained responses both for its subject and from Australia's Turkish community (*Daily Telegraph* 8 March 2005: 1; *Daily Telegraph* 11 March 2005: 32). The Australian government seemed willing to perpetuate the idea that the Turkish authorities were alone responsible for this affront to Australian sensibilities. Turkish officials were aggrieved that it should be thought that they were damaging grave sites, and pointed to Turkey's profound attachment to the site: 'This is our own historical heritage, and it is the heritage of other countries too, and we respect that heritage' (ABC 2005). It soon became clear that, while the roadworks were not conducted with sufficient concern for the site's integrity, Australia's Minister of Veterans' Affairs had requested improvements to the road in August 2004, with an eye to the 20,000 visitors expected for the ninetieth anniversary of the landings in 2005. The request included, according to a departmental official, 'improvements to the Anzac Commemorative Site and measures to reduce walking distances and ease traffic congestion' (Department of Veterans' Affairs 2005).

Clearly both sets of officials had something to answer for in accounting for the damage that had occurred. Australian criticisms of their government's handling of the roadworks issue also tended to assume a proprietary right over the battlefields, as they insisted on the government's obligation to maintain the battlefields for Australians past, present and future. The roadworks, they argued, far from facilitating tourism, destroyed the very thing that they had come to experience: the experiential 'sense of the past' had been compromised, especially the 'opportunity for future generations to gain an appreciation of what our forefathers experienced' (Sellars 2005). The extension of this logic was that the damage also threatened to compromise Gallipoli's ability to confirm Australia's own national mythologies for those who travelled. 'We are talking about Gallipoli after all,' insisted Cosmos Coroneos, President of the Australian Institute for Maritime Archaeology, as he made a plea for the preservation of the battlefields (Australian Institute for Maritime Archaeology 2005). Yet government officials were insistent that they had immediate obligations to Australians travelling to Gallipoli today. The Secretary of the Department of Veterans' Affairs pointed out that 'The issues for us include safety and whether we can enhance in any way what I would term the "Anzac Cove experience", which is a particular experience for Australian and New Zealand visitors' (Parliament of Australia 2005: 72). Government minister De-Anne Kelly was more explicit, claiming that modern pilgrims were as important as the landscape they came to experience. It was 'plainly unacceptable', she said, that people should travel to Gallipoli and yet find it difficult to attend commemorative services because of logistical problems. If this meant making a decision between preservation or provision of wider roads, Kelly was happy to refer the matter to 'the 20,000 people who want to come' (*Sydney Morning Herald* 24 April 2005). The alternative suggestion, that numbers attending the Anzac services should be limited, also received short shrift from Prime Minister Howard. 'I would not want to do that under any circumstances,' he responded. 'That would disadvantage Australia.' (*Age* 27 April 2005).

What did Prime Minister Howard mean, when he referred to a 'dis-advantage'? What contest did he imagine was being conducted in which there was advantage to be had by virtue of large numbers of Australians attending commemorative services? There is some clue, perhaps, in a growing Australian appreciation of the Turks' own interest and mythologies surrounding the Gallipoli Peninsula. In one way, this is easy to assimilate into Australia's narrative of Gallipoli: recognizing Turkish losses during the campaign allows them to become fellow sufferers. To be fair, however, travellers to Gallipoli are also exhibiting a willingness to acknowledge that the Turks were defending their homeland from invasion, and therefore have a justifiable pride in their victory. That level of Turkish interest is immediately appreciable to visitors who observe not just the proliferation of Turkish memorials, but the thousands of people who visit them. The numbers have increased tremendously, with

600,000 Turkish visitors in 2003, 1.2 million in 2004 and perhaps two million in 2005 (*Sydney Morning Herald* 3 March 2005: 1). There have been official prompts, with the marking of particular anniversaries and the Turkish government's desire that school groups should visit the peninsula as a priority. The development of the Peace Park received impetus from this didactic function, as Turkish Prime Minister Recep Tayyip Erdoğan embraced a mission (with help from private-sector funding) to 'turn Gallipoli Peninsula into an open and closed museum'. This was to happen as quickly as possible, the *Hürriyet Daily News* reported, as 'the Gallipoli Peninsula has become an important place for both domestic and foreign tourism' (*Hürriyet Daily News* 21 March 2005).

Such development presents its own problems in Turkey, where in the past fifteen years there have been increasingly public contests over Turkey's key national mythologies, as Islamist politics has sought to promote alternative versions of the Turkish past. One approach has been to look to the Ottoman past, in which Islam was accepted as the state religion, as a seven-century golden age of Turkish achievement, which went into decline with the advent of the republic after the First World War. A second approach to refashioning the Turkish past, as Esra Özyürek has shown, emerged during celebrations of the seventy-fifth anniversary of the republic in 1998. Here, Islamist politicians and media drew attention to the Islamic foundations of the republic, or at least Atatürk's favourable comments about Islam in the early years after 1923, before the secularist reforms that followed his consolidation of power. In doing this, Özyürek observes, Islamist politicians found space 'to critique the contemporary secularist officials as departing from the foundational principles and thus wrongly marginalizing Islamists both from the past and the present of the Turkish Republic' (Özyürek 2007: 121). This debate has implications for commemoration of the Çanakkale conflict. While the dominant secular narrative sees Çanakkale as a defence of the homeland preceding the establishment of the (secular) republic, Islamists have alternatively posited it as the last great victory of the Ottoman Empire, or part of a foundation narrative for a republic that is not necessarily entirely secular in character.

That struggle over the Turkish past also had its reverberations in Australia, as anxieties about roadworks were quickly coupled with broader anxieties about Turkish management and interpretation of the site. As the roadworks controversy broke in Australia, Sydney's *Daily Telegraph* noted that while Atatürk's words may have produced a close relationship between the two countries, 'It is yet to be seen how that may be affected by reports that nationalist Islamic politicians want to make Anzac Cove a shrine to Turkish military might' (*Daily Telegraph* 10 March 2005: 30). The *Daily Telegraph*'s reading of the situation was certainly sensationalized, but it was at least a reflection of a more general response. On the same day, Australia's Foreign Minister, seemingly to draw attention away from any culpability the Australian government might have had over the roadworks, assured the Parliament that:

> There is no suggestion that the Turkish government is going to somehow politicize the Gallipoli peninsula. There is no suggestion the Turkish government is going to turn it into some symbol of Turkish triumphalism, militarism and nationalism, as has been suggested in newspapers. I think it is very important that people be reassured that the Turkish government is working very closely with us to ensure that Anzac Cove and the Gallipoli peninsula are properly preserved. (Downer 2005: 75)

Brisbane's *Courier-Mail* nevertheless reported with alarm that 'The Anzac legend is being corrupted by unlicensed Turkish tour guides who claim the Gallipoli campaign was a holy jihad decided by the hand of Allah' (*Courier-Mail* 12 March 2005: 10). The report referred to a controversy already developing in Turkey, where Turkish historians and tourism officials were seeking stricter controls on who could act as guides on the peninsula. Their main concern was not what Australians were being told, but what Turkish citizens were learning on the peninsula, and they achieved a ban on all guides at Gallipoli that was not lifted until December 2008, when only accredited guides were permitted to work in the area. All of this suggests not only contestation within Turkey, but an ongoing unease in Australia about Turkish narratives of the campaign that deviate from a sense of a 'shared history' on Australian terms. At an extreme, this can result in a disavowal of alternate histories. Confronted with concerns about Turkish guides, New South Wales Returned and Services League president Don Rowe insisted that 'There is only one Anzac history, and that's the real one that has been thoroughly and meticulously documented' (*Courier-Mail* 12 March 2005: 10).

If Australians are uneasy about the politics of Turkey's Gallipoli/Çanakkale mythology, then there were also concerns in Turkey following Australia's response to the roadworks issue. An important strand of Turkish national mythology focuses on the continued defence of the nation from foreign designs. This took its potency particularly from the foreign incursions that were finally defeated in 1922, though it remained popular well into the 1980s to retail a joke about 'all Turks having to sleep with one eye open because someone is always waiting to take a piece of their country' (*Sydney Morning Herald* 14 October 1989: 92). The sentiment is easily applicable to the Gallipoli story: Prime Minister Erdoğan insisted that the victory at Gallipoli showed that 'in the most difficult of circumstances Turks had shown their determination to remain independent' (*Hürriyet Daily News* 11 August 2005). We should not be surprised then that there were those who saw in Australian attempts to list Anzac Cove on their Australian Heritage List, or to insist on some privileged rights regarding its management, a further installation on the theme. Writing to the *Hürriyet Daily News*, 'C. B.' of Istanbul certainly did:

I read in Aksam newspaper that Australia and New Zealand have requested that Anzac Cove be considered an independent territory, much like the embassy grounds of each country. Seems an innocent enough suggestion but, to me, a thoughtless and devious request. Turkey's position, in their eye, has not changed. They are as ignorant of the Turkey of today as they were when they arrived at Gelibolu peninsula during the major assault 90 years ago. It seems that some powers wish to cut up, slice up, separate and divide this country into smaller and smaller chunks. We have to be very careful and alert as our forefathers were 90 years ago. I used to feel very close and amicable with the above two countries' people but since the request noted above, my feelings are beginning to change ... I believe the West has never accepted Turkey's existence. Although Europe claims to be secular, it is very much a religious body. Behind the most welcoming of smiles lurks a negative prejudice against my country. (*Hürriyet Daily News* 1 May 2005)

Australian officials too became more aware of that particular sentiment as Prime Minister Howard met with Prime Minister Erdoğan immediately after Anzac Day in 2005. Here, Turkey affirmed its rejection of the prospect of a listing on the Australian Heritage List, concerned that it had the potential to compromise its sovereignty. Howard emerged speaking of other means by which to insist on Gallipoli's significance to Australians including, potentially, 'international possibilities'. He had made offers of financial and technical assistance in documenting Gallipoli's heritage values, and the two agreed on a 'joint historical and archaeological survey'. Australian officials now saw their task as 'to look at an appropriate mechanism for symbolic recognition' (Parliament of Australia 2005: 105). If by this they meant a possible World Heritage Listing, submissions to an ensuing Senate inquiry pointed out that not only did Australia have no formal power in this regard, but that achieving such a listing for Gallipoli was far from certain. When the two prime ministers met again in December 2005, Howard resumed the point: Australia wanted 'to ensure the protection of the historical aspects of the site', though the means by which it might be achieved were still under discussion (*Hürriyet Daily News* 9 December 2005).

In 2010 that problem of recognition still seems to be under consideration. In October 2008, Australia had appointed representatives to an archaeological review panel, and was awaiting action from Turkey. Still, we might judge some development in attitudes through a further controversy over roadworks in 2008. Amid reports that bones had been uncovered, an Australian on the site claimed that 'Turkish officials have not learnt from history. There is just a disregard, I feel, for the actual physical terrain and the history that that land represents' (*Canberra Times* 28 October 2008). Turkey's ambassador to Australia was angered by the comments, and returned to the unarguable point: 'Gallipoli is in Turkey ... The Gallipoli peninsula is an integral part of Turkey and any special conditions there are the result of agreements by Turkey, entered into voluntarily in the spirit of reconciliation and mutual respect' (*Hürriyet Daily News* 29 October 2008). On this occasion, the roadworks did not elicit the outrage one might have expected in Australia. Rather did it provoke support for the ambassador's point: Gallipoli is Turkish and of acknowledged cultural importance to Turkey (*Age* 30 October 2008: 19; *Herald-Sun* 28 October 2008: 19). Still there remains no conservation management plan for the Gallipoli Peninsula, and little if any progress on the once agreed design for the Gallipoli Peninsula Peace Park. A language of a 'shared history' at Gallipoli comes easily to politicians and diplomats, indeed to travellers and interested observers. Yet it remains difficult to appreciate what was so clear to the instigators of the Peace Park competition: there is much more than a shared history here. Rather is there a set of national mythologies and identities that intersect at key points, but which are not inherently homogeneous. There are politics specific to each, and in each national context those politics are contested. Gallipoli continues to serve national mythologies, despite overtures towards a shared history of suffering. An acknowledgement of the right to those individual histories and mythologies about the events of 1915, with their inconsistencies, points of divergence and tension, but which attach to the same site, must surely be the point at which to begin contemplating the future management of a site as much imagined as it is real.

References

ABC (Australian Broadcasting Commission) news, 10 March 2005. Online: www.abc.net.au/news/stories/2005/03/10/1319864.htm (accessed 5 October 2009).

Age (newspaper, Melbourne, Australia) 1922, 2004, 2005, 2008.

Argus (newspaper, Melbourne, Australia) 1916, 1937.

Australian Institute for Maritime Archaeology, Submission to Senate Inquiry into matters relating to the Gallipoli Peninsula, 10 June 2005. Online: www.aph.gov.au/Senate/committee/fapa_ctte/completed_inquiries/2004-07/gallipoli/submissions/sublist.htm (accessed 5 October 2009).

Başarın, H. H. and Başarın, V. (1993) *The Turks in Australia: Celebrating Twenty-Five Years Down Under*, Hampton: Turquoise Publications.

Bean, C. E. W. (1919) Report on Inspection of Graves, Gallipoli. National Archives of Australia (NAA): A2909, AGS3/1/3.

Bean, C. E. W. (1948) *Gallipoli Mission*, Canberra: Australian War Memorial.

Beck, G. (2004) 'Director's Foreword', *Office of Australian War Graves Journal 2003*, Canberra: Office of Australian War Graves.

Canberra Times (newspaper, Canberra, Australia) 2008.

Cenker, I. C. and Thys-Şenocak, L. (2008) 'Moving Beyond the Walls: The Oral History of the Ottoman Fortress Villages of Seddülbahir and Kumkale', in Paula Hamilton and Linda Shopes (eds), *Oral History and Public Memories*, Philadelphia: Temple University Press, 65–86.

Courier-Mail (newspaper, Brisbane, Australia) 2005.

Daily Telegraph (newspaper, Sydney, Australia) 2005.

Department of Veterans' Affairs (2005) Submission to Senate Inquiry into Matters Relating to the Gallipoli Peninsula. Online: www.aph.gov.au/Senate/committee/fapa_ctte/completed_inquiries/2004-07/gallipoli/submissions/sublist.htm (accessed 5 October 2009).

Downer, A. (2005) Speech in *Commonwealth Parliamentary Debates*, 10 March, 75.

Gallipoli Peace Park International Ideas and Design Competition (1997). Online: http://vitruvius.arch.metu.edu.tr/gallipoli/gallipoli_english.html (accessed 3 February 2009).

Gammage, B. and Williamson, D. (1981) *The Story of Gallipoli*, Ringwood: Penguin.

Gough, P. (2000) 'From Heroes' Groves to Parks of Peace: Landscapes of Remembrance, Protest and Peace', *Landscape Research* 25(2), 213–28.

Henderson, N., letter to Sir Fabian Ware, 11 February 1924. NAA: A458, P337/7.

Herald-Sun (newspaper, Melbourne, Australia) 2005, 2008.

Holt, T. and Holt, V. (2000) *Major & Mrs Holt's Battlefield Guide: Gallipoli*, Barnsley: Leo Cooper.

Howard, J. (2003) 'Address at the Launch of the Distinctively Australian, Chowder Bay Heritage Area, Mosman', 18 December. Online: http://pandora.nla.gov.au/pan/10052/20080118-1528/pm.gov.au/media/Speech/2003/speech632.html (accessed 5 October 2009).

Hürriyet Daily News (newspaper, Istanbul, Turkey) 2005. Online: www.hurriyetdailynews.com.

İğdemir, U. (1978) *Atatürk Ve Anzaklar/Atatürk and the Anzacs*, Ankara: Türk Tarih Kurumu Basimevi.

Inglis, K. S. (1998) 'Return to Gallipoli', in J. Lack (ed.), *Anzac Remembered: Selected Writings by K. S. Inglis*, Parkville: Dept of History, University of Melbourne, 43–62.

Keast, A. J. (1974) *Straws in the Wind: Recollections*, Canterbury, Vic.: A. J. Keast.

Macleod, J. (2004) 'The British Heroic-Romantic Myth of Gallipoli', in J. Macleod (ed.), *Gallipoli: Making History*, London: Frank Cass, 73–85.

McMullin, R. (2005) *Age*, 15 October, 7.

McQuilton, J. (2004) 'Gallipoli as Contested Commemorative Space', in J. Macleod (ed.), *Gallipoli: Making History*, London: Frank Cass, 150–8.

Özyürek, E. (2007) 'Public Memory as Political Battleground: Islamist Subversions of Republican Nostalgia', in E. Özyürek (ed.), *The Politics of Public Memory in Turkey*, Syracuse: Syracuse University Press, 114–37.

Parliament of Australia, Senate Finance and Public Administration References Committee (2005) *Official Committee Hansard*, 17 June. Online: www.aph.gov.au/Senate/committee/fapa_ctte/completed_inquiries/2004-07/gallipoli/hearings/index.htm (accessed 13 July 2009).

Scates, B. (2006) *Return to Gallipoli: Walking the Battlefields of the Great War*, Melbourne: Cambridge University Press.

Sellars, W. (2005) Submission to Senate Inquiry into Matters Relating to the Gallipoli Peninsula, 14 June. Online: www.aph.gov.au/Senate/committee/fapa_ctte/completed_inquiries/2004-07/gallipoli/submissions/sublist.htm (accessed 5 October 2009).

Sydney Morning Herald (newspaper, Sydney, Australia) 1989, 2005.

West Australian (newspaper, Perth, Australia) 20 April 1974.

Zaman (newspaper, Istanbul, Turkey) 2008–9. Online: www.todayszaman.com/tz-web.

Ziino, B. (2007) *A Distant Grief: Australians, War Graves and the Great War*, Perth: University of Western Australia Press.

Chapter 8

Narrating genocide on the streets of Kigali

Stephanie L. McKinney

Since the mid-twentieth century, tourism has been a growing industry, catering to a variety of markets and creating numerous subdivisions in the industry (Sharpley and Stone 2009: 9). For Rwanda, and many other developing nations, it offers a potentially lucrative source of income. Part of tourism's appeal comes from its dependence on the pre-existing resources that make a nation or a region unique. The 1994 genocide distinguishes Rwanda from other African nations and is a significant part of Rwanda's national identity. The tragedy is also potentially a basis for tourism, as Holocaust sites in Europe, particularly Poland, illustrate. Construing atrocity sites for tourists has led to a disconcerting relationship between trauma and consumerism, manifesting in what controversial historian N. G. Finkelstein describes as a 'Holocaust Industry' that manipulates Jewish suffering for financial and political gain (Finkelstein 2001). The amalgamation of trauma and tourism raises similar issues in Rwanda, where the infamy of the genocide raises enormous potential for Rwanda as a 'dark tourism' destination. Yet emphasizing the genocide also solidifies its role in Rwanda's national identity. As history is articulated for tourists, it formulates nationalist discourse and solidifies a distinct version of Rwandan genocide in public culture. This selective articulation emphasizes the role of the international community while obscuring the current government's culpability for the violence of 1994 and legitimizing its rule. Like all national discourse, this expression represents highly politicized remembering and forgetting, and it is embedded in the government-run Kigali City tour.

The full story of the atrocities committed in 1994 is not limited to the genocide, which consisted of the radical elements of the Hutu majority targeting the Tutsi minority for annihilation – and nearly succeeding. The history of violence between the Hutu and Tutsi began decades before the genocide when the Belgians, who acquired Rwanda from Germany after the First World War, granted independence in 1959. Upon their departure, the Belgians reversed the traditional cultural supremacy of the Tutsi minority, whom they had elevated and utilized as local authority during their reign, by placing the Hutu majority in power. Initially, discrimination against and persecutions of the Tutsi, including several massacres of Tutsi civilians, characterized Hutu control, especially under the rule of the Southern contingent of the Hutu power base, the Parmehutu. These periodic slaughters created a significant Tutsi diaspora, much of which settled in refugee camps in Uganda from the 1960s (Mamdani 2001: 160). There they eventually formed the Rwandan Patriotic Front (RPF), a military force composed of predominantly Tutsi refugees. In 1973, Northern Hutu leader Juvenal Habyarimana ousted the Southern Parmehutu government and remained president until 1994. While this shift in power largely ended the mass killing of the Tutsi until 1990, discrimination within Rwanda kept the Tutsi diaspora from returning and allowed the men of the RPF to hone their military skills by participating in Uganda's civil wars in the 1980s. By 1990, the RPF was a highly trained military force seeking to return to a homeland many members had never seen.

Discrimination against the Tutsi within Rwanda was not the only factor contributing to the genocide. By the mid-1980s, President Habyarimana faced enormous pressure from international agencies, particularly those that provided significant development aid to Rwanda, to democratize and end the discrimination against the Tutsi, as well as allow the Tutsi diaspora, including the RPF, to return (Uvin 1998: 62). This pressure was most intense when the collapse of the coffee market in the late 1980s brought economic crisis to Rwanda, already one of the poorest nations in the world. These internal problems fostered the re-emergence and growth of the Parmehutu, which was responsible for the discrimination against and slaughter of the Tutsi prior to Habyarimana's 1973 coup d'état. Habyarimana's willingness to negotiate the return of the Tutsi, including the RPF, helped fuel the anti-Tutsi extremism that had characterized the post-independence period. The fact that he was negotiating with the RPF, which was beginning to make incursions in 1990 to forcibly return to Rwanda, fed suspicions that the RPF intended a military takeover and that Habyarimana was not effectively thwarting it by negotiating their peaceful return. At the same time, the Tutsi-led slaughter of Hutu in neighbouring Burundi further fed anti-Tutsi sentiment within Rwanda (Des Forges 1999: 65). The RPF attacks in the 1990s led to reprisal killings of Tutsi civilians, foreshadowing the genocide and unambiguously illustrating the Hutu extremists' response to an RPF takeover (Kuperman 2004: 61). Thus, a tradition of prejudice, economic instability, regional conflicts, international pressure and RPF raids created a climate in which Hutu extremists easily recruited and trained unemployed young men to become the *Interahamwe*, the infantry of the genocide.

The full-scale genocide began on 6 April 1994 when the plane carrying President Habyarimana and Burundian President Cyprien Ntarymira was shot down as they were returning to Kigali after signing the Arusha Accords, a negotiated agreement that would have allowed the Tutsi in Uganda to return peaceably to Rwanda. Following the assassination, Hutu extremists began the slaughter of Tutsi civilians, as well as politically powerful Hutu moderates who might have thwarted the genocide. The willingness of ordinary Rwandans to enact the orders to kill supplemented the manpower of the *Interahamwe*, and ensured that the genocide occurred in all regions of Rwanda. It was a traumatic, national, experience. In the course of a hundred days, Tutsi seeking refuge in public spaces, such as churches, stadiums and schools, were brutally slaughtered with machetes, clubs and stakes. In other cases, villagers killed their Tutsi neighbours, who were often also their relatives.[1] All farming ceased in rural Rwanda as hunting and murdering Tutsi became the requisite 'work' of those Hutu willing or forced to participate in the genocide. In this process, approximately half a million Tutsi were butchered (Des Forges 1999: 15–16). In July 1994, the RPF defeated the Rwandan National Army and halted the genocide by taking Kigali and the nation, ending the only period of Hutu rule in the past eight centuries.

There are numerous tragic elements to the history of 1994. The Tutsi, while the primary targets, were not the only casualties of the genocide; there were casualties in the war between the Rwandan Army and the RPF, and local Hutu, who often found themselves embroiled in the conflicts, were also attacked. Additionally, these events sparked a refugee crisis in which an estimated two million Rwandans, primarily Hutu, fled the country. Hundreds of thousands of these refugees died, both from the atrocious conditions in the camps and from reprisal attacks by the RPF, who would cross into the Democratic Republic of Congo to avenge the slaughter of the Tutsi civilians (see Pottier 2002; Umutesi 2000). The extent to which civilians, not trained military personnel, carried out the brutal orders to slaughter Tutsi men, women and children distinguishes this genocide. The highly personal connections between perpetrators and their victims decimated communities and families, leaving some very difficult questions of culpability for the multiple tragedies that occurred in 1994.

These questions also extend to the current government, many members of which participated in the RPF victory. When the Tutsi diaspora returned, both as an invading army and as returnees from abroad, it reinstated Tutsi rule in Rwanda. This occurred most obviously with the 2000 election of former RPF commander Paul Kagame to the presidency. In the aftermath of so many heinous acts, this government faces the challenge of creating a national narrative, an interpretation that justifies and legitimizes its rule while distancing itself from the RPF's role in the events of 1994. The result has been a rendition of history purporting that Rwanda was a peaceful, harmonious nation before the Belgian colonists arrived after the First World War and made the previously fluid social categories of Hutu and Tutsi permanent ethnic identities. The RPF traditionally emphasizes the Belgian colonizers' creation of the division between the Hutu and Tutsi, most obviously through the implementation of identity cards. This ignores Rwanda's recent history, especially the Tutsi exploitation of Belgian favouritism, as they utilized Belgian assumptions about their racial superiority to expand their power over the Hutu, as well as internal power struggles prior to the Belgian arrival (Vansina 2004; Uvin 1998; Pottier 2002). In the RPF version, the genocide resulted from the discriminatory practices of the Belgians, which evolved into the extremism manifested in 1994. This account also extends the focus to external powers, emphasizing the utter impotence of the United Nations, as well as the machinations of international agencies and the French support of the Hutu. The Rwandan genocide is therefore construed as an international event in which Rwandans are once again victims of Western callousness (Dallaire 2003; Melvern 2000; Kroslak 2008). Such a focus on highly visible international factors ignores the domestic and regional features of the genocide. However, this selective version of the past constitutes the foundation for nation building in post-genocide Rwanda. For this reason, tourism, as one of the forums through which the RPF-led government disseminates its account of Rwandan history and the genocide, plays an especially vital role in the reconstruction of national identity. The stories of the genocide are on public display, not only for the international tourists, but also for Rwandans themselves.

Kigali City tour

The Kigali City tour is one forum through which the Rwandan genocide is culturally presented. The Rwandan Office for Tourism and National Parks (ORTPN), a division of the government, created the tour; therefore, it is a vehicle of the state and a forum for the production of nationalist discourse. Through the tour, the state defines what is unique and noteworthy about Rwanda. The majority of tourists in the country come to see the rare mountain gorillas; however, these ecotourists generally find themselves in Kigali, where some genocide sites have become a standard part of the tourist experience. Through the Kigali City tour, the genocide is implicitly highlighted, bringing dark tourism into the broader tourist experience and rearticulating it in the international audience's experience of Rwanda.

The presence of several genocide sites on the ORTPN's city tour, illustrate how these dark locales are interspersed among more traditional cultural sites. The tour includes the following, as described on the ORTPN website:

> **Richard Kandt's House:** The embryo of Kigali City.[2]
> **Old Kigali City:** The inner city.
> **Nyamirambo:** The section of Kigali City that never goes to sleep.
> **Kigali Institute of Science and Technology (KIST):** The military academy turned into an intellectual and technological centre.
> **Camp Kigali:** Another harsh reality of the Rwandan genocide: the site where the Belgian Blue Berets were killed at the onset of genocide.
> **Radio Television Libre des Milles Collines:** The seat of the Hate Radio.

Geological Museum: One-stop Centre where you can discover the Rwandan Minerals at a glance.

Kigali Memorial Centre (Gisozi): A glimpse of horrifying images of Rwandan Genocide.

Hero's Cemetery: Rwanda's Heroes must be honoured and respected.

Caplaki: The one-stop centre for Rwandan crafts.

Parliamentary Building: Where the laws of the country are enacted from.

Nyarutarama: The new and modern residential quarter. The future of Kigali City is bright.

Dancing Pots: Learn about the Batwa [Twa] people and participate in a traditional pottery workshop and dancing. (ORTPN n.d.)

These sites present an array of impressions and speak to several distinct periods in Rwanda's history. Several present Kigali as a contemporary urban centre: the inclusion of the Parliament, the KIST, an active nightlife and a contemporary neighbourhood emphasizes the modernity of Rwanda as it strives to become a commercial hub of East Africa. Since the majority of tourists to Rwanda are North American or European, as are 80 per cent of international tourists worldwide (Grosspietsch 2005: 14), these features aim to conform to Western ideas of progress. They represent Kagame's current emphasis on development and his efforts to make Kigali attractive to international business and investors to address the dire poverty in Rwanda.[3] These signs of growth provide a strong counter-point to the destitution that characterizes the rural areas.

Rwanda's colonial past is also highlighted in the city tour. The inclusion of Richard Kandt's house represents the beginning of Rwanda's early contact with the West. Both the German and Belgian colonizers touted the natural beauty and resources of Rwanda, emphasizing the unspoiled primitive nature of the land. The Geological Museum therefore highlights this aspect and an inherent call for preservation. In addition, the Dancing Pots studio is one of the few public recognitions of Rwanda's Twa population, an indigenous pygmoid people who comprise roughly 1 per cent of Rwanda's population. This venue gives them an outlet to sell their clay pots (which are largely devalued within Rwanda due to the availability of cheaper, lighter plastic containers) and provides tourists an opportunity to see pygmies, appealing to a colonial model of African 'otherness'. The visit to both Dancing Pots and the Caplaki market includes the requisite shopping opportunity, essential for transferring first-world wealth into third-world hands. Therefore, the tour represents contrasting images of Kigali: as a colonial gem, as the locus of genocidal violence and as a rapidly developing urban centre.

Camp Kigali

Prior to the genocide, Camp Kigali was the training ground for the *Interahamwe*, who would later orchestrate and supervise much of the killing in 1994. Today, parts of it are still used by the military and for public gatherings (Melvern 2004: 26). On the tour, it is as the location where ten Belgian soldiers with the United Nations Assistance Mission for Rwanda (UNAMIR) were killed on the first day of the full-scale genocide. The extremists targeted these soldiers in order to provoke Belgian withdrawal from the UN mission.[4] They were brutally slaughtered and dismembered, their remains placed in a pile for the mission commander, Lt Gen. Roméo Dallaire, to retrieve in one of the buildings now featured on the tour. The surviving structure testifies to the violence of their deaths (Fig. 8.1). The exterior is pockmarked with bullet holes; the interior of the room where the Belgian soldiers died is also marred by bullets and a chalkboard with anti-UN graffiti preserved. The rest of the rooms do not bear the same kind of physical reminders, but house an anti-genocide exhibit containing posters and statistics with general information about genocides throughout history. There is no narrative of the Rwandan genocide or the death of the Belgians, although English-speaking guides are often available to explain events.

Figure 8.1 Exterior of the building where Belgian UN troops were slaughtered at Camp Kigali.

The area outside this building also calls attention to the slaughtered Belgian troops. There are ten columns placed in a circle within a small garden; each of these grey stone pillars represents one of the soldiers who died, with the individual's initials, and cuts on the pillars representing the soldiers' age. Thus, it is possible to discern the identity of the soldiers, individualized through the personalization of the columns. Additionally, there is a plaque on the exterior of the building listing their names, as well as another inside with the soldiers' names and likenesses etched in brass. These representations differentiate the memorial from the numerous mass graves containing thousands of anonymous Rwandans. In their death, these soldiers maintained their identity, a dignity denied to most other genocide victims due to the sheer scale of the massacre. It is difficult not to see this memorial as a privileging of these identifiable white soldiers over the hundreds of thousands of anonymous Rwandans. Thus, even within the context of the Kigali City tour, the memorial serves as an embodiment of white privilege in Africa.

The Camp Kigali memorial is also an emblem for Belgian–Rwandan relations. Dedicated on 7 April 2000, the national Genocide Memorial Day, the private ceremony was attended by family members of the slain men, and Prime Ministers Guy Verhofstadt of Belgium and Bernard Makuza of Rwanda (Panafrican News Agency 2000).[5] During the dedication ceremony, Verhofstadt apologized to the soldiers' families, and vowed that the Belgian government would 'ensure that they did not die in vain' (Panafrican News Agency 2000). The deaths of these soldiers are incorporated into Belgian foreign policy through a promise of ongoing support for Rwanda, illustrating the role of memorials in contemporary diplomacy. Belgium has donated significant resources to Rwanda since its independence in 1959, contributing 1.5 million dollars to the ten-year anniversary memorialization alone (Hirondelle News Agency 2004). After the dedication, the Belgian Prime Minister visited the Kigali Memorial Centre to acknowledge the Rwandans killed. The recognition of mutual suffering through a common history shapes their future relationship against the backdrop of the genocide, emphasizing the cost to both nations. Thus, while contextualized in the city tour as a significant site, the Camp Kigali memorial also functions as a medium of diplomacy and defining relations between Belgium and Rwanda and emphasizes the intertwined histories of the two nations.

While a genocide site, the Camp Kigali memorial inevitably emphasizes the presence of the Belgians and speaks to Rwanda's colonial past. While these Belgian soldiers came to Rwanda as peacekeepers, the Western presence in Rwanda remains contested. This memorial reverses the traditional dynamics of power: rather than being an expression of superior power, Belgian military presence and the deaths of the soldiers represent the impotence of the West in the face of the genocide. The bullet holes throughout the building testify to the indefensible nature of the troops' position, allegorically representing the meagre UN response to an overwhelming conflict. The memorial also speaks to the momentary success of the *génocidaires*, and the triumph of extremism over global order.

There is a clear distinction between the representation of the Belgian presence in the outdoor display of columns and the building's interior. The outdoor feature of the memorial contains no direct reference to Belgium, although the tricolour of the Belgian flag appears on a large flowerpot placed near the stone pillars, as well as on the outdoor planters in front of the building where the Belgians died, creating a symbolic Belgian presence. These Belgian soldiers have once again 'claimed' a piece of Kigali through their deaths, though it is undoubtedly quite deliberate that there is not an actual Belgian flag flying over the hills of Kigali. Within the Camp Kigali building, however, the flags of Rwanda and Belgium stand side by side on either side of a plaque identifying the men killed. This connotes the dual loss of this tragedy, contextualized by the evidence of atrocious bloodshed.

The memorial at Camp Kigali represents the nexus of local, national and international narratives of the genocide. It also has a place in the Kigali City tour, contributing to the narrative of the city, and placing a macabre manifestation of the violence of the genocide in the definitional story of Kigali. In this context, Camp Kigali has the dual purpose of reflecting the extremism of the violence, and the failure of the UN to protect its own, much less Rwanda. Finally, the memorial offers a statement about the global nature of genocide, through both its incorporation of two nations' positions and the anti-genocide exhibit. It is a reinsertion of the Belgian presence in Kigali, albeit as post-colonial victims rather than colonial oppressors as the Belgians and Rwandans intertwine once again in a tragic past. This interrelation emphasized in the narrative of the genocide presented through the Kigali City tour offers no explanation as to the causes of the genocide while framing Rwandan history in terms of Belgian (in)action in the tradition of RPF discourse about the genocide.

Kigali Memorial Centre

If the Camp Kigali memorial illustrates the complexity of the international story presented for the tourist gaze, the Kigali Memorial Centre represents the national narrative of the genocide (Fig. 8.2). This is the best known of all the Rwandan genocide sites, a mandatory part of any dignitary's visit to Rwanda, and the most accessible memorial for tourists. The Kigali City Council hired Aegis Trust, a British non-government organization specializing in Holocaust education, as a consultant for the memorial, which opened on the ten-year anniversary of the genocide. While a museum, it also functions as a mass grave. In the aftermath of the genocide, new construction in Kigali continually unearthed corpses hastily buried in 1994, creating the need for a central, dignified burial site. This differentiates it from other sites, such as Auschwitz, which were the locus of slaughter, in that its significance as a genocide site

Figure 8.2 The Kigali Memorial Centre.

emerged after the fact. Currently, it houses the bones of an estimated 250,000 victims, giving the site multiple purposes as a means of defining history, and as an educational forum for the next generation, including Kigali's international tourists.

While the Centre serves as a documentation centre and develops educational programmes for Rwandan children, most tourists will experience it as a museum and graveyard. However, the educative component is inherent in these presentations as well. According to the Kigali Memorial Centre's official website, it is 'a meaningful tribute to those who perished, and a powerful educational tool for the next generation' (Kigali Memorial Centre n.d.). Since most tourists have limited knowledge of the events of 1994, the museum exhibits define, explain and contextualize the genocide for them. These include a three-part overview of the genocide, a children's exhibit and 'Wasted Lives', which details other genocides and similar atrocities, including the experience of the Hereo people under German colonialism, the Holocaust, Armenia, Cambodia and Bosnia. Like the Camp Kigali memorial, this exhibit frames the Rwandan genocide in terms of similar atrocities across several continents and centuries. This contextualization is a definitive move against the idea of African tribal barbarism as the root cause of the genocide (as well as other political violence), which is a common misconception often characterizing Western interactions with Africa.[6] By locating the Rwandan genocide among similar atrocities, the Kigali Memorial Centre's exhibit emphasizes the universality of the lesson. This contextualization suggests that the museum is not housing a display of African spectacle, but represents a far more universal phenomenon. At the same time, universalizing genocide is normalizing it, potentially limiting the efficacy of the preventative message.

The museum is also a key forum for articulating the government's interpretation of the genocide. Given the role of the Kigali City Council in the development of this museum, this is not surprising. The first room in the museum presents the history of Rwanda through panels displaying images of traditional dances and crafts. The next section describes Belgian rule, including a replication of the identity cards that officially defined every native Rwandan as Tutsi, Hutu or Twa. The display then moves to the Hutu Revolution in 1959, thus drawing a linear connection between the Belgians and the Hutu. From there, tales of the slaughter, photographs of victims and videos of survivor testimonies tell the story of the genocide itself. All of the narratives, whether written or recorded, are presented in Kinyarwandan, French and English. Thus, the very framing of the exhibits suggests the significance of the genocide to all who visit; it is not just a story for Rwandans, but for the international community as well. The Kigali Memorial Centre is one of the few places in Rwanda that deals with the causes of the genocide directly, and the very design of the museum reflects the numerous audiences who attend.

Beyond these visual renditions, the museum also includes physical artefacts from the genocide. A room of victims' preserved clothing is on the same floor as the explanatory exhibit. An adjacent room contains human remains, primarily skulls and other bones, enclosed in glass cases. In another part of the floor, videos of survivor testimonies play continuously among numerous informal family photographs of the victims. This exhibit emphasizes the lives, not deaths, of the individuals targeted during the genocide and addresses the desire to avoid framing the dead in the perpetrators' terms by refusing to reduce the targeted group to dehumanized remnants of a society where they no longer belong (Young 1993: 133). Thus, the Kigali Memorial Centre presents those so brutally dehumanized in highly individual terms. In doing this it also gives those who died individuality in a way that the display of anonymous bones inexorably refutes.

The Kigali Centre is the Rwandan museum tourists are most likely to visit since the others, including the National Museum in Butare, are not geographically close to Kigali, where tourists land, or the mountain gorillas' habitat, the fundamental basis of Rwandan tourism. As a result, while the Kigali Memorial Centre was constructed to accommodate Kigali's dead, it has far more prominence and purpose than the other memorials which also serve as mass graves. It serves the local population by continuing to bury the dead, documenting the genocide and educating Rwandan youth. It also has an explicit message for the international community, however, which is conspicuously absent from the other genocide sites due to their lack of explicit narration. Because it is the only iteration of Rwanda's past that tourists are likely to see, the genocide then becomes representative of the entirety of Rwandan history, reducing a rich and vibrant culture to its darkest hour.

Rather than incorporate the genocide in the recent national history, the Kigali Memorial Centre shifts the emphasis to the larger issues. As stated on the Aegis website, it is 'an international centre. It deals with a topic of international importance, with far-reaching significance, and is designed to engage and challenge an international visitor base' (Kigali Memorial Centre n.d.). This direct call to the visitor boldly asserts the museum's purpose by addressing the tourist and challenging him/her to confront the genocide as a global experience, reflecting the tendency of atrocity memorials to serve as both a lesson for contemporary audiences and a means of presenting hope for a different future (Ashworth 2002: 364). In this case, the display also mirrors the emphasis on the international community in the expectation that the international visitor will be 'engage[d] and challenge[d]' (ibid.) by the time spent in the Centre. This emphasis also posits the visitor as an agent of social change, inferring a call for action in an otherwise dark locale. The emphasis on the global nature of this kind of violence and persecution ignores the far more difficult issue of the national history, except for when it intersects with Western culpability.

Because the Kigali Memorial Centre is a centre for research and education, its purpose is constantly evolving. Currently, the Centre records oral histories of survivors, serving the potentially therapeutic function of allowing them to tell their stories while contributing significantly to the documentation of the genocide. It fulfils the drive for memory, defined by Pierre Nora: 'The imperative of our epoch is not only to keep everything, to preserve every indicator of memory – even when we are not sure which memory is being indicated – but also to produce archives' (1989: 15). Thus, it is serving not only memory but also national identity through the presentation of these manifestations of memory. If Patricia Boniface and John Fowler are correct in their argument that 'Museum buildings are one of the more powerful statements that a place can make about itself and how others would wish to see it' (1993: 104), then the genocide is indeed the prominent feature in Rwandan national identity. The Kigali Memorial Centre contributes graphic images of the genocide to the visitor's overall experience, counteracting the image of progress that the government actively promoted in other venues. Hosting genocide is an ignoble history for any nation, and partially explains the emphasis on the role of the West as both colonizers and apathetic bystanders. While the genocide is too visible in Rwanda's identity to ignore, clearly one way of mitigating the implications is emphasizing the role, both active and passive, of external agents. This shift reformulates the narrative into a model of Western perpetrator and African victim, a familiar dynamic for all concerned, and one legitimated by the examples presented. The Kigali Memorial Centre is the longest stop and most substantial part of the Kigali City tour, indicating its importance in the tourist experience and the primacy of the genocide in Rwanda's national identity.

Remembering and forgetting

The Kigali City tour is a display of both remembering and forgetting. Just as the emphasis on the slaughter of the Belgian UN troops subverts the previous use of Camp Kigali to train agents of genocide, other sites have one of their multiple identities brought to the forefront, while others are marginalized. For example, the building that housed the Radio Télévision Libre des Mille Collines (RTLM) is included on the tour. This radio station was the primary conduit of the Hutu extremists' anti-Tutsi propaganda, making the extremist anti-Tutsi rhetoric a highly visible part of Rwandan public culture. During the genocide, as well as spreading, and therefore normalizing, the Hutu extremists' point of view, it became one of the primary conduits for information among the *génocidaires* by airing suggested locations of Tutsi targets, their descriptions and licence plate numbers (Thompson 2007; Melvern 2004: 208). In addition, the *génocidaires* utilized the station to request supplies and report the progress of the genocide. The broadcasts of the RTLM are among the key signifiers of the impunity with which the extremists articulated their intent (Chalk 1999; Straus 2006). While it is well known to those versed in the history of the genocide, the average tourist is not necessarily aware of its significance prior to the Kigali City tour.

Unlike Camp Kigali and the Kigali Memorial Centre, both of which have obvious memorials outside the structures, there is no indication of the significance of this building from the outside (Fig. 8.3). It now hosts an array of businesses, displaying no obvious connection to its former role as the location of the RTLM. Its identification is entirely dependent the either on the visitor knowing its address or on a tour guide pointing it out. Its inclusion in the tour embodies the issues of authenticity and identity that tourist venues face. The radio station does not exist any more: the RPF destroyed it upon reaching Kigali. For tourists, however, this identity is reimposed, accentuating its function as a genocide site. This brings the genocide into the present, prioritizing a past identity over the present incarnation, which is otherwise indistinguishable from other similar buildings. Symbolically, the station represents another RPF victory over the hate-filled previous regime and illustrates the dangerous potential of free speech, which is not part of contemporary Rwandan culture. The resurrection of the building's pre-genocide identity allows for another narrative of RPF success, supporting the nationalist discourse of the RPF's heroic position during the genocide.

Also noteworthy in the Kigali City tour is the exclusion of the famous Hotel des Milles Collines. In the West, it is the best-known genocide site, largely due to the success of Terry George's film *Hotel Rwanda* (2004). The film details the story of hotel manager Paul Rusesabagina, who kept an estimated 1,268 Rwandans safe during the genocide under challenging circumstances. Prior to the genocide, this Belgian-owned hotel was the lodging of choice for visiting bureaucrats, diplomats and journalists. The

Figure 8.3 Building that formerly housed the RTLM.

UNAMIR also held meetings there in the days just before the genocide. For these reasons, the hotel has become iconic as Africa 'seem[s] to specialize in symbolic hotels which, for months or years, are microcosms of their countries' turbulent histories' (Wrong 2000: 16). However, despite its notoriety and central location in Kigali, it is not officially on the ORTPN city tour (although any Rwandan will point it out to Western visitors). This is a telling omission, particularly since it is the best-known genocide site in the public culture of the tourist groups most likely to visit Rwanda.

In spite of the Hotel des Milles Collines's identity as a genocide site, there is no recognition of this history in the hotel itself. Unlike the Camp Kigali memorial, the bullet holes resulting from the genocide have been patched, and the visible damage completely repaired (Lacey 2005). The hotel has remained functioning since the genocide, and the only tangible remaining connection is the presence of staff who survived the genocide along with the intended targets (Lacey 2005). While this site has all the makings of a tourist locale, there is a concerted effort by both the hotel owners and the government to keep its infamy secondary to its identity as an upscale hotel and conference centre. Part of the reason for this negative response to *Hotel Rwanda* within Rwanda is the fact that it was filmed in South Africa, and more particularly the positioning of Rusesabagina as a hero. The Kagame government has been especially virulent in discrediting his story, as mirrored in Kigali's main newspaper, the *New Times*, which describes him as an 'imposter humanitarian' and the charitable foundation he established 'a hoax' (Mugabo 2007).

Rusesabagina's critics view him as a collaborator, and the attention he received through the film as shameless self-promotion. This rejection of Rusesabagina corresponds with the omission of this internationally known genocide site in the city tour.

Like the issues around memorialization, the controversy around the narrative of Rusesabagina's actions reflects the contemporary political climate. Rusesabagina has been outspoken in expressing his concern about repression of any political opposition to the current government. Additionally, Rusesabagina's Hutu identity raises yet another challenge to ideas of heroism. With the wounds from the genocide so fresh, and the complexities of victimhood still not fully explored, many Rwandans are not yet willing to see a Hutu in a heroic light (Basiika 2006). At this time, the Hotel des Milles Collines is heavily identified with Rusesabagina, and accentuating its connection to the genocide and his story. In this case, the hotel is firmly implanted in the Western imagination, despite the attempts to supplant it within Rwanda. This process of 'forgetting' stands in direct opposition to the 'remembering' that occurs when the Kigali city tour highlights the former location of the RTLM, creating very different roles for these two significant sites in the tourist experience.

Conclusion

The inclusion and exclusion of genocide sites on the Kigali City tour constitutes its own narrative of Rwandan history, and one designed with the Western tourist in mind. Recounting a tale of loss and failure, these sites emphasize the tragedy of the genocide, particularly in the Camp Kigali memorial and the Kigali Memorial Centre, both of which graphically represent the brutality of events through their attention to the victims. The overarching narratives speak of the failures of the United Nations specifically, and the West more generally. This presentation of the brutal side of human nature suggests a promising market for the ever-increasing forum of dark tourism. Yet as Rwanda recognizes and emphasizes its own disturbing past, it cements the genocide in its national identity. This identification with the genocide cannot be separated from the tourist market, where consumers' assumptions about locations shape how they are displayed and defined. As a developing nation heavily dependent on tourism, Rwanda is in certain ways obligated to present the visions foreign visitors have travelled so far to see. Part of this expectation is graphic representation of the genocide, and in this, Rwandan tourist initiatives maintain expectations. While tourism has much potential in terms of development, this progress comes at a price for the host community, which begins to see itself as the tourists view it (Pearce 1988: 6). Furthermore, as long as the story must be told, it will have an essential role in shaping Rwanda's national identity, reflecting the concerns and issues of contemporary Rwanda as much as the history of the city of Kigali.

Both perpetrators and survivors of the Rwandan genocide are still living in Rwanda today, and this shapes public discourse around the genocide. Kagame's government had tactical reasons for discouraging open conversations about the genocide, which critics argue further feeds the divisionism still present in Rwandan society (Lemarchand 2000: 114). Yet memorialization is a process, and one that does not generally begin with inclusive narratives. For example, non-Jewish victims of the Holocaust began to receive significant attention in the late 1980s and early 1990s. Harold Marcuses's (2001) comprehensive study of the role of Dachau in German culture illustrates that the camp has had multiple meanings and places in the national narrative, some of which reinforced divisionism, indicating the problem with fixing a single narrative to a site or drawing definitive conclusions about meaning or audience interpretation. Both change over time, making memorials a valuable tool for gauging cultural perceptions of atrocities, both nationally and internationally. For example, the creation of both the Jewish Museum in Berlin, which opened in 2001, and Galicia Jewish Museum in Krakow, established in 2004, demonstrates a new phase in Holocaust representation as both museums seek to contextualize the Nazi genocide in the larger scope of Jewish history. These museums are in part a response to the sense that narratives of slaughter, rather than the richness of Jewish history and culture, dominated post-Holocaust Jewish identity as the Holocaust became more visible in many nations' public culture.

Rwanda is likely to go through a similar process, the course of which will be determined by Rwanda's political future. Currently, the discourse around the genocide is shaped by obscuring the culpability of the RPF in the bloodshed of 1994, and this government's need to create a national story that legitimizes its rule. It is difficult to imagine that narratives, such as Rusesabagina's, which have taken on a life of their own in the international context, will be successfully repressed within Rwanda, especially since they accompany Western tourists. There are also ongoing attempts to create a more inclusive dialogue, including the creation of the 'Heroes' exhibit by the Kigali Memorial Centre in 2009. This travelling exhibit details those who saved people during the genocide, including Hutu, and is a small step towards creating a public identity other than perpetrator for Rwanda's Hutu majority. At this point, it is designed for Rwandans; however, having been released in public culture, it is likely to expand to other realms. It also exemplifies the potential of dark sites to use their prominence as a tool for education, both nationally and internationally. The public discourse of the Rwandan genocide will undoubtedly continue to be as much a measure of contemporary politics as Rwanda's past, and tourism will remain a prominent venue for remembering and forgetting the events of 1994.

Notes

1   The best overview of the events during genocide is Prunier (1995). The most comprehensive documentation remains Des Forges (1999). There are also numerous survivor accounts, including Hatzfeld (2006).
2   Richard Kandt was a German naturalist who began to catalogue Rwanda's extensive wildlife and was an advocate for preservation during the German colonization. His residence is now a natural history museum.
3   For example, Starbucks recently agreed to build a coffee farmers' support centre in Rwanda to help farmers improve the quality of their coffee. Kagame has taken an active role in reaching out to international business to forward Rwandan development (Kimenyi 2007).
4   The Belgians were the most effective force in the UNAMIR, and the extremists rightfully calculated that their deaths would result in the Belgians pulling out of the mission, thereby rendering it highly ineffective. So although there were also soldiers from Ghana at Camp Kigali at the time the Belgians were killed, these soldiers were returned unharmed (Dallaire 2003: 239–40). The desecration of the bodies was so thorough that Dallaire was initially unsure of how many men had been killed (2003: 255–6).
5   Rwanda's political system has both a President and a Prime Minister.
6   Berkeley (2001) addresses the willingness of the West to view African political problems as tribal barbarism. The tendency of the press to portray the event as a tribal conflict is also illustrated in Meyer *et al.* (1996).

References

Ashworth, G. J. (2002) 'Holocaust Tourism: The Experience of Kraków-Kazimierz', *International Research in Geographical and Environmental Education* 11(4), 363–7.
Basiika, A. (2006) 'Why Rwanda Is Uneasy about Genocide Movies', *Monitor* (Kampala), 21 May. Online: http://allafrica.com (accessed 30 September 2008).
Berkeley, B. (2001) *The Graves Are Not Yet Full: Race, Tribe, Power and the Heart of Africa*, New York: Basic Books.
Boniface, P. and Fowler, J. (1993) *Heritage and Tourism in the 'Global Village'*, New York: Routledge.
Chalk, F. (1999) 'Hate Radio in Rwanda', in Howard Adelman and Astri Suhrke (eds), *The Path of a Genocide: The Rwanda Crisis from Uganda to Zaire*, New Brunswick: Transaction Publishers, 93–107.
Dallaire, Lt Gen. (ret.) R. (2003) *Shake Hands with the Devil: The Failure of Humanity in Rwanda*, New York: Carroll & Graf Publishers.
Des Forges, A. (1999) *Leave None to Tell the Story: Genocide in Rwanda*, New York: Human Rights Watch.
Finkelstein, N. G. (2001) *The Holocaust Industry: Reflections on the Exploitation of Jewish Suffering*, New York: Verso.
George, T. (2004) *Hotel Rwanda*, United Artists Films.
Grosspietsch, M. (2005) 'The Image of Rwanda as a Tourist Destination', Working Paper No. 4, Working Paper Series, Sustainable Development Tourism, Münster.
Hatzfeld, J. (2006) *Life Laid Bare: The Survivors in Rwanda Speak,* trans. L. Coverdale, New York: Other Press.
Hirondelle News Agency (2004) 'Seven Heads of State to Attend Genocide Commemoration', 2 April. Online: http://allafrica.com (accessed 7 October 2008).

Kigali Memorial Centre (n.d.) *The Memorial Centre*. Online: http://kigalimemorialcentre.org (accessed 4 June 2007).

Kimenyi, F. (2007) 'Rwanda Coffee Centre Underway', *New Times*, 2 December. Online: www.newtimes.co (accessed 9 September 2008).

Kroslak, D. (2008) *The French Betrayal of Rwanda*, Bloomington: University of Indiana Press.

Kuperman, A. J. (2004) 'Provoking Genocide: A Revised History of the Rwandan Patriotic Front', *Journal of Genocide Research* 6(1), 314–49.

Lacey, M. (2005) 'Dramatic Role in '94 Horror Haunts Hotel', *New York Times*, 28 February. Online: www.lexis-nexis.com (accessed 15 June 2007).

Lemarchand, René (2000) 'Hate Crimes: Race and Retribution in Rwanda', *Transition* 9.1 and 2: 114–32.

Mamdani, M. (2001) *When Victims Become Killers: Colonialism, Nativism and Genocide in Rwanda*, Princeton: Princeton University Press.

Marcuse, H. (2001) *Legacies of Dachau: The Uses and Abuses of a Concentration Camp, 1933–2001*, Cambridge: Cambridge University Press.

Melvern, L. (2000) *A People Betrayed: The Role of the West in Rwanda's Genocide*, London and New York: Zed Books.

Melvern, L. (2004) *Conspiracy to Murder: The Rwandan Genocide*, London and New York: Verso.

Meyer, G., Klak, T. and Koehl, T. (1996) 'The Inscription of Difference: News Coverage of the Conflicts in Rwanda and Bosnia', *Political Geography* 15(1), 21–46.

Mugabo, C. (2007) 'Paul Rusesabagina Creates Hoax Charity to Enrich Himself', *New Times*, 22 October. Online: http://allafrica.com (accessed 30 September 2008).

Nora, P. (1989) 'Between Memory and History: Les Lieux de Mémoire', in 'Memory and Counter Memory', *Representations* 26, 7–24.

ORTPN (n.d.) 'Kigali City tour'. Online: www.rwandatourism.com/cityTour.htm (accessed 9 September 2008).

Panafrican News Agency (2000) 'Slain Belgian Peacekeepers Memorialized in Kigali', 7 April. Online: http://allafrica.com (accessed 20 September 2008).

Pearce, P. L. (1988) *The Ulysses Factor*, New York: Springer-Verlag.

Pottier, J. (2002) *Re-Imagining Rwanda: Conflict, Survival and Disinformation in the Late Twentieth Century*, New York: Cambridge University Press.

Prunier, G. (1995) *The Rwanda Crisis: History of a Genocide*, Columbia: University of New York Press.

Sharpley, R. and Stone, P. R. (2009) *The Darker Side of Travel: The Theory and Practice of Dark Tourism*, Bristol: Channel View Publications.

Straus, S. (2006) *The Order of Genocide*, New York: Cornell University Press.

Thompson, A. (2007) *The Media and the Rwandan Genocide*, London: Pluto Press.

Umutesi, M. B. (2000) *Surviving the Slaughter: The Ordeal of a Rwandan Refugee in Zaire*, trans. Julia Emerson, Madison: University of Wisconsin Press.

Uvin, Peter (1998) *Aiding Violence: The Development Enterprise in Rwanda*, West Hartford: Kumarian Press.

Vansina, J. (2004) *Antecedents to Modern Rwanda: The Nyiginya Kingdom (Africa and the Diaspora)*, Madison: University of Wisconsin Press.

Wrong, M. (2000) *In the Footsteps of Mr. Kurtz: Living on the Brink of Disaster in Mobutu's Congo*, New York: HarperCollins.

Young, J. E. (1993) *The Texture of Memory: Holocaust Memorials and Meaning*, New Haven: Yale University Press.

Chapter 9

Remembering and forgetting: South Asia and the Second World War

Yasmin Khan

In 2009 a news story broke in the Indian press: a Second World War George Cross medal awarded to Naik Kripa Ram posthumously in 1946, a member of the 8th battalion, 13th Frontier Force Rifles, was up for auction at a Mayfair-based London auction house for £25,000. The auction was halted when Kripa Ram's widow, Brahmi Devi, who had received the medal on her dead husband's behalf from the Viceroy Lord Wavell at the age of 13, complained that the medal was stolen from her. Countering her story, a Delhi dealer claimed to have purchased it from her for the sum of 20,000 rupees (approximately £250). The Chief Minister of her state, Himachal Pradesh, intervened, and the subsequent police investigation blocked the auction of the item while a campaign in India gathered momentum to press the British authorities to return the medal to the elderly widow (*Times of India* 2010; *Outlook magazine* 2009).

The story of this medal has a greater resonance within the context of India's challenging and asymmetrical relationship with the Second World War, the subject of this chapter. Medals, as repositories of memory and meaning, have taken on new value in a global marketplace. The story later emerged of many Indian soldiers and their families selling their medals. Latent but clearly noticeable strands of nationalism entered the picture once political capital could be made of it, pitting Brahmi Devi against the London-based auction house. Reportage of the case escalated, was made a cause célèbre, and the sale of the medal was ultimately stopped.

Undivided India's involvement in the Second World War was extensive: in 1941 the country faced the prospect of occupation, and Japanese aircraft bombed the eastern coastline. In campaigns in North Africa, the Middle East, South East Asia and in India's north-eastern Burmese frontier region, 87,000 Indian military personnel were killed. Thirty Indians won Victoria Cross medals (Fig. 9.1). The mobilization of an army 2.5 million strong (the largest volunteer army in world history) profoundly altered the society, economy and political life of the country: factories became geared to the production of new foodstuffs, new consumer goods became available, some industrialists profited greatly, while urban consumers suffered devastating price fluctuations due to

Figure 9.1 Twenty-year-old sepoy Kamal Ram is awarded the Victoria Cross in New Delhi, 1944, by Commander in Chief, Claude Auchinleck.

wartime food shortages (most terribly in the Bengal famine of 1943). One million Indians laboured to build the ports, railways, airstrips and roads needed in the war effort (Fig. 9.2). The state was also moving forward with developmental plans which paved the way for Nehruvian state planning (Jackson 2005; Bayly and Harper 2005).

Old hierarchies of class and race were challenged as American and African soldiers were stationed in India and members of the old colonial order had their ideological and racial superiority challenged. Today in the Kirkee war cemetery outside Bombay one can find the graves of soldiers from the West Africa Engineers, the Gold Coast and Nigeria Regiments. Japanese and Germans in India were interned and Jewish and Polish evacuees arrived in Indian cities from Europe. British and Indian soldiers were in closer contact than ever before and this created an intricate interaction of racial politics; some heightened racism existed alongside increasing anti-imperialism. As Clive Branson, a soldier with strong communist sympathies wrote, 'The slogan of India for the Indians is universally popular' (Branson 1944). On the other hand, civil–military clashes attended resurgent tensions. The colonial regime tried to control and direct the news: the 1943 Defence of India Act rules meant that a short propaganda film had to be shown before every film in the cinema. Axis and Allied propaganda messages competed on the airwaves (Bhattacharya 2001).

Figure 9.2 Production of Second World War armaments in India, 1943.

In short, the Second World War in India had a very widespread impact on many aspects of Indian daily life, political, economic, cultural and social, and this ranged from 'life and death' issues of war and the loss of life of combatants, to a more diffused but serious sense of everyday life on the Indian 'home front' being constrained and shaped by India's engagement in a global war with its epicentre in Western Europe. Indians were affected by wartime conditions not only as combatants, but also as merchants, nurses, transport workers, labourers, merchant seamen and prostitutes.

Yet, despite all this, India has a mixed relationship with wartime commemoration, marked by silences and ambivalence. This is in striking contrast to European war 'industries' that seek to keep war memories alive through seemingly ceaseless publishing, memorials and museums. Here, I briefly seek to trace a genealogy of Indian wartime commemoration. I point out, in particular for those less familiar with South Asia, that European-style war memorialization has been largely absent from contemporary Indian life. Considering the scale of India's wartime involvement there are striking absences of commemoration and commentary. Indeed, although there has been no shortage of studies of the 1940s by historians of India, these are very rarely framed in the context of war. They are *abstracted* from war; the war becomes conspicuous by its absence or, if mentioned, is something intangible, located far away and not really impinging upon or involving Indians. Classic studies of the 1940s in India have not framed it as a wartime story. The political story of Gandhi's Quit India movement and the celebration of the Indian National Army (INA) have taken precedence over any more holistic interpretations of war and memory, leaving those who died during the war suspended in time and marginalized in popular and state narratives. The comparison with African history, where there has been a long tradition of understanding wartime memory and involvement and the links between wartime participation and nationalism, is striking (Killingray and Rathbone 1986; Killingray 1996). There has also been little visibility of the war in popular culture: few Bollywood films or novels examine India's wartime as a subject, compared with the Partition of 1947 in which there has been extensive elite interest since the 1980s and numerous editions of poetry, plays and novels alongside art-house cinematic and Bollywood depictions (Talbot and Singh 2009; Khan 2007).

War memorials certainly have no innate value or benefit, indeed they may be used in suspect and pernicious ways, of more use for contemporary political ends than for healing or peaceful purposes. I am not arguing for a retrieval of wartime memory in a celebratory way or suggesting that this should be restored to history: I am interested in disentangling some of the reasons for these silences and how we may also be able to cut across the grain to understand post-colonial wartime narratives beyond the dichotomies of resistance or collaboration, nationalism or imperialism. In particular, the stilted efforts to commemorate the war by the British establishment and the Imperial War Graves Commission (later Commonwealth War Graves Commission) suggest the ways in which India's Second World War has slipped between competing national narratives and has not been 'useful' to state projects in either the UK or India. These elisions and absences, then, suggest perhaps just how important state backing for Second World War commemoration has become on the international stage, and the way that memories of extensive wartime engagement can become fragmented and disjointed without contemporary political stimulus. It is the absences then, in India's Second World War memories, which are as interesting as the presence of war memorialization and commemoration.

Critical studies of war memorialization have stressed the interplay of the needs of state and society, and the struggle to articulate war memories in a national setting; some highlight the political use of war memory and a 'top-down' statist direction of memorialization and remembrance to serve the needs of the state. Others point to the relationship of such 'invented traditions' with the psychological need for mourning and 'bottom-up' pressures on the state exerted by those traumatized by war. Some historians would argue that war memorialization has been a hegemonic, statist project (Hobsbawm and Ranger 1992) which has involved statist projections of national ideals on an unsuspecting public. Others have regarded states as having to accommodate and adapt to the popular needs of mourners and the transformation of local and regional memories into national ceremonies and memorials (Ashplant *et al.* 2000; Winter and Sivan 2007). The latter approach is more sensitive to the interwoven processes of memory and memorialization, and lends itself to more nuanced readings of memorialization and a diachronic understanding of time. It destabilizes memorialization as something linear or straightforward and reveals the subtle interplay of memory and memorialization, the fluidity of memory in relation to a sturdy national framework which seeks to project a timeless, stable memory. For this reason, within post-colonial studies there has been a robust critique of Pierre Nora and his project of *lieux de mémoire* in France, which sought to 'fix' the locations of important national memories in a rigid, nation-centred French history (Sengupta 2009; Nora 1989).

Starting with this conceptual framework, South Asian approaches to the memories of the Second World War (particularly given the level of India's involvement and the number of casualties from India) are curious. The memorialization of the Second World War in South Asia clearly does not fit well into the discursive needs of *either* state *or* society. India's involvement in the Second World War is marked by ambiguity and silences, with neither social groups nor state agencies initiating a re-evaluation of this wartime experience.

The South Asian experience points to the ways in which hegemonic state memories can overshadow and shape direct experiences of death and destruction in wartime and, in particular, how narratives of national liberation from colonial rule may 'override' local wartime memories because of the need to commence 'nation-statist' initiatives immediately on independence (Roy 2007). The decolonization process, and shifting sovereignties, have meant that in South Asia the Second World War has been boxed into a peculiarly detached and abstract kind of memory which is either shot through by militarism, conservatism and 'Raj time nostalgia' for a more hierarchical era, or identified with an era of radical, Congress-led resistance under the leadership of Gandhi's Quit India movement. War-related cultural heritage is dictated by a global marketplace and a Eurocentric story, as the story of Naik Kripa Ram's medal may suggest. Memories and memorialization of the 'Freedom Movement' and of the Partition and accompanying violence and displacement have not fragmented sufficiently to allow the war to emerge as a broader and more serious subject of investigation, despite sustained assaults on nationalism and the project of national history in India over the past two decades from the Subaltern Studies collective. This may say more about the relationship between Indian state and society in the 1940s and 1950s than it does about memorialization per se. Simultaneously, racially defined, Eurocentric readings of war have overlooked the drain on resources and manpower that the war placed on the British Empire. Island histories driven by the anxieties of postwar Britishness have supplanted acknowledgement of the wider debts of war to India (Gilroy 2005).

This chapter sets out some tentative explanations for why this war has been 'forgotten'.

The nationalism paradigm

There is still ambivalence in India about memories of an anti-fascist war in which many in the leading Indian political party, the Indian National Congress, were reluctant and unenthusiastic participants. The Congress had resisted the way that India was unilaterally entered into the war without the consultation of Indian political opinion. The British administration roundly interned Congress leaders, who spent long years in jail. The British government regarded the Quit India movement of 1942 as pernicious and opportunistic given the Allies' weakness in South East Asia at the time. The ways in which the Indian National Army, a group of soldiers led by Subhas Chandra Bose, broke away from the Indian Army to join the Japanese campaigns, created resentment among those who regarded it as pro-fascist anti-imperialism (Fay 1993). The Indian National Army trials left a bitter legacy and revealed a controversial set of contradictory ideological impulses within the Congress Party itself. These issues remain controversial to this day.

The Indian National Congress Party governed India with almost unchallenged authority from independence in 1947 until 1967 and has remained important thereafter (it is still the party of government today). The Indian National Congress Party also shaped the writing of history and memorialization after 1947 under the leadership of Nehru, the first Prime Minister (d. 1964), for instance by commissioning school textbooks and museums. Yet the class and political interests of the Congress were detached from wartime engagement: the Congress had opposed the war, and the core leadership of the Congress were behind bars for most of its duration. Many autobiographies and histories written in the 1950s and 1960s which made up the canon of Congress historiographies, therefore, jump from 1942 to 1945 with little detail or insight about the social challenges and changes that had been taking place during this time (for example the autobiography of A. K. Azad, 1959). It was not only the Congress high command which was in prison. Many of the grassroots leaders were also arrested and therefore detached from the social and economic transitions and pressures of wartime India.

In particular, the widespread celebration of the INA in India – Bose's image can still be seen painted on buses, on posters and on many book covers – means that the politics of wartime commemoration is not one any Indian state leadership would profit from. Again, there was a close nexus between the Congress and the INA. Nehru himself acted as defence barrister for the accused INA officers tried in a sensational public trial in 1946. At the same time, Indian communists' support for the war was used as a stick to beat them with in electoral campaigns after 1947. Many Indian communists, caught between conflicting ideological impulses, suffered 'an agonizing choice' during the war, particularly once Germany attacked Russia (Sarkar 1983). Anti-fascist internationalism was superseded in India by Congress nationalism and by the resurgence of right-wing militant groups. Many Indians, with very good reason, blamed the war for the cataclysmic Bengal famine of 1943 in which up to three million people may have perished, for rising food prices, for increasing divisions between Muslims and Hindus and – at the time – for exploitation of women by soldiers. In Britain, by contrast, a small-islander nationalism was part and parcel of the war effort, and the broad consensual internationalist agenda of the left was rarely in the ascendancy.

In short, Indian soldiers and their wartime activities did not easily fit into dominant national or global narratives, either in the UK or in South Asia. It was in this way that the history of the war could sink between the seams of different historiographical impulses that would otherwise validate the war and place it firmly within a reading of national and international history.

Partition and the creation of the separate states of India and Pakistan in 1947

The calamities of the Partition of India (during which perhaps 250,000 to one million were killed and 12 million displaced as refugees) affected directly those Punjabi communities where military recruitment had been extensive. The Sikh community was divided into two by the line which divided Punjab and millions of Punjabis of all religious faiths on both sides of the border now had to address more urgent practical questions as refugees establishing homes and new livelihoods. There was wide-scale death and destruction in 1947 and many who had lost husbands or sons in the war, particularly from Punjab, may have suffered from further loss of life within their family in the massacres accompanying Partition. Mourning the partition dead and mourning the war dead had the potential to collapse into each other and blur into a single set of memories of loss, rapid change and grief. This blurring of partition and war grief may have been particularly likely among a public scarred by wartime prices and famine, and deeply ambivalent about remembrance of a war fought without nationalist acquiescence. In addition, administrative changes meant that practical decisions about war memorials after the end of the war became entangled in the difficult administrative handover during 1946–7. As the Imperial War Graves Commissioner in India and South East Asia reported in March 1948, everything was in 'the melting pot' because of decolonization and the transfer of power (CWGC 1948).

The military personnel who had participated in the war had been living and working together in regiments made up of mixed communities of Muslims, Hindus and Sikhs. The Indian Army's regimental esprit de corps and sense of a shared past was broken by the separation of the two new states which overlapped with the demobilization at the end of the war and the creation of Pakistan. Muslim soldiers were despatched to Pakistan and non-Muslim soldiers to India, breaking up the networks of the old Indian Army. By 1948 these former allies were fighting each other during the first war in Kashmir and learning to perceive the opposing state as the enemy. In the later wars between India and Pakistan (1965, 1971) sometimes old colleagues and officers faced each other as enemies and even had responsibility for taking old friends as prisoners of war.

The issue of commemorating the dead of the Second World War was further complicated by the fact that names of Muslim soldiers could not necessarily be earmarked as 'Pakistani' casualties; who could say if a pre-partition Muslim killed in wartime service 'belonged' to either India or Pakistan? Similarly, was a non-Muslim soldier who had been born in a place now in Pakistani territory to be counted as an Indian war casualty?

Pakistan Armed Forces Day remembers so-called *shaheeds* or martyrs for the state; but this day only commemorates wars dating back to 1948 and does not include the Second World War within its remit. The two countries are still locked in a cold war over Kashmir and have become nuclearized (with the constant threat of hot conflict, as in 1999 and 2001). They are not 'postwar' states: war is still a real threat and presence in South Asia. Unfortunately while the two states remain non-signatories to the Comprehensive Test Ban Treaty and the Non-Proliferation Treaty, unreconstructed, realist perceptions of warfare run through state perceptions and agencies to shape popular and sanctioned readings of war and peace in the South Asian context.

The Commonwealth War Graves Commission and India's war

Many within the British administrative hierarchy wanted to glorify the role of Indian soldiers in the war immediately after the end of hostilities. A decisive factor in the nature and formation of war memorials in India was, of course, the role of the Imperial War Grave Commission. Its Vice-Chairman Fabian Ware was addressing the Government of India on the question of how to commemorate fallen Indians in 1944, before the war had even ended (CWGC 1948). It was decided that Indians who died in non-operational areas in India would not have the full 'war grave' treatment. They would forego a full individual war grave but would have their names on a collective monument erected at the end of the war. The numbers of these personnel were estimated to be around 100,000 at the end of the war. Interestingly, some members of the Indian government wanted 'decentralized memorials' either at regimental depots, or in the provincial capitals. In a country the size of India this held some logic. They were firmly overruled by the War Department in India, which responded:

> It is the intention of the Government of India to discourage local memorials in order that the full support of the Provincial Governments and of the public may be concentrated on the national war memorial. (CWGC 1945)

This was fully in keeping with anti-federal centralized strategies of state development and state memorialization, which emerged in the postwar years of Indian government (Khan 2011). In 1949, both the Indian and the Pakistani governments agreed to centralized memorials to be established in Delhi and Karachi respectively.

One of the striking things about the debates in the Commission files is the focus on the memorials above all else, and their detachment from vernacular, local sensibilities. Public access to the memorials, or the points of view or feelings of the bereaved, were not taken into consideration in any way. These state-sanctioned memorials were driven largely by the need to match what was being done elsewhere in the Empire-Commonwealth, or former Empire-Commonwealth, and the anxiety of India and Pakistan to not be outdone by the respective 'rival' power. Again this speaks of state-centric notions of memorialization which were neither organic, substantive nor representative of local concerns with the memory of the war, but imposed externally by the Commission. As a note from London revealed:

> it is politically a matter of urgency that some progress is made on these two memorials … we are faced with the position that there is nothing to show in the Home Countries of what the Commission is actually doing in the commemoration of their war dead. (CWGC 1948)

In 1952 Indian, Pakistani and British representatives met at the Commission Headquarters in Grosvenor Gardens, London, and agreed that the memorials would be identical in every way, except for language. (Incidentally, this provided a revealing insight into the importance of the two scripts of Hindi and Urdu to the visual identities of the two new states, which were used for the same spoken language, Hindustani.) In 1957, the question of memorialization was resolved by erecting two identical memorials to the war dead in Delhi (India's capital) and Karachi (then Pakistan's capital) with the same 27,000 names inscribed on them both in Hindi (seen as the language of India) and Urdu (Pakistan's national language). Two large books of remembrance were also unveiled. *The Hindu* reported the event:

> A large and distinguished gathering, including members of the diplomatic corps, witnessed the smart turn-out of men forming the combined Indian armed forces guard of honour and those of the British contingent who had specially flown to Delhi to do honour to the memory of the soldiers and airmen of the Indian army who gave their lives during the last war. (*The Hindu* 1957)

Although this was an appropriate way of negotiating the complex question of how to remember these men, there was a definite irony about the choice of the linguistic inscriptions. Many of the deceased men would not have known Hindi or Urdu and would have been more familiar with languages like Punjabi or Tamil. These memorials were capturing these deceased soldiers for the respective nations; the flags and symbols of the new nation-states used at the unveiling ceremony in 1957 were the flags and symbols of two nations which by the 1950s were in conflict with each other.

Nevertheless, the agreement to erect two 'mirroring' memorials was reached quite easily and amicably: at the time, there were far more pressing concerns in both states regarding historical memorialization and institutionalization of the nationalist histories and origins of both states. In the early years of independence there were many decisions to be made on remodelling urban architecture and spaces: the Jallianwalah Bagh memorial to commemorate the killing of unarmed civilians in Punjab in 1919 was established in 1961, and British monuments and relics were being actively removed throughout the 1950s and 1960s, especially in Uttar Pradesh and Bengal. More than 400 protestors were arrested across Uttar Pradesh in 1957 for demanding the removal of all remaining British statues and monuments (Heathorn 2009). The Second World War was far less politically potent or useful to either nation-state or Indian politicians. It is striking, however, that 1957, the year that the Commission established war memorials in India and Pakistan, was also the centenary of the Indian uprising of 1857, which was a cause of some anxiety and concern among British officials, who feared for diplomatic relations if the celebrations in India were too overtly nationalistic (Heathorn

2009). The timing of the unveiling of the memorials, marking a shared Commonwealth-Imperial 'heroic memory', may have been far from coincidental and viewed from London as a counterweight to the tone of the 1857 commemorations which, it was feared, would be fervently anti-British.

The new war memorials prioritized the international gaze. The subaltern South Asian was entirely excluded from the memorialization, in particular the very families the memorial was supposedly intended to represent. As a member of the Commission stationed in India and South East Asia wrote in 1955, 'It is anticipated that the numbers of visitors who will wish to see the names will be infinitesimal. The relatives of the greater number of those commemorated will be too poor to afford the trip to either cemetery, and, in fact, will know nothing about the Memorial' (CWGC 1955). Furthermore, in a discussion about whether the memorial books should be accessible to the public, colonial stereotypes about Indians make a stark and ugly appearance: 'No visitor will be allowed to handle it [the memorial book] himself since they will probably have dirty hands and soil it' (CWGC 1955). These memorials were emphatically not intended to provide comfort, honour or a place of pilgrimage for the families of the dead.

Other complexities of memorialization intersected with ambiguous borderlines of race, nationality and class. German prisoner of war graves continued to be maintained in India and there were at least 38 German bodies buried five and a half miles outside Dehra Dun at Prem Nagar, close to a large partition refugee camp. The German government enquired about this in 1952. There, a heap of gravel and a cactus marked each grave until gravestones were established (IOR 1952). In 1953, the remains of 360 Italian prisoners of war scattered all over India, in Poona, Meerut and Bangalore, were exhumed and centralized in the Bombay Catholic Cemetery (IOR 1953). The treatment of Anglo-Indians became a vexed one at the Commission in the late 1940s: should those with some European parentage be given independent graves like other European soldiers buried in the subcontinent? Ultimately, this was decided on a question of domicile, but as one of the Commissioners, Colonel Chettle, expressed it, 'I am afraid we are going to get into a bit of a muddle on this question' (CWGC 1946).

Underlying all these difficulties was the issue of attributing national identities to individuals who had more transnational identities, and marking bodies with a national stamp, at a time of decolonization, imperial decline and rising nationalism. As Elizabeth Buettner has traced, the British Association for Cemeteries in South Asia (BACSA) has worked persistently since 1947 to preserve cemeteries holding British remains which date to the earliest years of European power in the subcontinent. She argues that 'Cemeteries serve as a barometer signalling how both ex-colonizers and the ex-colonized have assessed colonial spaces, artefacts, and empire more generally after decolonization' and that the post-1947 record of BACSA, which is manned by many former colonial officials and their families, was 'augmenting a narrative of empire imbued with nostalgic overtones' by insisting on pristine spaces of memorialization in India, and well-preserved European graves, at exactly the time that decolonization was taking place (Buettner 2006: 1, 9). The attempts of the War Graves Commission can also be viewed as part of this attempt to project British power onto a decolonizing space, using wartime memories. It underscored a shared Imperial-Commonwealth enterprise and offered chances for retired colonial officials to revisit former territories and relive their former experiences.

Significantly, however, in the UK, the former imperial metropole, there was no memorial to any of the Indian or Commonwealth troops who perished in the war. There was some talk of it in 1949: General Claude Auchinleck, who was a staunch and consistent defender of the Indian soldiers he had commanded, personally pressed for a monument or a memorial in central London. Auchinleck had the backing of the editor of the *Daily Mail* and other Indian Army generals in the UK and discussions on the memorial reached cabinet level. Auchinleck suggested it would be 'a mark of gratitude from the British people to those soldiers who served Britain and the empire for 200 years'. It would be a monument for men who 'fought and fell in our wars all over the Old World'. A statue of a sepoy was proposed, or maybe a series of orientalized figures, modelled on the 'chief classes enlisted in the Indian Army' (IOR 1949). The Government of India was agreeable, as long as it was consulted on the form of the memorial and any wording. But no committee was formed, no funds were raised, the site for the memorial remained undecided and without a more sustained backing, the General's idea fizzled out and the file was closed in 1949.

In the UK, postwar reconstruction and regeneration quietly erased the Indian contribution which was at odds with a story of plucky small-island British heroism and seemed anachronistic in the heady days of postwar British modernism and architectural innovation. For the British, the Second World War Indian was represented in two ways. On the one hand stood the idealized subaltern soldier: courageous, bold, coming to the help of the motherland but in a secondary and auxiliary role. At the other extreme, was the Indian nationalist: pro-Gandhi, and therefore unprincipled in his prioritization of Indian nationalism over global freedom from Nazism, ignorant of the dangers of fascism and selfishly abandoning Britain in its hour of need. These two stereotypes were reproduced in the media and in the official documents of civil servants and politicians (Webster 2005: 19–54). The more subtle realities of negotiating racial and class lines in Britain of the 1940s are obscured by these cut-out dolls. Yet, this dual perception of Indians is a persistent and effective paradigm. A polarized and simplistic impression of wartime India persists, when it has been remembered at all.

Idioms and cultures of remembrance

There are also greater questions to consider here of remembrance and death: could the Commission, for instance, really provide a model which made sense in an Indian context and for Indian people? There was a risk in the post-colonial context of the Commission being seen as an agency of extended imperial influence in India (early requests made by the Indian government to change its name from the Imperial to the Commonwealth War Graves Commission were only heeded in 1960). The different funerary rites of Hindus (which involve cremation rather than burial) imposed one immediate difference. The Commission model operated in a particular idiom with the ideal of establishing 'English Country gardens' in graveyards around the world (Longworth 1967). Despite attempts to devolve power to local branches of the Commission, the Commission's work remains highly centralized. There was some continuity between the work of the Commission and a tradition of funerary architecture, graveyards and statuary in British India which stretched back to the eighteenth century, including the British memorials to those killed in the 1857 uprising. How could this legacy of remembrance be made meaningful for South Asians? At the same time, the former colonies had to carry the cost of the maintenance of graves and memorials themselves, in 1952 at the cost of five rupees per grave. Indeed, in 1972, Pakistan withdrew from the Commission, primarily for financial reasons.

The dead in South Asia have always been remembered, but in multiple and specific ways: in the private space of the family home, through prayer and death anniversary rituals, through the presence of ghosts and family storytelling, through publications and announcement of death anniversaries in newspapers (Parry 1994; Saunders and Aghaie 2005). This suggests a different interpretation of public and private space, while also allowing for interflow and disconnection between local and collective memories. Memories of the war dead are preserved by families but these have not become public, state centred or part of a hegemonic, integrated national narrative. The Second World War poses a particular problem because many volunteers did not come from areas of traditional recruitment where other family members had seen active service, in contrast to the First World War. Soldiers themselves had to negotiate their complex hybrid identities as both autonomous individuals and employees in the most coercive of the Raj's agencies, as both colonizer and colonized (Singh 2009). Their 'heroism' and societal explanations for their work were not necessarily scripted for them, in the way that First World War stories and war movies had chalked out the ground for European and American soldiers in myths and celebrations that both preceded and followed after the time of war (Bourke 1999). In Pakistan there was some difference to India: the continued presence of European officials, the institutionalization of the army in political life and the role of men such as Ayub Khan (who was President of Pakistan from 1958 to 1969 and had seen active service in Burma in the 1940s as second in command of the 1st Assam Regiment) meant that war memorialization had more prominence than in India (for instance, it featured in the autobiographies of many prominent and politically powerful individuals such as Ayub Khan himself (Khan 1967)). Regimental histories, reinforced through continued bilateral training programmes at Sandhurst, had a higher prominence in the national pecking order.

When the Second World War is remembered in India it tends to be through regimental initiatives and veterans' groups. Small memorials, plaques and museums do exist. The coastal city of Vishakhapatnam, for instance, which was bombed during the war by the Japanese, has a museum funded by the Royal Indian Navy which displays artefacts associated with the war including an unexploded Japanese bomb. In 2007 at Bathinda in Punjab a memorial was unveiled to commemorate all who died in wars 'sacrificed for the motherland' since the First World War (*Tribune* 2007). Often these local initiatives have also been linked to appeals by veterans' groups to receive better pensions or recognition from the Indian or British state. The Ex-Services League of Punjab and Chandigarh for instance has been campaigning for grants from the British government, exemption from the UK visa fee and payments to former prisoners of war, with their chairman, Lieutenant-Colonel Chanan Singh Dhillon, petitioning that 'the Indian government didn't strike a deal with the UK government in 1947 for Indian sacrifices' (*Tribune* 2001). There has been encouragement to this cause because of the recent high profile of the Gurkha Justice campaign that has been seeking pensions and the right for former Gurkha soldiers to settle in the UK.

There is a direct link here between those who have links to the Indian diaspora overseas. The Punjabi diaspora has a significant presence in the UK and Canada. Indian war veterans now based in the UK are more actively networked into British public/state remembrance and have been included (increasingly in recent years) in the hyperactive British culture of remembrance, attending public remembrance services and taking part in the BBC online 'People's War' which records memories of veterans and those affected on the 'homefront'. It is telling that the Memorial Gates Trust, which lobbied for several years to create a monument to memorialize the contribution of the five million Commonwealth soldiers from South Asia, Africa and the Caribbean who volunteered to serve in the First and Second World Wars, was only successful in 2002. The memorial erected in their honour on Constitution Hill in London was the first marker of recognition in the UK. Gradually, though, exhibitions, documentaries and films are beginning to tell the story of the Commonwealth contribution to the war effort. Still, to date scholarly and public attention to the South Asian role in the First World War has been far advanced and more subtle in its development (Ahuja 2009).

An ageing community of Indian veterans in the UK are 'remembering' the war in a way which is channelled through the British media and are taking part in a general culture of remembrance which is quite different to that of South Asia itself. It could be argued that without a thorough reappraisal of the nationalist lens through which many in the UK regard the war, and without a careful unpicking of the meaning of the war to Indians, this recovery of the wartime role of Indians, Africans and former members of the Commonwealth does nothing more than add spice, variety and legitimacy to a discourse which is based on an uncritical conceptual premise in the first place. In other words, it expands our understanding of participation in the war, and emphasizes that it was not simply a European event, without asking what this meant to different participants, or how coercive or exploitative this relationship may have been.

Conclusion

The South Asian experience points to the ways in which hegemonic state memories can overshadow the direct experiences of death and destruction in wartime and, in particular, how narratives of national liberation from colonial rule may 'override' wartime memories because of the need to commence 'nation-statist' initiatives immediately on independence. Notwithstanding the spatial appropriation of memorial sites by South Asians, and their malleable, changing meanings for local people, the Commission's attempts to mark the war in India have met with little success. The war is associated with many different, cross-cutting memories in South Asia, many unpleasant and disturbing, in particular the Bengal famine. This case would therefore seem to support the notion that state support is crucial in the generation of public memory, and that without the support of a powerful elite even very brutal or disruptive episodes in history can be 'forgotten' in public life, even if they are well remembered in manifold other ways. This is even stranger in the Indian case as many of those most seriously affected by the war - regular soldiers, labourers, peasant agriculturalists, women – are exactly the groups which recent historiography has championed and attempted to restore to agency in history.

Simultaneously, in the UK, the circle of British memorialization has been widened to acknowledge a Commonwealth role in the war, and this undermines narrow British interpretations of the war as an 'island story'. Nonetheless, this widening of the 'memorial circle' does nothing to move forward or critically explain South Asians' role in the war if it does not ask questions about the complicated layers of pride, ambiguity and coercion which lie beneath the surface of this involvement. The story of the sale of an Indian war medal to a British collector at an inflated price is suggestive of the asymmetrical power relations that marked India's involvement in the Second World War. The resulting furore in India is also, however, indicative of a global commercialization of wartime commemoration and the competing demands on state-sanctioned memories of war today.

References

Ahuja, R. (2009) 'South Asian Experiences of the World Wars: New Evidence and New Approaches', International Workshop, SOAS/German Historical Institute/Zentrum Moderner Orient, London, May.

Ashplant, T. G., Dawson, G. and Roper, M. (2000) *The Politics of War Memory and Commemoration*, London: Routledge.

Azad, A. K. (1959) *India Wins Freedom*, Bombay: Orient Longman.

Bayly, C. and Harper, T. (2005) *Forgotten Armies: Britain's Asian Empire and the War with Japan*, London: Penguin.

Bhattacharya, S. (2001) *Propaganda and Information in Eastern India, 1939–45: A Necessary Weapon of War*, London: School of Oriental and African Studies and Curzon Press.

Bourke, J. (1999) *An Intimate History of Killing: Face to Face Killing in Twentieth Century Warfare*, London: Granta.

Branson, C. (1944) *British Soldier in India: The letters of Clive Branson*, London: Communist Party of India.

Buettner, E. (2006) 'Cemeteries, Public Memory, and Raj Nostalgia in Postcolonial Britain and India', *History & Memory* 18(1), 5–42.

CWGC – Commonwealth War Graves Commission Archives (1945), Government of India War Department to Principal Staff officers, India, 7 May. A/171.

CWGC – Commonwealth War Graves Commission Archives (1946) 26 August. A/171.

CWGC – Commonwealth War Graves Commission Archives (1948) 2 March. A/171.

CWGC – Commonwealth War Graves Commission Archives (1955) 20 September. A/171.

Fay, P. W. (1993) *The Forgotten Army: India's Armed Struggle for Independence, 1942–1945*, Michigan: University of Michigan Press.

Gilroy, P. (2005) *Postcolonial Melancholia*, New York: Columbia University Press.

Heathorn, S. (2009) 'The Absent Site of Memory: The Kanpur Memorial Well and the 1957 Centenary Commemoration of the Indian "Mutiny"', *German Historical Institute Bulletin*, Supplement 1, 73–116.

Hindu, The (1957) 'War Memorial', 17 November.

Hobsbawm, E. and Ranger, T. (eds) (1992) *The Invention of Tradition*, New York: Cambridge University Press.

IOR – India Office Records, British Library (1949) War Staff Papers, IOR L/WS/1/962.

IOR – India Office Records, British Library (1952) German POW graves in India, IOR R/4/115.

IOR – India Office Records, British Library (1953) Italian POW graves in India, IOR R/4/103.

Jackson, A. (2005) *The British Empire and the Second World War*, London: Hambledon Continuum.

Khan, M. A. (1967) *Friends, Not Masters: A Political Autobiography*, New York and Oxford: Oxford University Press.

Khan, Y. (2007) *The Great Partition: the making of India and Pakistan*, New Haven and London: Yale University Press.

Khan, Y. (2011) 'Performing Peace: Gandhi's Assassination as a Critical Moment in the Consolidation of the Nehruvian State', *Modern Asian Studies* 45 (Special Issue 01), 57–80.

Killingray, D. (1996) '"If I Fight for Them, Maybe Then I Can Go Back to the Village": African Soldiers in the Mediterranean and European Campaigns, 1939–45', in P. Addison and A.Calder (eds), *Time to Kill: The Soldier's Experience of War in the West*, London: Picador.

Killingray, D. and Rathbone, R. (eds) (1986) *Africa and the Second World War*, London: Palgrave Macmillan.

Longworth, P. (1967) *The Unending Vigil: A History of the Commonwealth War Graves Commission, 1917–1967*, London: Constable.

Nora, P. (1989) 'Between Memory and History: Les lieux de mémoire', *Representations* 26, 7–24.

Outlook magazine (2009) 'Come Bear the Cross', 21 December. Online: www.outlookindia.com/article.aspx?263237 (accessed 10 December 2010).

Parry, J. (1994) *Death in Banaras*, Cambridge: Cambridge University Press.

Roy, S. (2007) *Beyond Belief: India and the Politics of Postcolonial Nationalism*, Durham, NC: Duke University Press.

Saunders, R. and Aghaie, K. (2005) 'Introduction: Mourning and Memory' *Comparative Studies of South Asia, Africa and the Middle East* 25(1), 17–29.

Sarkar, S. (1983) *Modern India: 1885–1947*, New Delhi: Macmillan.

Sengupta, I. (2009) 'Introduction: Locating lieux de memoire: A (Post)colonial Perspective', *German Historical Institute Bulletin*, Supplement 1: 1–11.

Singh, G. (2009) 'Appealing to the "Beneficent Sarkar": Loyalty, Hierarchy and Rank and File Dissent in the Colonial Indian Military, 1914–1917.' Paper presented at 'South Asian Experiences of the World Wars: New Evidence and New Approaches', workshop convened in London, May.

Talbot, I. and Singh, G. (2009) *The Partition of India*, Cambridge: Cambridge University Press.

Times of India (2010) 'George Cross "Sale" on Internet', 11 August. Online: http://timesofindia.indiatimes.com/city/chandigarh/George-Cross-sale-on-internet/articleshow/6290174.cms (accessed 10 December 2010).

Tribune (2001) 'UK Memorial for War Veterans', Chandigarh, 20 November. Online: www.tribuneindia.com/2001/20011120/punjab1.htm (accessed 10 December 2010).

Tribune (2007) 'War Memorial Unveiled', Chandigarh, 28 May. Online: www.tribuneindia.com/2007/20070528/punjab1.htm (accessed 10 December 2010).

Webster, Wendy (2005) *Englishness and Empire, 1939–1965*, Oxford: Oxford University Press.

Winter, J. and Sivan, E. (2007) *War and Remembrance in the Twentieth Century*, Cambridge: Cambridge University Press.

Part III

The politics of reconstruction

Chapter 10

Reconstruction over ruins: rebuilding Dresden's Frauenkirche

Tony Joel

Debates over the reconstruction of Dresden's Frauenkirche, the city's landmark Church of Our Lady destroyed by aerial bombing in 1945, exemplify the conflicts inherent in the treatment of war-related cultural heritage. This chapter traces the shifting dynamics of a half-century-long debate over how the Frauenkirche site could and should be conserved, and the impact that struggles over war memory and commemoration have on cultural heritage. Initially, only some local citizens' determination to rebuild the church prevented this particular ruinous site from being cleared away with all the other rubble from Dresden's almost entirely destroyed historic Old Town (*Altstadt*). Over time, however, the Frauenkirche ruins emerged in their own right as an arresting antiwar symbol and one of the foremost sites of politicized war memory and commemoration in divided Germany. Of course, the two roles that the ruins had come to fulfil – either facilitating the church's future reconstruction, or functioning as an increasingly prominent site of memory deserving of conservation in its unaltered state – were incompatible. Moreover, principles endorsed by the International Charter for the Conservation and Restoration of Monuments and Sites – popularly known as the Venice Charter of 1964 – could not resolve the issue one way or the other. By the 1980s, severe decomposition of the ruins demanded action. Then, with the advent of Germany's reunification in 1989-90, the kind of heritage to be preserved at the site came under reintensified scrutiny and debate. This created fresh opportunity for the church's potential reconstruction, and a local citizens' action group (*Bürgerinitiative*) successfully appealed for worldwide support to rebuild Dresden's Frauenkirche. Debates over war-related cultural heritage are loaded with the politics of the past and present. In Dresden, we see that the political imperatives of the state, the agency of individual stakeholders and changing political contexts over time each influences debate over whether to preserve, reconstruct or redevelop war-damaged sites.

Destruction of the Elbflorenz

Allied aerial bombing heavily damaged over 130 German cities and towns of varying size and military-industrial strategic importance during the Second

World War. Estimates of the associated civil death and devastation are imprecise, but commonly accepted figures include some 600,000 German civilians killed, around 900,000 others wounded and a further 7.5 million 'de-housed' after 3.5 million dwellings were destroyed (Sebald 2003: 11; Hastings 1979: 352; Moeller 2006: 27; USAAF 1945–6: 5–6). In addition to such sobering statistics, myriad landmark buildings and artefacts of inestimable historical, architectural and cultural worth were lost, too. Germany abounds with constant reminders of the bombing-war, from memorials, museum exhibitions and local remembrance days to various other state-centred and socially engineered forms of public commemoration. Cityscapes across the nation, furthermore, still bear witness to the destructive effects of area-bombing. Whether it be the derelict vestiges of bombed-out buildings that remain standing or, conversely, modernized skylines emblematic of the massive postwar reconstruction that has taken place, many German town-centres serve as implicit tokens of the Western Allies' strategic bombing offensive against the Nazi homeland. Among this impressive catalogue of civil devastation, the 13 February 1945 firebombing of Dresden is widely recognized as both the zenith of the European bombing-war and a *sui generis* case of German wartime loss and suffering. Indeed, through the politics of war memory and commemoration Dresden promptly garnered a postwar reputation as the paradigmatic German *Opferstadt*, or victimized city sacrificed towards the war's end.[1]

Several factors account for why the destruction of Dresden remains particularly controversial. One is the lateness of such a heavy attack on the hitherto virtually ignored city, which, when combined with the unmistakably civic nature of the designated target-area, raises serious questions about the operation's military-strategic justification. The unknown but certainly excessive civilian death toll continues to be a powerful motivator in private and public memory (Reinhard *et al.* 2005; Addison and Crang 2006; Joel 2009). The raid's devastating effectiveness – largely due to the successful creation of a much sought-after but rarely achieved inner-city firestorm – not only produced this human catastrophe, but also erased virtually all of the city's historico-culturally rich buildings. Perhaps more than any other factor, this explains why Dresden became a byword for German wartime loss and suffering that resonated on the international stage.

Dresden's rich cultural reputation can be traced back to the sixteenth century, when Saxony's ruling Wettin dynasty had settled on Dresden as its royal seat (*Residenzstadt*). In the early eighteenth century, under Elector Augustus II (the Strong) and his son and successor Augustus III, the picturesque capital sprawling along both sides of the River Elbe first gained real repute as a leading centre of architectural splendour and high culture. Inspired by the great northern Italian Renaissance cities, both electors invested substantial resources into transforming their *Residenzstadt* into an internationally revered *Kulturstadt*, or city of culture. Dresden amassed an envious collection of some of Europe's finest examples of (neo)baroque architectural design and its opulent galleries housed masterworks by Raphael, Bernado Bellotto Canaletto, Titian and Rembrandt among others. In 1802, the celebrated German author Johann Gottfried Herder was moved to write: 'Bloom, German Florence, with your treasures of the art world!'[2] The popularized version became Elbflorenz (Florence of the Elbe).

In the heart of the Elbflorenz lay the Saxon capital's most celebrated building and arguably German Protestantism's most impressive architectonic achievement, George Bähr's 1743 masterwork, the Frauenkirche. The church's symbolic importance to Dresden is based on historical, architectural, cultural and spiritual grounds, and Dresdeners have long bestowed an exalted status not only on the building but also on the site itself. The first church in the Elbe Valley surrounding present-day Dresden was built in the eleventh century as a missionary church to convert the local Sorbian population to Christianity (Friedrich 2005: 13; SFD 2005: 11; FDO 2009). Its full name was the Unserer-Lieben-Frauen-Kirche, conveniently abbreviated to Frauenkirche. The following century, the Romanesque church was relocated to the site that roughly 600 years later would be occupied by Bähr's baroque replacement. Meanwhile, Dresden's original Frauenkirche underwent periodic extensions reflecting both early and late gothic-inspired architectural trends. By the late seventeenth century, however, the church had become so badly dilapidated it was virtually beyond repair. Coincidentally, around this time Augustus the Strong made some controversial decisions. In 1697, to realize his ambition to become a king (and greatly expand his sphere in influence), Saxony's ruler successfully sought election to the newly vacated throne of the adjacent Polish kingdom. To qualify, however, first he had been forced to convert to Catholicism. Being ruled by a Catholic dividing his time between Dresden and Warsaw challenged the faith and very sense of identity of the elector's Saxon subjects. It had been under the House of Wettin that Martin Luther was protected in Wittenberg, leading to Saxony earning its cherished reputation as the 'birthplace of the Reformation'. Augustus the Strong nonetheless promoted religious tolerance and reassured Saxons they would not be forced to follow his lead and convert to Catholicism. In 1714, however, he ordered the closure of Dresden's decrepit Frauenkirche. Following its demolition, by 1722 planning was underway for a replacement to be constructed on the same site and Bähr, as the city's official master builder, was commissioned to undertake the project.

Augustus the Strong, a renowned patron of the arts who played a pivotal role in Dresden garnering its reputation as the Elbflorenz, showed genuine interest and regularly received Bähr to discuss progress. He nonetheless declined repeated requests to help fund the ambitious project, steadfastly maintaining it should be a municipal venture. Between 1726, when the foundation stone was laid, and Augustus the Strong's death in 1733, construction costs were completely funded by the city council, Saxony's

Protestant Church consistory, and the city's populace. Despite also converting to Catholicism in order to inherit the Polish throne, Saxony's new Elector Augustus III proved far more receptive than his father to the idea of contributing to the new Frauenkirche in his beloved birthplace. He donated tens of thousands of talers, a most crucial gesture because it allowed Bähr to complete the cupola in sandstone rather than copper or wood, facilitating his vision of making the church appear as if it were carved out of 'a single stone from top to bottom'.[3] Notwithstanding Augustus III's considerable contribution, upon its completion in 1743 Dresdeners looked upon the Frauenkirche as a municipal accomplishment and the object of unmatched civic pride. It served, then, as a powerful statement of both Saxon Protestant self-assertion and Dresden's municipal wealth. The construction of such an impressive building, moreover, continued several centuries of history and tradition by having a Frauenkirche on this exact site (Fig. 10.1).

For centuries Dresden's cultural significance was appreciated not only outside the city itself but indeed beyond Germany. And not even five years of Nazi barbarism and total war prevented some quarters of the enemy from publicly articulating hopes that this one particular German city would survive undamaged. With impeccably bad timing, the reputable *Manchester Guardian* declared on 12 February 1945: 'We may hope the Saxon capital is spared the worst. Only Germans need care for Berlin, but Dresden, with the charm of its streets and the graciousness of its buildings, belongs to Europe' ('West and East' 1945). Within 48 hours, and after the city had avoided any serious damage throughout the first 65 months of the war, 1,083 British and American aircraft dropped 1,952 tons of high explosives and 1,477 tons of incendiaries onto central Dresden, destroying 13 square miles of the pristine *Altstadt* and adjacent residential quarters in a single night (Bergander 1998; Neitzel 2006). American novelist Kurt Vonnegut, who witnessed the raid while interned in a local slaughterhouse as a prisoner of war, later recalled Dresden in his 1969 acerbic timewarp classic *Slaughterhouse-5* as having resembled a virtual moonscape (Vonnegut 2000).

The bombing and firestorm heavily damaged, if not wholly destroyed, practically all of Dresden's splendid Renaissance-inspired and (neo)baroque gems. Initially, however, there was hope of a miraculous exception. Despite being located within the designated target-area, it seemed that somehow the Frauenkirche had survived. Yet, whereas the church's exterior appeared remarkably unscathed, the intense heat had warped the internal wooden support beams holding up its massive sandstone dome, affectionately known to locals as the 'Stony Bell' (*Steinerne Glocke*). Owing to unbearable structural damage, mid-morning on Thursday 15 February 1945 (around 36 hours after the raid had commenced and some 22 hours after it had concluded), the Frauenkirche imploded into a mountain of rubble (*Trümmerberg*) covering an area 71 x 74 metres on the ground and reaching 17.6 metres into the air (SFD 2005: 128). Just as it had been Dresden's last major public

Figure 10.1 George Bähr's 'Stony Bell'. Dresden's reconstructed Frauenkirche.

building to succumb, so, too, would the Frauenkirche be more or less the last to reappear.

Dresden had lost its pre-war character, charm, identity and reputation as the Elbflorenz, and, according to W. G. Sebald (2003: 11), with an average of 42.8 cubic metres of rubble per person (based on the city's pre-war population of roughly 600,000 inhabitants) Dresdeners faced one of the most monumental reconstruction tasks in postwar Europe. Its location in the German Democratic Republic (GDR) made Dresden's rebuilding difficult for several reasons, not least the state's lack of funds and chronic shortage of materials (Jokilehto 1998a). Also, the new government's communist ideals were fundamentally opposed to the architectural grandeur synonymous with the former Saxon *Residenzstadt*, which in some cases such as the ornate Zwinger complex arguably even crossed the line into folly. As Robert Goeckel (1992) explains, moreover, Church and state shared an awkward relationship in the GDR, making the reconstruction of houses of worship especially problematic.

Nonetheless, over time many of Dresden's most prominent buildings including the state theatre (Staatstheater), academy of fine arts (Kunstakademie), town hall (Rathaus), state opera house (Semperoper), the Protestant Church of the Holy Cross (Kreuzkirche) and the Catholic cathedral endearingly known as the Hofkirche either were restored, renovated, or reconstructed. The gradual reappearance of such buildings could be considered tangible manifestations of the GDR's national anthem *Auferstanden aus Ruinen* (literally 'risen out of the ruins'). Conversely, there were some striking examples of neglect and even inexplicable demolition. Dresden's only surviving gothic church, the Sophienkirche, for instance, had been gutted by the firestorm but local historic monument conservationists secured its structurally sound exterior walls thereby making renovation/reconstruction possible. In 1962, however, GDR leader Walter Ulbricht ordered the church's demolition, purportedly declaring that 'a socialist city had no need for a gothic church' (quoted in Köppe 2010). The Sophienkirche was just one such example of several bombed-out but salvageable churches demolished at the state's behest in Dresden and across the GDR more generally. Whilst spared from demolition, Dresden's badly damaged former royal palace (Residenzschloss) remained secured yet neglected until the mid-1980s. It was, along with the Frauenkirche ruins, one of Dresden's two foremost sites whereby neither rebuilding nor redevelopment had occurred four decades after the war. Whereas the exterior of the former Residenzschloss was largely intact, the Frauenkirche site was nothing more than a pile of sandstone rubble framed by the two small sections of wall – part of a stair-tower, and a segment of the choir – still standing. Ostensibly there was little discernible difference between the Frauenkirche ruins and the millions of cubic metres of rubble surrounding them. Yet, it was no mere coincidence that this particular site was conserved in its ruinous condition while the rest of central Dresden was cleared for the GDR's socialist-inspired redevelopment and 'rebirth' of the city.

Inadvertent conundrum

For over 200 years Bähr's inimitable 'Stony Bell' had crowned Dresden's internationally adored Elbe skyline. Locals therefore widely anticipated, indeed expected, the Frauenkirche would feature among the city's first major rebuilding tasks. As early as August 1945, when the Cultural Department of the Saxon State Administration (*Landesverwaltung Sachsen – Kulturabteilung*) convened its first postwar Salvage and Reconstruction Meeting, the Frauenkirche was prioritized among Dresden's six most historico-culturally significant buildings (SFD 2005: 95). Somewhat fortuitously, the church had been comprehensively restored – cosmetic rejuvenation of the interior and structural reinforcement of the exterior – during the Third Reich. Despite its subsequent destruction this effort was not in vain because the project's meticulous documentation survived (Nadler 1992: 25–7). The Frauenkirche, then, was not only probably the single most popular choice but also theoretically a most feasible candidate for rebuilding. Local supporters conceived novel fundraising ideas to help finance reconstruction including 'donation angels' (*Spendenengel*) for Christmas trees as early as 1945 and a specially commissioned 'reconstruction lottery' (*Wiederaufbaulotterie*) three years later (SFD 2005: 98–9). As custodian of the land and ruins, the Protestant Church in Germany (*Evangelische Kirche in Deutschland*, EKD) initially announced its support in principle for rebuilding the Frauenkirche. Declaring that it was in no position to help fund such a project, however, the EKD handed over responsibility for conserving the ruins to Dresden's Institute for the Preservation of Historic Monuments (*Institut für Denkmalpflege*).

Under the watchful eye of head curator Hans Nadler, in the immediate postwar years the Institute conducted some preliminary rubble-clearing at the Frauenkirche site (Nadler 1992: 25–34; 2001: 91–2). In a prescient move that proved crucial a half-century later, all such work was carefully carried out in preparation for reconstructing the church – as far as possible – according to the principles of anastylosis, which essentially involves reassembling existing but dismembered parts. (Here it is worth noting that Nadler's insistence on adhering to anastylosis predated the Venice Charter by almost two decades.) Salvaged sandstone blocks were painstakingly catalogued and stored off-site, but with neither Church nor state offering financial support it soon became apparent the project would not get off the ground. By the early 1950s, Nadler and his colleagues stopped planning for imminent rebuilding and instead turned their attention to preserving the ruins indefinitely. Securing the Frauenkirche ruins served a twofold purpose. First, their existence safeguarded the site against possible redevelopment (an ongoing threat as evidenced by the sudden demolition of the far-more-intact Sophienkirche) before the church's reconstruction could be achieved. Second, it was recognized from the outset that if the Frauenkirche were to be rebuilt 'authentically' according to anastylosis principles then incorporating the ruins would be absolutely vital. Accordingly, as one of its leading curators Heinrich Magirius later reflected, throughout the entire GDR era Dresden's Institute for the Preservation of Historic Monuments guarded the Frauenkirche ruins 'like its most treasured possession'.[4]

In the early Cold War period, 13 February was prominent in the GDR's public memory calendar. State-centred commemorative politics saw East

German communist officials appropriate the anniversary of Dresden's destruction as an occasion to openly portray the capitalist Western Powers – including the Federal Republic of Germany, accused of being the successor-state to the Third Reich – as aggressive warmongering imperialists (Margalit 2002; Neutzner 2005; Joel 2009). On the one hand, by holding the Nazis ultimately responsible for everything that had happened during Hitler's War, the loss and suffering associated with Dresden could be evoked as a warning of the inherent evils of fascism. On the other hand, annually commemorating the Dresden raid as a pernicious act of wanton destruction meant that those directly responsible could be depicted as 'Anglo-American terror-bombers', a term ironically enough borrowed from Nazi Propaganda Minister Joseph Goebbels, who had accused the Western Powers of using 'terror-bombers' to erase German identity through the physical destruction of Germany's cultural heritage. The Frauenkirche ruins, increasingly prominent as all other rubble was cleared away, emerged as Dresden's undisputed foremost bombing-related site of memory. As a corollary, the ruins became imbued with powerful anti-fascist and antiwar symbolism. In German, an important distinction can be made between a *Denkmal*, meaning a memorial or monument, and a *Mahnmal*, which denotes a special kind of memorial/monument that serves as a reminder or warning to present and future generations. Although it was never the intention of those conservationists responsible for guarding over it, the ruinous Frauenkirche site categorically developed into an antiwar (and anti-fascist) *Mahnmal*.

By the 1960s, then, Dresden's cultural heritage conservationists had unwittingly created a kind of Hamlet-esque conundrum: to rebuild, or not to rebuild. It was a quandary not only facing the many supporters who had so vehemently advocated reconstructing the Frauenkirche since the war's end. It equally concerned anyone who now believed that such an arresting site merited preservation in its existing ruinous state. For the church to reappear the ruins would have to be monumentally disturbed, yet the fact that they had materialized into an important *Mahnmal* in their own right simply could not be overlooked. Paradoxically, preserving the ruins indefinitely would prevent the realization of ever seeing the 'Stony Bell' once again crown Dresden's Elbe skyline. There was no forgetting that this widely held dream was the only reason why this particular site had been protected instead of being cleared away with the rest of Dresden's rubble. And it was this development, in turn, which had inadvertently enabled the remnants of the Frauenkirche to manifest themselves as arguably the most (in)famous antiwar site of memory in divided Germany, thus creating a cultural heritage impasse.

Around this time, in May 1964, the Second International Congress of Architects and Technicians of Historic Monuments was held in Venice. The most immediate objective of the resultant Venice Charter was to arrest the widespread mistakes still being made in restoration and reconstruction practices across war-ravaged Europe. Through its advocacy of key concepts such as preserving monuments in their historical setting, privileging 'authenticity' by distinguishing between genuinely restored objects and rebuilt replicas, and strictly limiting reconstructions according to anastylosis principles, the Venice Charter had ramifications for the debate over rebuilding the Frauenkirche. Whereas some of the Charter's concepts could be used in support of conserving the ruins, paradoxically other aspects contained in its 16 articles could be invoked as endorsements for rebuilding the church. Supporters of conserving the ruins as a *Mahnmal*, for instance, needed to look no further than the Charter's preamble. It states that, when it comes to historic monuments that are 'imbued with a message from the past', we all share a responsibility 'to hand them on in the full richness of their authenticity' (Jokilehto 1998b, appendix). The Frauenkirche ruins certainly evoked an important warning from history about the horrors and futility of modern total war, and there was real danger of losing this message if the remnants were to be incorporated into (or consumed by) a reconstructed church. Any generation that did not pass on this message-laden site of war memory in the full richness of its authenticity, so the argument followed, must be viewed as having failed to meet its cultural heritage obligations. Given that only a small section of one stair-tower and a segment of the choir remained standing, furthermore, critics could argue that an over-reliance on introducing new materials meant that in this case reconstruction could not possibly qualify as anastylosis and so a rebuilt Frauenkirche would be nothing more than a replica. Conversely, Article 7 of the Charter could be read as vindication for demands to rebuild the church, on its original site, at the ruins' expense:

> A monument is inseparable from the history to which it bears witness and from the setting in which it occurs. The moving of all or part of a monument cannot be allowed except where the safeguarding of that monument demands it or where it is justified by national or international interest of paramount importance. (Jokilehto 1998b, appendix)

At first glance this passage ostensibly supports preservation of the ruins as bearing witness to the history of National Socialism, the Second World War and the church's own destruction. Upon closer inspection, however, it actually contains some crucial points for advocating reconstruction. Whereas the ruins symbolized only one specific era and had functioned as a *Mahnmal* for barely a quarter-century, the site had a consistent history as a Frauenkirche (in various incarnations) for three-quarters of a millennium. Almost throughout Dresden's history *in toto* this site and a functioning church had been inseparable. In terms of universal significance, furthermore, supporters of the Frauenkirche could insist that the ruins' 'accidental' functionality as a *Mahnmal* was of secondary importance to their 'real' purpose of facilitating the rebuilding of a renowned and much loved historical landmark church. The Venice Charter thus could be interpreted either in support of preserving the *Mahnmal* as a site of war memory and commemoration, or as mounting an equally persuasive case in support of reconstructing the church over the ruins. Dresden's Frauenkirche thereby offers a graphic illustration of how the Venice Charter can effectively cancel itself out, reinforcing the intrinsic difficulties of prescribing particular cultural heritage action through charters in an environment in which meaning and significance are open to interpretation and consequently a matter of considerable debate.

Time for action, of one kind or another

For advocates of rebuilding the Frauenkirche the situation was looking rather dire by the 1980s. The previous decade (coinciding with détente and improved relations with Bonn), East Berlin had intensified its interest in preserving and promoting German national cultural heritage (Koshar 2000: 269–83; Fulbrook 1991: 299–306). In July 1975, the GDR Parliament (*Volkskammer*) had enacted influential new cultural heritage conservation laws and tens of thousands of objects slated for attention were registered on special lists at the local, district and state level (Hinze 1985). This exhaustive programme finally delivered funding to reconstruct Dresden's world-renowned Semperoper, and when opening the rebuilt opera house on 13 February 1985 – the milestone fortieth anniversary of the firestorm – GDR leader Erich Honecker (1985) announced that the Residenzschloss would be Dresden's next major reconstruction project. The Frauenkirche, however, did not feature on the state's itinerary. The EKD's synod likewise still could not be persuaded to help fund the church's reconstruction. Many Dresdeners nonetheless maintained hope that one day a project somehow might come to fruition, and local conservationists continued to safeguard the site accordingly. The ruins, meanwhile, continued to grow in stature as an antiwar *Mahnmal*. From 1982 onwards, annually on 13 February, the Frauenkirche site was the focal point of mass gatherings designed partially as silent candlelit remembrance of the bombing victims and, in what was extremely rare for the GDR at the time, public demonstrations of passive resistance against the state. As each year passed, rebuilding the Frauenkirche seemed increasingly unlikely.

After four decades, weathering had taken its toll. Experts testing the Frauenkirche site before construction commenced on a nearby luxury hotel the Dresdner Hof (nowadays the Dresden Hilton) discovered advanced decomposition in some of the more concealed parts of the ruinous sandstone mountain. The hazardous site was cordoned off immediately in the interests of public safety. It clearly was no longer an option simply to leave – or 'passively' conserve – the ruins in their deteriorating condition; major activity of some kind or other was required. This could have entailed, on the one hand, securing the ruins' continued existence in their unaltered state, or, on the other hand, incorporating them as much as possible into an 'authentically' reconstructed Frauenkirche. Either way, however, funding posed seemingly insurmountable hurdles in the late 1980s. Without Church or state intervention the costs of rebuilding remained unattainable. Even reinforcing the ruins would have required considerable funds, and in the impecunious GDR allocating large sums of money to the upkeep of what essentially was a pile of rubble just was not feasible. Almost certainly, without meaningful change to the status quo, the Frauenkirche would not have been rebuilt and the ruins would not have received the attention necessary to prevent further deterioration and eventual collapse. Then suddenly in the autumn of 1989, the *Wende* – the profound socio-political 'turn' of events that caused the GDR's collapse and culminated in Germany's reunification – unexpectedly created fresh opportunity.

The *Ruf aus Dresden* and World Heritage listing

In late November 1989, a fortnight after the fall of the Berlin Wall, a select group of influential Dresden residents gathered at the home of local art-dealer Heinz Miech. Agreeing the time was politically ripe to launch a new campaign to rebuild the Frauenkirche, they established a *Bürgerinitiative* and elected Ludwig Güttler, arguably Germany's leading trumpet virtuoso, as spokesperson. The group immediately established contact with EKD authorities, endeavouring to 'get the Church to come on board'.[5] They hoped that, in light of the state's collapse, the synod might change its longstanding attitude and make a sizeable monetary contribution to the campaign. And, even if financial assistance was not forthcoming, obtaining the EKD's permission to continue campaigning alone would at least circumvent any future legal battles over ownership and usage of the land and ruins. The synod announced it would not stand in the way if the *Bürgerinitiative* attracted the necessary funds from elsewhere, but declined to become involved. Underpinning the EKD's polite but apathetic response were not only financial concerns, though these were critical. The synod also pointed out that the Frauenkirche no longer had a community and central Dresden simply did not need another Protestant church. Postwar city-planners had largely abandoned the traditional concept of centrally located housing in favour of Stalinist gigantism and exaggerated spaciousness. The altered urban landscape meant that the Kreuzkirche (with over 3,500 seats) and the nearby Annenkirche – two churches reconstructed within the first postwar decade – easily could accommodate Dresden's reduced number of inner-city Protestant churchgoers. On practical grounds, then, the EKD considered rebuilding the Frauenkirche to be indulgent.

Similarly, initial contact with Dresden City Council met with polite but firm rejection. While maintaining dialogue with both the synod and council in late 1989, the *Bürgerinitiative* realized that wider support would be crucial and thus decided to make an ambitious global appeal for help. Güttler suggested that, in order to harness the heightened emotions that would envelop the forty-fifth anniversary of the city's destruction, February 1990 was the opportune moment to publicly launch the *Ruf aus Dresden* – a call from Dresden for worldwide financial assistance to rebuild the Frauenkirche. Accordingly, the official *Ruf* released to the media contained a strong international dimension. In part it appealed for a campaign to reconstruct the Frauenkirche as a 'Christian Centre of World Peace in the new Europe' (Jäger 1992: 98–100). This concept could help to thwart criticism that central Dresden did not need another 'conventional' Protestant church, which would leave a rebuilt Frauenkirche without a community. It was, moreover, an assurance that even if the admonishing site of memory gave way to an august house of worship, the lessons from Dresden's wartime fate would not be forgotten. The *Ruf aus Dresden* also appealed for international support under the rubric of reconciliation. Indeed, a month prior to publicly launching their campaign the *Bürgerinitiative* sent private letters to Queen Elizabeth II and United States President George Bush Sr as the respective heads of state of the two nations directly responsible for Dresden's destruction, and reconciliation was the key theme underpinning the letters' request for moral and financial support.[6]

The *Ruf aus Dresden* also addressed that most crucial issue of authenticity. The *Bürgerinitiative* – boasting as a member the spritely octogenarian Hans Nadler some four decades after he had played such a pivotal role in safeguarding the ruins – was supremely confident that the church's reconstruction could be accomplished in accordance with the principles of anastylosis. There were the two segments of wall still standing, salvaged sandstone blocks to reuse, untold other objects concealed underneath the mountain of rubble to be recovered during the site's excavation, and meticulous documentation to facilitate a faithful and 'authentic' reconstruction. The *Ruf aus Dresden* even went so far as to declare that, upon its completion as an internationally backed project, the Frauenkirche 'should be included on UNESCO's World Heritage List' (quoted in Jäger 1992). This claim made in reference to one specific building (that did not even exist at the time!) was particularly bullish given that a 1989 GDR proposal that Saxony's entire capital be inscribed in the World Heritage List under the title 'The Baroque Ensemble of Dresden' had been rejected. The International Council on Monuments and Sites (ICOMOS) recognized Dresden's 'great cultural value' but the proposal to inscribe the ensemble was rejected on the basis of the World Heritage Committee's earlier ruling over another war-ravaged city painstakingly restored: Warsaw (UNESCO 2003: 87). For several years in the late 1970s, the Committee debated whether reconstructed sites such as the Polish capital qualified as authentic. When, in 1980, it inscribed the Historic Centre of Warsaw as 'an outstanding example of a near-total reconstruction of a span of history covering the 13th to the 20th century', the Committee announced that it would remain an exceptional case and no other reconstructed sites would be considered on the grounds of authenticity and integrity (quoted in UNESCO 2010b; see also Cameron 2008).

The Warsaw ruling, then, ostensibly precluded either Dresden or a reconstructed Frauenkirche from World Heritage recognition. In 2004, however, an expanded proposal encompassing not only the city but also the surrounding Elbe Valley was inscribed on the World Heritage List as a 'continuing cultural landscape'. An ICOMOS expert mission that visited the proposed site in September 2003 did not ignore the problematic cultural heritage issues stemming from Dresden's wartime destruction. Furthermore, it acknowledged the capacity of a reconstructed Frauenkirche – nearing completion by this stage – to contribute to the overall authenticity and integrity of the site:

> The historic city centre was bombed at the end of the Second World War, but the remaining buildings continue to have an important role in the panorama ... The most damaged building of the monumental group was the *Frauenkirche*. Around 40% of the original stones have been recovered, and the work is based on exceptionally complete records ... While recognizing the unfortunate losses in the historic city centre during the Second World War, the Dresden Elbe Valley, defined as a continuing cultural landscape, has retained the overall historical authenticity and integrity in its distinctive character and components. (UNESCO 2010a)

Joy was short-lived, however, when five years after its inscription the Dresden Elbe Valley became only the second site ever to be deleted from the World Heritage List. The controversy centred on state and city officials' decision to build the Waldschlösschenbrücke, a four-lane bridge over the River Elbe designed to alleviate Dresden's traffic congestion but arguably at the cost of upsetting the valley's aesthetic equilibrium. UNESCO immediately announced its concerns that the bridge would 'irreversibly damage the Outstanding Universal Value and integrity' of the World Heritage Site. When the project went ahead anyhow, UNESCO responded by listing the Dresden Elbe Valley as an Endangered World Heritage Site and three years later, in June 2009, ultimately decided to remove the site from the World Heritage List (UNESCO 2010a). Whereas the reconstruction of war-damaged buildings had not disqualified Dresden on the grounds of authenticity, moves to add another modern man-made construction to the valley's 'continuing cultural landscape' ultimately proved one step too far (Fig. 10.2).

Criticisms of, and support for, the Frauenkirche rebuilding project

Calls for a post-reunification reconstruction of Dresden's Frauenkirche met with criticism on scientific, aesthetic, moral and pragmatic grounds.

Figure 10.2 'The Dresden Elbe Valley'. Vandalized sign still bearing witness to the short-lived status of Dresden and its surrounding area as a 'continuing cultural landscape' on UNESCO's World Heritage List.

Notwithstanding the idea of it serving as a 'Christian Centre of World Peace' in the new post-Cold War Europe, opponents could adopt the EKD synod's view that central Dresden simply did not require another Protestant church. From a Christian perspective, furthermore, given all the poverty, hunger, illness and associated misery in the world such an extravagant project could be dismissed as pure hedonism. And renewed calls to rebuild the church once again raised questions over whether the ruins should be conserved as a site of war memory and commemoration rather than being replaced by what arguably would be little more than a mere replica. A number of questionable examples of supposedly 'authentic' reconstructions of historico-cultural landmarks destroyed by wartime bombing already existed in Germany, and the influential German Foundation for Monument Protection (*Deutsche Stiftung Denkmalschutz*, DSD), a private Bonn-based initiative established in 1985, declared itself fundamentally opposed to all such endeavours. In 1991, the DSD became particularly alarmed by growing calls to rebuild Dresden's Frauenkirche and Berlin's Stadtschloss, the war-damaged but reparable Hohenzollern city palace located on Unter den Linden that had been controversially demolished in 1950 because East German officials disapprovingly viewed it as a symbol of class oppression and Prussian militarism. In response, the DSD released a statement explaining its disapproval of these projects:

> The erection of reproductions of lost monuments can only be of importance for the work in the present day. Such copies cannot be monuments recalling great achievements of the past in their full sense and keeping alive the memory of historic processes with their heights and depths. Conservationists are responsible only for historical evidence which cannot be reproduced and must warn when there is a threat to the possibility for remembrance in the public arena. (Quoted in Friedrich 2005: 77)[7]

Furthermore, as Martin Gegner's earlier chapter in this volume explores in detail, an alternative approach to war-related cultural heritage could be found in (West) Berlin where the Kaiser-Wilhelm-Gedächtniskirche, the heavily bomb-damaged nineteenth-century church, was conserved in its ruinous state and complemented by the construction of an adjacent modern replacement. Rather than simply replicating past architectonic achievements, then, a new work was created that in due course developed its own cultural heritage value as a unique example of 1950s architectural design. And the remnants of the original church were preserved as probably (West) Berlin's foremost antiwar *Mahnmal*. Theoretically there was no reason why this approach could not have produced similarly impressive results at the Frauenkirche site. In Dresden, however, it represented an unacceptable compromise because advocates of rebuilding always had set their hearts and minds on seeing an 'authentic' reconstruction of the city's beloved landmark. For this to eventuate, of course, the ruins had to be incorporated (or sacrificed) and the Frauenkirche had to rematerialize on the exact site it had previously occupied for centuries. Neither a nearby replica nor an adjacent replacement would be satisfactory. As a commentator exclaimed in the influential *Frankfurter Allgemeine Zeitung* a week after the public launch of the *Ruf aus Dresden*: 'So long as this dome of the Church of Our Lady no longer crowns the city, not only will Dresden have a gaping wound, but also every Dresdener, regardless of where they live now, will have a bleeding heart' (Zimmermann 1990).

Despite heated debate, the *Ruf aus Dresden* soon proved successful in creating an irresistible groundswell of (inter)national support to rebuild the Frauenkirche. Considerable donations came from all corners of the globe, in particular the United States and Britain where some inspired individuals respectively established the charity organizations Friends of Dresden and the Dresden Trust. Having opposed the idea during the GDR era, in February 1992 the Dresden City Council announced it would cover 10 per cent of the total rebuilding costs (Friedrich 2005: 87). The 'reunification chancellor' Helmut Kohl was personally responsible for a very substantial early donation that helped to kick-start the fledgling project. In December 1989, Kohl had travelled to Dresden to hold closed talks with his new GDR counterpart Hans Modrow about strengthening German–German relations following the *Wende*. Upon arrival, however, Kohl was overwhelmed by an unexpected groundswell of popular support and as a show of gratitude made an impromptu public address. Employing the Frauenkirche ruins as an arresting backdrop, an inspired Kohl for the first time publicly articulated his vision of 'the unity of the nation'. He later reflected on this particular occasion as his 'key experience' of the entire reunification process (Kohl 2005: 1020). In April 1990, a sum of approximately €750,000 was raised after Kohl requested that all guests attending an event at Bonn's Beethovenhalle celebrating his sixtieth birthday donate to the Frauenkirche rebuilding project in lieu of personal gifts to him (SFD 2005: 117).

Other major donations followed. During her state visit to Germany in 2004 Queen Elizabeth II, whose first cousin Prince Edward the Duke of Kent was intimately involved in the rebuilding project as royal patron of the Dresden Trust, hosted a gala event at the Berlin Philharmonic to raise funds for the final stages of the church's reconstruction. The lavish evening was not the Queen's only engagement with the Frauenkirche and Dresden commemorative politics. During her brief but controversial visit to Dresden in 1992, when Elizabeth II attended a special reconciliation service conducted in the Kreuzkirche but refused to apologize for the city's wartime destruction, her motorcade had (purposely) passed the Frauenkirche ruins. Thereafter the Queen maintained a personal interest in the rebuilding project as evidenced by the 'four-figure contribution' she made to the Dresden Trust from her own privy purse (Heimrich 1995). The most significant ongoing financial commitment was provided by Dresdner Bank. Despite having kept its city of origin in its name, for decades the bank had been based in Berlin and Frankfurt-am-Main and during the Cold War it operated as a Western financial institution. The Frauenkirche rebuilding project thus represented the ideal chance for the bank to re-establish itself in Dresden and across the former GDR territory. Furthermore, underpinning such a popular war-related cultural heritage venture certainly would have been a welcome public relations boon at a time when Dresdner Bank's reputation was coming under increased scrutiny for having been the 'bank of choice' for the SS and other Nazi organizations during the Third Reich's occupation of much of Europe (Young 2006).

Fundraising, of course, was not restricted to such prominent public figures and institutions. Notwithstanding the sizeable contributions made at both local and international levels, between February 1990 when the *Ruf* was launched publicly and the rebuilt church's (re)consecration in October 2005, the overwhelming majority of funding was collected across reunified Germany in a truly national effort. Many Dresdeners and local businesses donated to the appeal, while across Germany for the whole 15 years the fundraising campaign persisted through a variety of methods. Public concerts and other festive gatherings were staged. The federal government commissioned commemorative stamps and coins. The EKD raised ongoing donations, as did numerous churches (of all denominations) across Germany. Such an emphatic response as occurred at all levels suggests that the (inter) national community shared the local positivistic view that the reappearance of Dresden's spectacular Frauenkirche held far stronger historico-cultural appeal than the continuing conservation of a haunting antiwar *Mahnmal*. Furthermore, the rebuilding project's registered logo encapsulates the ambiguity inherent in this chapter's title. On the one hand, it depicts the long-held intention not merely to replace the ruins with the church, but rather to incorporate them as a feature with the 'authentically' rebuilt church rising above. On the other hand, however, this image is emblematic of how the fight to reconstruct the Frauenkirche ultimately won out over the battle to preserve the ruinous site of memory. On both accounts it was, indeed, literally a case of reconstruction over ruins.

Controversies during reconstruction

Even once underway the Frauenkirche rebuilding project was not without controversy. Questions were raised on matters as diverse as reconstruction techniques employed, the handling of building materials and even the commissioning of an anachronistic musical instrument. Adopting modern engineering and building techniques could be justified according to the Venice Charter. Articles 2 and 10, for instance, approve of having recourse to modern techniques wherever traditional practices may prove inadequate. Nonetheless, employing at least some period technology when rebuilding the Frauenkirche could have helped to reinforce the project's claims of being a faithful reconstruction of Bähr's eighteenth-century masterwork. When coupled with the necessary introduction of so many new building materials, however, in the eyes of purists the project's heavy reliance on computerized engineering and modern construction methods could be seen as undermining its 'authenticity'.

A notable controversy, the so-called Dresden organ dispute, erupted midway through the rebuilding project after a French company was commissioned to design and build a new instrument for the Frauenkirche. The German-born, New York-based researcher Günter Blobel had been the driving force behind the American charity Friends of Dresden. Blobel (2005: 39–41) recalled how, as a boy fleeing from the advancing Red Army in early February 1945, he had trekked through Dresden with his mother and siblings. Coming from a small Silesian village, Blobel remembers being awestruck by the silhouette of the Saxon capital's Elbe skyline and was especially impressed by the dome of the Frauenkirche. He wished to stay in Dresden but they had to keep trekking westward, so his mother promised they would return as soon as possible. Just days later, however, the Blobels heard news of Dresden's destruction and a distraught Günter realized he would never get the chance to revisit the Elbflorenz. This experience left such an indelible impression on Blobel that a half-century later he not only established the charitable organization but, moreover, upon winning the 1999 Nobel Prize for medicine donated his entire award of some €800,000 to the project. Blobel, however, made this magnanimous gesture while under the misapprehension that the church's original Silbermann organ would be replicated. Instead, the decision was made to install a larger 4,873 pipe organ with a stoplist range reaching well beyond that of its predecessor in order to cater for post-baroque compositions. Arguing that the modern Strasbourg-made organ would be an anachronism and an insult to Saxony's celebrated eighteenth-century organ builder, an outraged Blobel henceforth distanced himself from the remainder of the Frauenkirche rebuilding project (Paul 2004: 57–8).

Finally, perhaps the most intriguing aspect of the entire reconstruction process concerns the use of original stones from the destroyed church. Not all salvaged stones could be reused, because compression testing revealed that some were badly decayed and engineering computations warned that too many old stones in any given area could cause structural weakness. For two reasons, however, incorporating as many original stones as possible was crucial: first, to adhere to anastylosis reconstruction principles; and, second, to achieve the desired effect of making the ruins a prominent feature of the rebuilt church. Therefore, Bernd Kluge (2002) explains, engineers used the IBM software suite CATIA (Computer Aided Three-dimensional Interactive Application) to arbitrarily determine the placement of original stones. Their darkened appearance due to over 200 years of natural patination means that these original blocks can easily be identified among the new lighter sandstone blocks (Fig. 10.3). (Coincidentally, this effect adds a nice touch by mirroring Dresden's official city colours of black and gold.) Moreover, the contrast between the golden colour of the new stones and the original blocks' blackish patina is in keeping with the Venice Charter's proposal that the introduction of new materials must always be clearly visible in reconstructions. But the arbitrary nature of the original stones' placement around the church raises serious questions about the artificial creation of what Mark Jarzombek terms 'embedded memory' (2004: 55–6). And what, if anything, should be done in future when decades or centuries of natural patination take their course and the difference between the original eighteenth-century stones and the majority of 'new' blocks is no longer discernible?

Conclusion

Dresden's Frauenkirche is an illuminating case study of how the production of war heritage constitutes an evolutionary and quite often organic process. For almost a half-century after its wartime destruction, debate over whether to rebuild this historico-culturally rich landmark building was shaped and

Figure 10.3 Arbitrarily determined 'embedded memory'? The black patina formed on original stones reused in the rebuilding of the Frauenkirche constrasts starkly with the light golden colour of the new sandstone blocks.

reshaped by the politics of the past and present. Over time the situation had become further complicated by the fact that the ruinous site – only preserved during the city's postwar rubble clearance in order to facilitate the church's 'authentic' reconstruction – materialized into an important antiwar site of memory and commemoration. This development posed a cultural heritage conundrum: rebuilding the church meant disturbing the ruins and thus robbing future generations of an important relic of the Second World War; conversely, preserving the ruins indefinitely would prevent Dresdeners from ever healing the gaping wound in their city's heart. Looking to the Venice Charter could not provide a definitive solution, for its articles could be interpreted as supporting either side of the debate. The case of the Frauenkirche thereby illustrates the difficulty of prescribing particular actions through charters when contemplating whether to reconstruct, conserve, or possibly even redevelop culturally significant sites decimated by war. For decades a chronic shortage of funds exacerbated by a lack of support from church and state authorities had put paid to the idea of reconstruction, anyhow. Then, in the wake of the GDR's sudden collapse, a new call from Dresden for global help to rebuild the Frauenkirche as a 'Christian Centre of World Peace in the new Europe' met with spectacular success. Donations flooded in at local, national and international levels over the next 15 years as the rebuilding project progressed, albeit not without controversy. In accordance with the principles of anastylosis, the two remaining segments of wall were incorporated and many original blocks were (arbitrarily) placed all over the church. That stark contrast between the older, darker stones and the light golden colour of the new sandstone blocks is very impressive and informed visitors receive a jarring visual reminder of the city's destructive past. It remains to be seen, however, whether this impact is lost as natural patination eventually envelops the church's exterior and if memories of the war likewise fade with the passage of time.

Notes

1   In German, as Jost Dülffer (1999: 300) explains, conceptually the noun *Opfer* contains both a passive (victim) and a voluntary (sacrifice) connotation.
2   'Blühe, deutsches Florenz, mit Deinen Schätzen der Kunstwelt!' (quoted in KAS 2006). This and all subsequent translations of the original German are my own unless otherwise stated.
3   'von Grund aus bis oben hinauf gleichsam nur ein einziger Stein' (quoted in Magirius 1992: 13–14; Gretzschel 2006: 30).
4   'gehütet wie seinen Augapfel' (Magirius 1990: 3).
5   'die Kirche mit ins Boot zu bitten' (quoted in SFD 2005: 114).
6   A verbatim transcript of the letter sent to Queen Elizabeth II is in possession of the author.
7   The DSD eventually had a change of heart and became supportive of the Frauenkirche rebuilding project. For an interview in which its chairman Gottfried Kiesow justifies the change in attitude, see Mayer (2010).

References

Addison, P. and Crang, J. (eds) (2006) *Firestorm: The Bombing of Dresden, 1945*, London: Pimlico.

Bergander, G. (1998) *Dresden im Luftkrieg: Vorgeschichte – Zerstörung – Folgen*, revised edition, Würzburg: Flechsig.

Blobel, G. (2005) 'Der Himmel wurde feuerrot', in S. Burgdorff and C. Habbe (eds), *Als Feuer vom Himmel fiel*, Munich: Deutscher Taschenbuch Verlag.

Cameron, C. (2008) 'From Warsaw to Mostar: The World Heritage Committee and Authenticity', *APT Bulletin* 39(2–3), 19–24.

Dülffer, J. (1999) 'Erinnerungspolitik und Erinnerungskultur – Kein Ende der Geschichte', in Hamburger Institut für Sozialforschung (ed.), *Eine Ausstellung und ihre Folgen: Zur Rezeption der Ausstellung 'Vernichtungskrieg. Verbrechen der Wehrmacht 1941 bis 1944'*, Hamburg: HIS Verlagsges.mbH.

FDO, Frauenkirche Dresden Online (2009) 'Baugeschichtliche Zeittafel', Leben in der Frauenkirche. Online: http://www.frauenkirche-dresden.de/zeittafel.html (accessed 24 August 2009).

Friedrich, A. (2005) *The Frauenkirche in Dresden: History and Rebuilding*, trans. R. Nitschke, Dresden: Michel Sandstein Verlag.

Fulbrook, M. (1991) *Fontana History of Germany, 1918–1990: The Divided Nation*, London: Fontana Press.

Goeckel, R. F. (1992) *The Lutheran Church and the East German State: Political Conflict and Change under Ulbricht and Honecker*, Ithaca, NY: Cornell University Press.

Gretzschel, M. (2006) *Die Dresdner Frauenkirche*, Hamburg: Ellert & Richter Verlag.

Hastings, M. (1979) *Bomber Command*, London: Michael Joseph.

Heimrich, B. (1995) 'Der Stellvertreter in Dresden', *FAZ*, 13 February, 12.

Hinze, A. (1985) 'Zweckmäßiger, wohnlicher und schöner?', *Süddeutsche Zeitung*, 13 February, 8.

Honecker, E. (1985) 'Es geht heute um das Überleben der Menschheit und um die Existenz unserer Erde', *Neues Deutschland*, 14 February, 3.

Jäger, H.-J. (1992) 'Die Bürgerinitiative: "Gesellschaft zur Förderung des Wiederaufbaus der Frauenkirche Dresden e.V." ', *Dresdner Hefte* 32(4), 97–101.

Jarzombek, M. (2004) 'Disguised Visibilities: Dresden/"Dresden"', in E. Bastéa (ed.), *Memory and Architecture*, Albuquerque: University of New Mexico Press.

Joel, T. (2009) 'Dresden as *Opferstadt*? The Politics of Commemorating Destruction, 1985–2005', PhD thesis, Deakin University.

Jokilehto, J. (1998a) 'International Trends in Historic Preservation: From Ancient Monuments to Living Creatures', *APT Bulletin* 29(3–4), 17–19.

Jokilehto, J. (1998b) 'The Context of the Venice Charter (1964)', *Conservation and Management of Archaeological Studies* 2, 229–33.

KAS, Konrad Adenauer Stiftung (2006) 'Dresdner Barock.' Online: www.kas.de/proj/home/events/92/1/year-2006/month-3/veranstaltung_id-18688/index.html (accessed 4 November 2009).

Kluge, B. (2002) 'Die Planung des Wiederaufbaus', *Dresdner Hefte* 71(3), 26–35.

Kohl, H. (2005) *Erinnerungen. 1982–1990*, Munich: Droemer.

Köppe, T. (2010) 'Kirchensprengung: Dresden', Kirchensprengung und -abriss in der Deutschen Demokratischen Republik. Online: www.kirchensprengung.de/Dresden.htm (accessed 5 June 2010).

Koshar, R. (2000) *From Monuments to Traces: Artifacts of German Memory, 1870–1990*, Berkeley: University of California Press.

Magirius, H. (1990) 'Die Frauenkirche darf nicht in Schönheit sterben', *Die Welt*, 13 February: 3.

Magirius, H. (1992) 'Zur Gestaltwerdung der Dresdner Frauenkirche', *Dresdner Hefte* 32(4), 4–16.

Margalit, G. (2002) 'Der Luftangriff auf Dresden. Seine Bedeutung für die Erinnerungspolitik der DDR und für die Herauskristallisierung einer historischen Kriegserinnerung im Westen', in S. Düwell and M. Schmidt (eds), *Narrative der Shoah. Repräsentationen der Vergangenheit in Historiographie, Kunst und Politik*, Paderborn: Ferdinand Schöningh.

Mayer, A. (2010) 'MDR – Kultur FIGARO Interview (with Gottfried Kiesow): "Lebende Denkmale erhalten, nicht Tote exhumieren!"' MDR.de Kultur. Online: www.mdr.de/kultur/2115039.html (accessed 20 April 2010).

Moeller, R. G. (2006) 'The Politics of the Past in the 1950s: Rhetorics of Victimisation in East and West Germany', in B. Niven (ed.), *Germans as Victims*, New York: Palgrave Macmillan.

Nadler, H. (1992) 'Der Erhalt der Ruine der Frauenkirche nach 1945', *Dresdner Hefte* 32(4), 25–34.

Nadler, H. (2001) 'The Battle to Conserve: Securing the Ruins of the Frauenkirche', in A. Clayton and A. Russell (eds), *Dresden: A City Reborn*, Oxford: Berg.

Neitzel, S. (2006) 'The City under Attack', in P. Addison and J. Crang (eds), *Firestorm: The Bombing of Dresden, 1945*, London: Pimlico.

Neutzner, M. (2005) 'Vom Anklagen zum Erinnern: Die Erzählung vom 13. Februar', in O. Reinhard, M. Neutzner and W. Hesse (eds), *Das Rote Leuchten: Dresden und der Bombenkrieg*, Dresden: Edition Sächsische Zeitung.

Paul, C. (2004) *Dresden's Frauenkirche: A Symbol of Reconciliation*, trans. C. Müller, Meissen: Sächsische Zeitung.

Reinhard, O., Neutzner, M. and Hesse, W. (eds) (2005) *Das rote Leuchten. Dresden und der Bombenkrieg*, Dresden: Edition Sächsische Zeitung.

Sebald, W. G. (2003) *Luftkrieg und Literatur*, Frankfurt-am-Main: Fischer Taschenbuch Verlag.

SFD, Stiftung Frauenkirche Dresden (ed.) (2005) *Die Frauenkirche zu Dresden: Werden – Wirkung – Wiederaufbau (Ausstellungskatalog)*, Dresden: Michel Sandstein Verlag.

UNESCO (2003) 'Dresden Elbe Valley: Advisory Board Evaluation', World Heritage List. Online: http://whc.unesco.org/en/list/1156/documents/ (accessed 5 June 2010).

UNESCO World Heritage Centre (2010a) 'Dresden Elbe Valley', World Heritage List. Online: http://whc.unesco.org/en/list/1156 (accessed 3 June 2010).

UNESCO World Heritage Centre (2010b) 'Historic Centre of Warsaw', World Heritage List. Online: http://whc.unesco.org/en/list/30 (accessed 30 April 2010).

USAAF, United States Army Air Force (1945–6) 'The United States Strategic Bombing Surveys (Summary Reports: European War; Pacific War)', Air University Press. Online: http://aupress.au.af.mil/Books/USSBS/USSBS.pdf (accessed 4 November 2009).

Vonnegut, K. (2000) *Slaughterhouse-5*, London: Vintage.

'West and East,' (1945) *Manchester Guardian*, 12 February, 4.

Young, M. (2006) 'Hitler's Willing Bankers', Spiegel Online International. Online: www.spiegel.de/international/0,1518,401575,00.html (accessed 25 April 2010).

Zimmermann, M. (1990) 'Ruine oder Kirche? Frauenkirche, Schloß, Neumarkt – Dresdener Denkmalprobleme', *FAZ*, 17 February, 2.

Chapter 11

Symbols of reconstruction, signs of divisions: the case of Mitrovica, Kosovo[1]

Frank Schwartze

Parallel to the European integration process of the late twentieth century, the world also saw the collapse of the Federal Republic of Yugoslavia, accompanied by war and destruction. The dissolution of Yugoslavia began with Macedonia's demand for independence in 1991 and the declaration of independence by Slovenia in the same year followed by a short ten-day war. The subsequent separation of the new states of Croatia, Bosnia and Herzegovina took place amid years of massive armed conflicts which could only be stopped by the Dayton Agreement signed in 1995. Conflict between the autonomous republics and the Yugoslav Army as well as between the different paramilitary groups and the autonomous republics claimed thousands of lives and led to a process of systematic destruction and ethnic cleansing. The violent dissolution of Yugoslavia, which at least from the outside was considered to be a multi-ethnic state of various nations and religions, made Europeans aware of the diversity and regional inner conflicts in the Western Balkan region. It also exposed the limits of a joint cultural identity as a basis for a peaceful co-existence.

The dissolution of the loose political union between Serbia and Montenegro in 2006 left the future status of the province of Kosovo unresolved. Kosovo formally still belonged to the Republic of Serbia, and its declaration of independence in February 2008 remains controversial. The city of Mitrovica in the north of Kosovo is a kind of open interface within this conflict.[2] Due to the constant tensions in this area, Mitrovica is certainly one of the most dangerous cities in Europe. The city, which since 1999 has been divided along the Ibar River between an ethnic-Serb-majority north (approximately 16,400 inhabitants) and an ethnic-Albanian-majority south (approximately 66,000 inhabitants), is one of the most recently divided cities in Europe. The cultural identity of Kosovo, as of Mitrovica itself, is marked by constant ethnic clashes between the two communities. The destruction of the living environment and cultural heritage as well as the houses and symbols of value to both communities serves as a central means for the implementation of political goals, in order to push through territorial claims.

In the case of Mitrovica two examples show how the development and protection of cultural identity can be handled in different ways. First is the endeavour to implement a kind of symbolic unity and identity through architectural means such as the new bridge across the river Ibar. Second, efforts have been directed towards creating a possible means of co-existence between different ethnic groups by redeveloping the Roma settlement 'Roma Mahala'. Both examples show in different ways that the construction or reconstruction of monuments or settlements must fail if they are not able to be fully integrated into everyday life or gain an important symbolic character for the community. The case of the Kosovo conflict also makes obvious the discrepancy between the aims of international interventions and their means of implementation.

Kosovo and Mitrovica – a short overview

The conflict in the Kosovo region has a more than 20-year-long history. In 1989 the Serb government under its president Milosevic restricted the autonomy of the province, which it had gained in 1974, and commenced a process of systematic oppression of the Albanian majority. Serbian was implemented as the sole official language, teaching in the Albanian language was eliminated, and the Albanian population was progressively excluded from public office and administration. The Albanian opposition to the removal of autonomy as well as the growing level of oppression led to serious violent clashes. At the same time, the development of an Albanian self-administration with its own education and healthcare system emerged as a reaction to exclusion from the public services.

In the second half of the 1990s the conflicts intensified. As a result of the massive displacement of the Albanian population from Kosovo and in order to prevent a humanitarian catastrophe NATO commenced a military operation against Serbia (Kosovo war 24 March 1999 – 10 June 1999), which on 10 June 1999 led to the withdrawal of the Yugoslav Army from Kosovo and the deployment of an International Kosovo Force (KFOR). With the implementation of the UN resolution 1244 dated 10 June 1999 the province was placed under the supervision and protection of the UN interim administration in Kosovo (UNMIK). In February 2008 the Kosovo Parliament unilaterally declared its independence, which up to the present has still not been accepted by the Serb government. Today the state, which is mostly populated by Albanians, is a divided country. The new state with an Albanian majority under the supervision of the international community and the European Union is trying to establish a multi-ethnic state which will guarantee the same rights for all population groups living in this region. The north of the state which is dominated by a Serb population rejects independence and wants to belong to the state of Serbia. All over the country individual Serb-dominated enclaves can be found, which up to the present are under the protection of the international KFOR. The main task of the international military forces, besides the protection of the population, is the protection of cultural heritage belonging to the individual population groups. Before the NATO invasion in 1999 this meant mainly Albanian and Islamic cultural sites which had been systematically destroyed. Today it is the Serbian Orthodox churches and monasteries which have to be protected by the KFOR troops.

Mitrovica is located 45 kilometres north of Kosovo's capital Pristina which is situated at the northern end of the country's central valley and flanked by the Bajgorë/Bajgora mountains. The town itself is situated in a wide open plain at the confluence of the rivers Sitnica and Ibar. Before the war Mitrovica was a one-company town which prospered economically due to the development of the mining and metallurgy complex 'Trepca', one of the biggest companies of socialist Yugoslavia. At its peak in 1988 almost 23,000 people from the region worked in the Trepca complex, which apart from its mines possessed a lead smelter as well as facilities for zinc metallurgical works.

The development of the city is closely linked to the construction of the railway and the industrialization of the twentieth century. The origins of the city go back to the medieval settlement Trepca located in the mountains to the east of today's Mitrovica. Today only ruins remain of this settlement which developed together with the mining industry in that region. Since the thirteenth/fourteenth century Trepca had been inhabited by Saxon miners but also by a Slavic population. At nearby Stari Treg, a Turkish colony ('Turkish Terpca') had been established in the fourteenth century. The ruins of the thirteenth-century Roman Catholic Church of St Peter can still be found there. Around 1600 the Mitrovica that is recognizable today emerged, consisting of 300 houses, a hostelry ('han'), a Turkish bath and a mosque, though it was a place of little significance within the Ottoman Empire, on the route from central Bosnia to the south (Vavic 1965: 5). With the construction of the railway running from Mitrovica to the city of Skopje and further to the Mediterranean Sea (1873) the city became a centre of trade. After the turn of the century it prospered even more with the expansion of the railway further north to the city of Kraljevo.

The industrialization of the region began in 1930 with the opening of the mines in Stan Tërg/Stari Treg up in the mountains and the lead smelter in Zvecan, a settlement three kilometres north of the town. After the Second World War the growth of the town was more and more determined by the development of the mining complex. In the north of the town the construction of apartment buildings for miners was underway by the early 1940s. From 1948 to 1960, in only 12 years, the number of inhabitants doubled from 13,900 to 26,100. With the establishment of a fertilizer plant (1964), zinc production (1967) and a battery factory (1974) in Mitrovica, the town itself became industrialized. The population in the town doubled again and by 1981 claimed 52,900 inhabitants, together with another 35,000 inhabitants in the surrounding villages. Although Trepca was the main employer in the area, the company itself was in serious debt, productivity had been declining in relation to the level of employment for some time and the company had been making a loss since the early 1980s. The decline of Trepca took place in the context of the decline of heavy industry across Europe, and the closure of many mines during recent decades. (Schwartze and Harvey 2004)

The urban development of Mitrovica is a good example of a form of Fordist modernization mainly supported by one large industrial complex. Large, multistorey buildings from the 1960s and 1970s along the major axis which leads towards the city centre at the river crossing dominate the image of the town. Here also starts the pedestrian area, featuring the once biggest department store of the Kosovo region as well as a large sports hall and a high-rise building for the former state bank. Photographs from the 1970s show a large number of shops and cafés on the ground level of the modern buildings, and give the impression of a modern industrial city with well-developed conveniences. Mitrovica probably was 'once the most Yugoslav city' in Kosovo (ESI 2008). In the mines and factories Serbs worked closely together with Albanians and other Yugoslav ethnic groups, and there was no other urban region where so many Serbs spoke Albanian. The monument which rests on a hill above the city symbolizes the mining tradition of the city and at the same time is a symbol of a lost unity – two columns which carry an oversized lore (mining cart).

This is the legacy of the city which, compared to other cities of the region, cannot boast a large number of cultural sites. An article by Kosovarian think tank IKS about the role of cultural heritage in connection with the question of whether the heritage of Mitrovica should be considered 'a shared asset or a liability' lists nine still existing cultural heritage sites, including the Hamam, the Roman Catholic Church of St Peter and one traditional residential house which managed to survive the destruction of the past ten years. Nineteen cultural sites had been heavily damaged in the course of the violence in 1999 and four other buildings, including another mosque (the Ibar Mosque, located directly at the town bridge), as well a traditional stone house (Kulla) and a house of prayer, had been completely destroyed (IKS 2009: 4). The heaviest wave of destruction took place in Mitrovica one week after the NATO intervention concluded. During the night of 20 June 1999 one of the biggest settlements of the Roma in the former Yugoslavia – the Roma Mahala – was pillaged and destroyed by the Albanians, although the exact circumstances could not be fully clarified. The approximately 8,000 inhabitants fled to the north. Five years later during the unrest in March 2004 the Serbian Orthodox Church of St Sava in the south of the city, which was safeguarded by the KFOR troops, was set on fire. Several villages inhabited by Serbs were also burnt down. This outbreak of violence – the heaviest in Kosovo since 1999 – cost the lives of nineteen people, among them eight Serbs, and drove about 3,000 Serbs from their houses. In light of these incidents, and bearing in mind the demand of the 2006 Kosovarian law on cultural heritage that insists on recognition and valuing of the cultural values of every ethnic community in Kosovo within the context of diversity and tolerance, IKS came to the conclusion that 'Promoting cultural tolerance has been an impossible exercise' and 'Cultural heritage as a common value remains a distant goal' (IKS 2009: 2).

Since the NATO intervention in 1999 and the escalation of violence, Mitrovica has been a divided city. The Serbs and Roma fled to the north, the Albanians to the south. The Trepca factory with its various facilities had to be closed down after the intervention and has not been reactivated since that time. With the division of the city many citizens lost their cultural identity. The Serbian Orthodox church and cemetery are located in the south of the city; the Muslim cemetery lies in the north. Funerals cannot take place any more and visitors need military protection. The north of the city represents the biggest of the Serbian-dominated enclaves in Kosovo and with the neighbouring region in the north there is a direct link with the Republic of Serbia. In the industrial sector Mitrovica has practically no jobs to offer. The soil is polluted by heavy metals, and due to the city's division the north especially cannot survive economically on its own and receives significant support from the Serb government. Since 1999 the Serb government has been ensuring the provision of communal services, granting the citizens high additional payments to their wages as well as subsidized employment. Consequently, in the north of Mitrovica two-thirds of the monthly income come directly from Belgrade, and as far as economic and political decisions are concerned, the north is dependent on the government in Belgrade.

The south is poverty-stricken. Here the average monthly income per person is not more than 38 euros (ESI 2004b). The economic decline accompanied by the hopeless political situation has led to even more ethnic tensions. Since 2003, after a long period of observation, the UNMIK has been trying hard to bring the two sides together and reach a political solution. In the north of the city a municipal administration under the direction of the UNMIK was established, which was meant to implement the responsibilities of local government in accordance with the regulations in Kosovo as a whole. These endeavours aimed at finding a solution in connection with the future structure and status of Kosovo as a sovereign state by solving the political, economic and social problems of Mitrovica and minimizing the conflict. Their efforts ended in the unrest of March 2004 which started in Mitrovica and from there spread across the entire Kosovo region. On 17 March 2008, one month after the declaration of Kosovo's independence, Mitrovica saw the latest outbreak of violence, during which an international policeman was killed, and 42 international policemen as well as 22 KFOR soldiers were seriously wounded.

The bridge of Mitrovica

Bridges are a symbol for crossing borders (Fig. 11.1). They mark the borderline near rivers which divide states and regions. Newly built bridges across former border rivers, such as for instance bridges between Germany and Poland, act

Figure 11.1 Bridge of Mitrovica.

as symbols of European reunification. In his book *Bridge over the Drina*, which was published in 1962, Yugoslav Nobel Prize winner Ivo Andric told a story of co-existence and conflicts between the various ethnic groups, Christians and Muslims, and Turkish and Austrian rulers, in his home country Bosnia. This bridge only exists in his mind: it crosses the river Drina in the heart of Bosnia and is a symbol for existing borders and hopes for a peaceful co-existence in a multi-ethnic society. This story about the bridge is also a story about the region and its history. The people in the city and this bridge there have been strongly connected for centuries. Their fates are so closely linked to each other that they cannot exist or be expressed separately. That is why Andric's story about the creation and fate of the bridge is at the same time a story about life in the city with its different people – men and women (Andric 2003: 19).

The story ends with the blasting of the bridge in 1914 after the assassination of the Austrian heir to the throne in Sarajevo which precipitated the First World War. The war, which ended in 1918, destroyed the Austro-Hungarian Empire, giving way to the formation of the first Yugoslav national state as the 'Kingdom of the Serbs, Croats and Slovenes', renamed in 1929 the 'Kingdom of Yugoslavia'. The Socialist Federal Republic of Yugoslavia founded after the Second World War in 1948 by Tito represented a multi-ethnic nation-state which at least from the outside united (or forced to unite) the various nations and cultural groups. The idea of creating a 'Yugoslav socialist civilization' (Miroslav Krleža) also meant a constant debate on pressing national questions, which in the 1960s were considered to have been solved. The national conflicts were glossed over with a socialist standard lifestyle and became more or less a taboo. Consequently, 'this was a state, where a democratic and critical approach to solve its problems did not take place and where these national conflicts finally led to the break-up of the state in 1990/91' (Roksandić 1994: 135f).

Like the bridge across the Drina which serves as a symbol of the idea of co-existence in a multi-ethnic society, the Mostar bridge is a symbol of the dissolution of the Yugoslav state as well as the segregation of its different nationalities in the late twentieth century. The bridge spans the River Neretva in Mostar, which is the biggest town of the Herzegovina region in the south of Bosnia and Herzegovina. The city once was culturally influenced by Bosniaks, Croats, Serbs as well as Albanians and Turks, and the bridge, built in 1566, was more than a link between two riverbanks. As the Croatian author Predag Matvejević observed, here the Orient and Occident met (Matvejević 2008). On 9 November 1993 the bridge was demolished by mortars and the town as a multi-ethnic place ceased to exist. Since that time two different living environments have existed – a Croatian in the west and a Bosnian in the east. The Mostar bridge was rebuilt between 2002 and 2004, after UNESCO in 1998 had decided to support its reconstruction. According to UNESCO, the Old Bridge was destroyed for its symbolic value. For this same reason UNESCO promised to rebuild it (UNESCOPRESS 2004). Its reconstruction was meant to demonstrate, as Mounir Bouchenaki, Director General for Culture at UNESCO stated, that 'the Organization has been able to bring past enemies together and reconcile them around monuments that have strong symbolic value and help them cooperate to restore a cultural heritage that is both an integral part of their shared history and a measure of their common future' (UNESCOPRESS 2002). Mostar is still a divided city, but the reconstruction of the bridge set an example against hatred and intolerance. We might still be wary of its efficacy as a symbol: it was not the people of Mostar who set this example, but the international community, perhaps because the people 'did not have the strength to fight for their bridge, as they have already grown more and more apart from each other' (Matvejević 2008: 365).

In 2001, the international administration of Kosovo decided to follow this example by constructing a new bridge across the River Ibar in the centre of Mitrovica. The bridge was built on the initiative of the first UN envoy in Kosovo, Bernard Kouchner, and was supposed to set an example for future peace in the region. Construction workers had been recruited equally from the Albanian as well as the Serb population, which was meant to be a symbol of peaceful cooperation. The distinctive, dynamically curved arch which dominates the character of the bridge, as well as its night-time illumination, are elements of an iconic construction intentionally designed to serve as a symbol. The French KFOR troops based in the area around Mitrovica call it Pont d'Austerlitz.[3] Apart from its architectonic features, this name may also be seen as the wish to succeed in this particular mission – like Napoleon at Austerlitz.

Compared to the literary bridge across the Drina or the real bridge in Mostar, the bridge of Mitrovica does not reflect the close linking of a people's life of a particular town to a building of particular meaning. It is a geopolitical symbol, created by the international community, which is not directly linked with the particular place. As if to confirm this, a series of violent and warlike clashes repeatedly took place there and were widely reported in the media. For the local population the bridge has become a no-go area. Especially in the first years it was monitored by the so-called 'Bridge watchers' on the Serb side in the north. They registered and prevented any crossing of the bridge from the southern side. As far as everyday life in both parts of the city is concerned, the bridge is not playing a significant role any more. It is not the centre of the city as it used to be, but is located at its very end. Everyday life has shifted away from the bridge. The areas at both ends of the bridge are more or less deserted, and only on nice summer evenings when people are sitting at the waterside promenade, can one still imagine that this once used to be a central place in one of Yugoslavia's most important industrial cities. So only the 'Internationals' were able to use the bridge and it became what initially had not been planned: the symbol of a divided city which is still being monitored today.

Roma Mahala

Another symbol of the difficult situation in Kosovo is the redevelopment of the Roma Mahala, the Roma settlement of the city which had been totally destroyed in 1999. Today it remains the largest undeveloped area of a city in the former Yugoslavia (Djurik *et al.* 2002: 113). Its destruction during the night of 20 June 1999, which French KFOR troops based only a few hundred metres from the Roma Mahala failed to prevent, was partly an act of politically motivated violence seeking to drive all non-Albanian ethnic groups out of Kosovo in order to better justify the establishment of an independent state. The UN later described the event as a systematic attack against ethnic minorities (Auer and Kanzleiter 2006) (Fig. 11.2).

Of the previously 150,000 Roma two-thirds were driven out of the country together with Serbs and other ethnic minorities. Today only about 30,000 Roma still live in the Kosovo region, many of them in temporary refugee camps. At the beginning the refugees from the Roma Mahala had found accommodation at three refugee camps in the north of the city of Mitrovica where they were allowed to stay for one year. Due to protests by the World Health Organization and various NGOs two of the three camps had to be closed in the meantime. The main reason was the major health risk for the camp population posed by high levels of soil contamination from the lead

Figure 11.2 Destroyed buildings in Roma Mahala, 2004.

smelter at nearby Zvecan. A number of families had already been living in these temporary camps for ten years. Up to the present the reconstruction of the Roma Mahala has not been put into practice, so that the situation of the Roma is especially tense in a European region which is under the administration of the United Nations – Kosovo (Auer 2007).

The former settlement of Roma Mahala covered about 21 hectares to the south of the River Ibar only a few hundred metres from the city centre. The football stadium divided the Roma Mahala from the city centre. It was, like most of the Roma settlements in the autonomous republics of Yugoslavia, a separate ill-equipped settlement in an urban residential area. The settlement had been in existence since the end of the nineteenth century, though in 1976 the Yugoslav government for the first time officially stipulated the terms for private property. From the 1950s the area of settlement became more densely populated with the erection of two- and three-storey residential houses, and the flood-prone banks of the River Ibar were used for urban development. Before the beginning of the war, between 8,000 and 10,000 inhabitants lived in 750 houses here. They were 90 per cent Roma but also Albanians from Kosovo and other ethnic minorities like the Ashkali and the Egyptians, which were Albanian-speaking ethnic groups probably of Egyptian origin. The settlement was densely built-up, characterized by small dead-end roads and structured by cohabitation in extended families. It featured a vegetable market, a hairdresser, a tailor, a teahouse, fast-food stalls and several small shops, as well as several bars and restaurants. These were complemented by several social institutions including a kindergarten, a town hall, a walk-in clinic and an animals' home. Accounting for about 25 per cent of jobs, the biggest employer was the Trepca mine (Davanzo *et al.* 2004). Former residents tend to reflect positively on their quarter despite its high density and its structural deficiencies: 'We were many. We were Roma, but among us there were a great number of people who had gained a certain wealth.' (Auer and Kanzleiter 2006).

The international community's assessment of the quarter's condition before the war, however, had never been a positive one. The report which formed part of the recovery plan described conditions there ranging from 'ad hoc' to 'unregulated impediment'. The informality of the settlement was the main obstacle and problem of the officially planned redevelopment. Due to the fire and the change of administration, the UNMIK and the city council in Mitrovica had very little information available. The destruction of the remaining foundation walls by the city council made the investigation of ownership before 1999 even more difficult. The only bases for investigation were inventory photographs of the time before the tear-down and documents from the land registry of the Yugoslav era, 1978, as well as a satellite photograph and oral testimonies of former inhabitants. The Danish Refugee Council (DRC), which in 2003 with a special team of city planners took over the task of redeveloping the area with the aim of creating an urban environment, said, 'The primary objectives of the zoning process are the … urban ambience, which does not exist in the current layout of the Roma Mahalla' (Davanzo *et al.* 2004: 4).

The planned redevelopment, considered the biggest urban redevelopment project within Kosovo, was pushed through by the international community against the will of the local administration and public opinion in the south of Mitrovica. At the beginning the municipal administration did not show much desire to cooperate and argued that the development of the communal land by the Roma was partly illegal. Later it emerged that the construction of a shopping centre as well as a recreation area on this compound had been planned anyway. The area of the settlement was attractive because of its central location, and so an agreement could be reached only after the international community had given in to the demands of the municipal administration and granted it one part of the area of the former Mahala. Apart from the openly negative attitude towards the redevelopment itself as well as the competing economic interests, the various ideas about how the area should be redeveloped were the main obstacle to project planning and realization. Before the DRC had taken over the planning procedure the municipal planning administration had provided a first redevelopment plan which in its first stage had foreseen the construction of apartment houses for those refugees who could not present any formal documents proving a former landownership. In a second stage the construction of detached houses was planned for those who could prove the possession of former property (Mulliqi 2006). The city planners accused the

Roma of not having been willing to accept the municipal administration and its formal authority and of rejecting any form of face-to-face discussion, but had acted only through their international representatives. One representative of the Roma explains the resigned behaviour of the refugees with the following words:

> You [planners and administration] do not understand our mentality and that we do not want to live in those apartment blocks. We want to go back, but to the place where we once used to live. We only want that everybody gets his house where he once used to live. We do not want to be put into blocks and lose our land, in order to build a recreation park in the Mahala which you say you need. (Gushani 2006)

Despite their announced participation in the DRC's 'Manual for Sustainable Returns' the Roma did not feel sufficiently involved in the redevelopment process. They continue to argue that the redevelopment plan had been decided over their heads and that they had not been involved in a sufficient way, according to their needs and ideas. Five years after the redevelopment plan was adopted 440 people have been placed in four apartment blocks as well as in a number of one-storey and multistorey houses. According to one occupier, however, some of the houses are already standing empty again, as the owners have left for Western Europe. Generally speaking, the area is not very attractive, as apart from a police station, a walk-in clinic and a modest playground, there is little public infrastructure (Fig. 11.3).

Figure 11.3 Roma Mahala, August 2009.

Despite the unhealthy conditions in the refugee camps in the north of the city only a few former inhabitants of the settlement decided to return to Roma Mahala. One reason is the social benefits which are guaranteed in the north of the city of Mitrovica, but not so much in the Albanian part. Another reason is the level of security: 'The families we spoke to do not intend to live in the flats they are being offered. Nobody wants to live in the south of Mitrovica. They all fear that they might be attacked by their Albanian neighbours again.' (Gesellschaft für bedrohte Völker 2006). In recent years the Roma who fled to Western Europe have often been deported to Kosovo as the security situation in the Kosovo region has improved, but also under the pretence of creating a multi-ethnic Kosovo. Many international observers, however, came to the conclusion that the refugees, who should be protected, suffer most from this situation. Bearing in mind the fact that the international community over a period of ten years was not able to accommodate securely a few hundred internally displaced Roma and Ashkali, the question arises how the return of several tens of thousands people who will be 'resettled' in the Kosovo region in the next few years will be managed. Apart from the security issue in the Roma Mahala, for the former inhabitants it is also a major question whether redevelopment will make the Roma Mahala an attractive place to which to return. Efforts to push through the aesthetic and planning-related standards of the international investors in connection with the redevelopment as well as consideration for the economic interests and technocratic ideas of the municipal administration have so far prevented establishment of a new and better Roma Mahala according to the wishes and needs of its inhabitants. A former member of the UN expressed their disappointment in an interview: 'I am so unhappy that there were no people who were trying to make this an interesting area … Why didn't anybody came up with some great ideas? Why don't we make this the nicest and biggest Roma settlement? Why don't we make great buildings, funny buildings? Things that illustrate their culture and ideas? Why don't we make an interesting culture house? Instead we make this an awful building that is never clean … We can do something. I am sure if you make them a little bit more responsible' (Anonymous UN Employee 2009).

A Roma Mahala redeveloped in this way might have looked like 'Gypsy Hill', one of the biggest Gypsy settlements in the Republic of Moldova (Fig. 11.4). Here in the town of Soroca, 170 kilometres north of the capital Chisinau and near the border to the Ukraine, Roma families have been settling for decades, and their houses stand for a cultural identity unaffected by norms or regulations. This also includes the possibility of building and owning a house without necessarily living in it, as the house is primarily seen as a symbol and place of family cohesion and not a permanent place of residence. This totally different idea of living and staying based on the principle of non-sedentarism which is part of the Roma culture, does not seem to have been included in the redevelopment plans of the Roma Mahala and continues to inhibit restoration of Mitrovica's Roma community.

Figure 11.4 Gypsy Hill Soroca.

Conclusion

The example of the Roma Mahala clearly shows that the destruction of settlements as part of ethnic cleansing is more than just the destruction of buildings and other people's property. It is also the destruction of the cultural structures of identity. The reconstruction of these structures in the sense of a habitat is only possible if both the financial conditions and a high level of social self-determination can be guaranteed, the latter being of even greater importance. The bridge of Mitrovica had been intended as an identity-establishing symbol. But like the Roma Mahala it shows that this idea cannot be realized without being embedded in a social-cultural context. Consequently, the bridge remains the symbol of an unresolved conflict. Initially this had not been the idea of the international community, and it shows that buildings or monuments cannot act as representatives of their own identity but only as a part of identity constructions which are the result of the social reality. The reconstruction of destroyed monuments like the bridge in Mostar can serve as a role model and lead to an open debate about things lost. But its meaning derives from the past.

So what could be an identity-establishing symbol of reconstruction for both parts of the city? If we accept that it is social reality out of which symbols may arise, one possible joint symbol in the case of Mitrovica could be the football club KF Trepca. Named after the Trepca mine, the club in the mid-1970s played in the first league of Yugoslavia. This makes it a symbol of the co-existence of various groups of the population and it has survived in the memory of the people until today (ESI 2004a). Like the story about the bridge across the Drina, the football club is a story about the common history of this town and consequently could serve as something like a connecting factor for a common process of development in the future. This is an approach which only to a limited extent would be perceptible to the outside world. But in the longer term certain material symbols might derive from this idea, and the Trepca Stadium, the biggest in the entire Kosovo region, not far from the Roma Mahala, could be such a symbol. The acceptance of different social realities could also be the key factor to allow the Roma Mahala itself to become a symbol of a successful reconstruction. Whether an integration of all ethnic groups will be successful or not remains to be seen. Implementing a way of peaceful co-existence is an absolute necessity. This makes Mitrovica a litmus test for the international community which now has to prove that it is able to reach its objectives not only symbolically but also in reality.

Notes

1   The author wishes to thank Paula Hentschel for her support in the research and final editing of the chapter.
2   The chapter uses the English notation Mitrovica, rather than the Serbian or Albanian language: Митровица/Mitrovicë.
3   All streets and places in Kosovo get their own name by KFOR, in order to make orientation and communication easier for the international armed forces.

References

Andric, I. (2003 [1962]) *Die Brücke über die Drina*, Frankfurt am Main: Suhrkamp Taschenbuch.

Anonymous UN Employee (2009) Interview given to the author at Pristina July 2009.

Auer, D. (2007) 'Roma in Europa', Bonn: Bundeszentrale für politische Bildung. Online: www.eurotopics.net/de/archiv/magazin/gesellschaft-verteilerseite/roma_in_europa_2007_09/debatte_roma_in_europa (accessed 30 March 2009).

Auer, D. and Kanzleiter, B. (2006) 'Vergessene Opfer. Die Vertreibung der Roma aus dem Kosovo', Radio feature on Deutschlandfunk, broadcast 21 November.

Davanzo, V., Stefani, B., and Surdulli, B. (2004). 'Return to Roma Mahalla /Mitrovica, Draft urban proposal'. Danish Refugee Council.

Djurik, R., Becken, J. and Bengsch, A. B. (2002) *Ohne Heim ohne Grab-Die Geschichte der Sinti und Roma*, Berlin: Aufbau Verlag.

Draft Urban Plan-GAR-007 (2004) Danish Refugee Council.

ESI (European Stability Initiative) (2004a) 'The Footballers' Story', Berlin. Online: www.esiweb.org/index.php?lang=en&id=48&movie_ID=2&language=english (accessed 11 December 2009).

ESI (European Stability Initiative) (2004b) 'People or Territory', Berlin. Online: www.esiweb. org/index.php?lang=en&id=156&document_ID=50 (accessed 11 December 2009).

ESI (European Stability Initiative) (2008) Berlin, May. Online: www.esiweb.org/index. php?lang=de&id=298&city_ID=54 (accessed 11 December 2009).

Gesellschaft für bedrohte Völker (2006) 'Flüchtlingslager Osterode', 18 September. Online: www.gfbv.de/inhaltsDok.php?id=820 (accessed 1 October 2009).

Gushani, S. (2006) Interview on Deutschlandradio representing the refugees of Roma in Mitrovica.

IKS (Kosovar Stability Initiative) (2009) 'Mitrovica's Heritage: Shared Asset or Liability?' Online: www.iksweb.org/repository/docs/policy_brief_cultural_heritage.pdf (accessed 5 December 2010).

Matvejević, P. (2008) 'Die Alte Brücke in Mostar –Verbindung von Ost und West [The Old Bridge in Mostar – Connection between East and West]', *Phantom der Freiheit* 1–2, 361–6.

Mulliqi, X. (2006) 'Integrating City of Mitrovica', 42nd ISoCaRP Congress. Online: www. isocarp.net/Data/case_studies/907.pdf (accessed 1 October 2009).

Roksandić, D. (1994) 'Nationale Konflikte in Titos Jugoslawien—ein Tabu?', in R. Streibel and P. Bettelheim (eds), *Tabu und Geschichte: Zur Kultur des kollektiven Erinnerns*, Vienna: Picus Verlag, 100–28.

Schwartze, Frank and Harvey, Joanna (2004) *Mitrovica Local Development Plan*, Mitrovica: UNMIK.

UNESCOPRESS (2002) 'Reconstruction of the Mostar Bridge to Begin in June'. Online: www. unesco.org/bpi/eng/unescopress/2002/02-avis20e.shtml (accessed 16 April 2010).

UNESCOPRESS (2004) 'Inauguration of the Mostar Bridge'. Online: http://portal.unesco.org/ en/ev.php-URL_ID=21743&URL_DO=DO_TOPIC&URL_SECTION=201.html (accessed 16 April 2010).

Vavic, Milorad (1965) *Saveza socijalistickog radnog naroda in Kosovska Mitrovica*, Opstinski odbor.

Chapter 12

Reconstruction as exclusion: Beirut

Esther Charlesworth and Anitra Nelson

Beirutland

The politics of defining and managing cultural heritage is critical. During the recent reconstruction of Beirut, the value of protecting the city's cultural heritage was contested by a politico-economic elite represented by Rafiq Hariri (and, later, his son Saad). A businessman who made his fortune in the Gulf in the 1970s, Hariri became Lebanon's Prime Minister (1992–8 and 2000–4). This chapter argues that Beirut's rich cultural heritage has been redefined and managed according to Haririan political and economic needs. After decades of intermeshing internal and external conflicts highlighted in the Lebanese Civil War (1975–90), efforts to inspire and control national unity centred on recreating the Beirut Central District to stress its millennia-long mercantile and trading history (Fig. 12.1). This emphasis accorded with the state as an agent for private entrepreneurship handing the responsibility for supervising the reconstruction to Solidere, a private firm with strong Haririan links.

This chapter explores how damaging exclusive control of cultural heritage can be: from razing cultural heritage to destroying or isolating more diverse interpretations and appreciations of cultural heritage, and limiting open democratic access to, and decision-making over, such heritage. The central question remains: 'Whose cultural heritage?' Mocking the stated aims of preserving and recovering Lebanon's rich cultural history, substantial heritage was destroyed during 'reconstruction' leaving a mere, and partial, spectacle of history, a 'Beirutland'. A sentinel principle for preservers and managers of cultural heritage is to protect against such exclusive ownership, definition and management and, instead, to understand and respect cultural heritage in diverse, interdisciplinary ways.

Paris of the Mediterranean

Beirut's history stretches further back than the few millennia most recent analyses mention. There were settlements in Beirut 65,000 years ago (Makdisi 1997: 679). It has a long history as a trading node in the region. By the

Figure 12.1 Beirut Central District after the war, 1995.

nineteenth and twentieth centuries it was considered a culturally tolerant merchant post (Nagel 2002: 717–19). Indeed, when the 'Civil War' (1975–90) started in earnest, Beirut had been a lively immigration centre and flourishing port referred to variously as the 'Paris of the Mediterranean', 'Paris of the Orient' and the 'Switzerland of the Middle East' (Shwayri 2008: 70).

After the French created an independent Lebanon in 1943 deep divisions simmered between pro and anti-Arab nationalists, residents from diverse ethnic and religious backgrounds, colonialists, and the immigrants and refugees flowing in and out. Nevertheless, Martinez-Garrido (2008: 1) writes that 'community intermixing was characteristic of the city centre'. One of the defining spatial markers of the Civil War was a city rent in two east and west, right down its heart by the 'Green Line', which separated Christian and Muslim communities. Clearly, enduring social tensions and planning challenges needed addressing by national political authorities in the reconstruction of Lebanon and its capital Beirut once the Civil War abated.

Solidere, a private firm, was established in 1992 to supervise the reconstruction of the exclusive Beirut Central District (BCD). This chapter briefly outlines the Civil War in Beirut and discusses how this private capital became the vehicle for its reconstruction. We argue that the Beirut reconstruction story is a clear example of cultural heritage becoming hostage to a politico-economic elite with interests contrary to wider and more diverse interpretations of cultural history. Solidere's exclusive and partial neocolonialist approach has damaged, and limited access to, Beirut's cultural heritage. The conclusion is that preservers of cultural heritage must maintain the integrity of 'sentinel' principles which guide professional conduct directed at working for broad public interests and diverse interpretations of history.

This raises the problematic yet significant role of architects and allied professionals such as planners in the reconfiguration of the partitioned city. In a 1995 promotional Solidere video, the background image and parlous beat of a heart monitor dominated the reconstruction narrative. The metaphor of rebuilding the city's 'heart' as akin to a surgical operation on a 'diseased body' also dominated the planning and rationale behind much of the rebuilding strategy to revive the concept of architects as 'pathologists' (Charlesworth 2006). Unfortunately, forcing the heart metaphor into a form that paralleled reality leads pointedly to the concept of 'rejected heart'!

Civil war

The conflicts embraced in the catch-all phrase 'the Lebanese Civil War' were in fact localized in region, time and warring factions. Many political historians have discussed the causes (e.g. Khalaf 1993; Tueni 1992; Hourani 1995; Salibi 1998). For instance, immigrants from Palestine and their continuing struggle with Israelis was one contributing factor. In an interview with one of the authors (13 October 2001), Beirut architect Ayssar Arrida offered a succinct and simplified chronology, which indicates various complications:

- 'The Two Year War' (1975–6), triggered by Palestinian-Christian Phalange clashes in inner Beirut.
- 'The Invasion' (Al-Ijtiyah) – an Israeli invasion (1982), which included a three-month siege and continuous bombing of Beirut, even though the Israelis claimed, initially, to have entered Lebanon only for a few kilometres to create a 'security zone'. The invasion 'ended' with an Israeli withdrawal from Beirut to south Lebanon, creating that so-called 'security zone' within Lebanon, policed by the Israeli-allied SLA (South Lebanon Army) militia till 2000, when the Israelis totally withdrew.
- 'The War of the Mountains' (1983) saw Christians and the Druze fighting over Mount Lebanon (Shuf Mountain), displacing Christians into what became known as Al-Sharquiyyeh (the Eastern Part). Christian militias, the LF (Lebanese Forces), allies of the Israelis during the Invasion, fought with the Druze in the power vacuum once Israel withdrew.
- 'The War of Liberation' (Harb al-Tahrir) (1988–9) against Syria 'declared' by Prime Minister Michel Aoun (March 1989) ended in ceasefire resulting in the Taif Agreement (1989) leading to the end of the Civil War (1991).
- 'The War of Annihilation' (Harb al-Ilghaa) (1990) was a clash between an Aoun-led Lebanese Army and the Christian militia of Samir Geagea.

Other struggles included: the War of the Refugee Camps ('Harb al-Moukhayyamet'), waged between different Palestinian groups; the War of Tripoli; the War of Zahleh; the battle of Ashrafiyyeh; and the Battle of the Hotels. Struggles involved intra-Christian fighting, intra-Muslim fighting, intra-Shia fighting and Shia–Druze fighting, as well as Palestinians and Druze versus Christians and Syrians, and Syrians and Druze versus Christians. Many accounts describe localized fighting or fighting on one or two fronts simultaneously for a few months to a couple of years.

There were lengthy periods of relative calm between events and mini-wars, but tensions at internal frontlines were constant. The impacts of Israeli–Palestinian conflicts exemplified the influence of regional powers as the Palestine Liberation Organization operated out of refugee camps. Thus the Civil War was imposed as well as internal. Indeed Lebanese commonly referred to the 'Civil War' as *Al-Hawadeth*, Arabic for 'the events' and a 'war of others' (Tueni 1992). Many Lebanese felt like witnesses as well as victims of these 'events'. In an interview with Arrida (13 October 2001) he reported that common usage of 'when it was happening' represents 'a combination of denial either of reality and/or responsibility' and 'the fact that we were "in it" but, at the same time, felt it was beyond our control'.

Divisions and destruction

Human casualties were enormous for a national population of just three or four million: 170,000 killed and 300,000 wounded (Khalaf 1993). Another 500,000 residents were displaced. By 1990, as civil warring abated, at least one million permanently emigrated, taking their talent and money with them. The violence heavily damaged Lebanon's cities, ports and countryside too. The first two years of the Israeli invasion witnessed the most extensive damage to buildings and physical infrastructure, including strategic facilities such as Beirut's international airport, sewer systems, electrical grid and telephone lines. Reconstruction costs mounted to billions of dollars. The implications were far wider than simply economic. Makdisi (1997: 666) has pointed to 'the very heavily damaged city center, which for more than fifteen years remained an emptied-out site marking the graveyard of national dialogue and reconciliation'.

Disastrous events continued well after 1991. For instance, the July–August 2006 Israeli war on Lebanon left 1,200 dead and over 5,000 injured, with the poorest areas worst off and 'massive physical destruction of civilian infrastructure and public services and utilities' (UNDP 2009: 7). In another example, after sectarian struggles between the Druze and Hizballah (Party of God) throughout Lebanon, and between Alawites and Sunnis in the north, in May 2008 Hizballah and the Shia opposition gained control of Beirut International Airport; heavy fighting with government forces resulted in hundreds injured and 85 deaths (Campaign for Good Governance in Lebanon 2008).

As conflict raged, Lebanese people retreated into religious neighbourhood communities that relied on strong internal bonds between members for support (Nagel 2002: 720–1). Divisions took on spatial, material forms solidifying developments emerging from the late 1950s in which Christian nationalists congregated in the east and Sunni pan-Arabian Muslims to the west of a 'Green Line' (Fig. 12.2) which came to divide Lebanon's urban heart, public spaces, historic harbour and Martyr's Square (Calame and Charlesworth 2009: 37–60). Thus central city spaces where diverse communities had engaged with one another socially in a 'monocentric' public place pre-war were either eliminated or became characterized by segregated communities during the Civil War (Martinez-Garrido 2008: 2). That is why, during the reconstruction, a 'city as heart' metaphor was promoted, though the reality was to seem more like urban surgery.

Reconstruction politics

Transforming a culture of warring and sectarianism to a culture of reconciliation was not the priority of the political elites dominating postwar reconstruction in the mid-1990s. Arguably, the dual national challenges had been, on the one

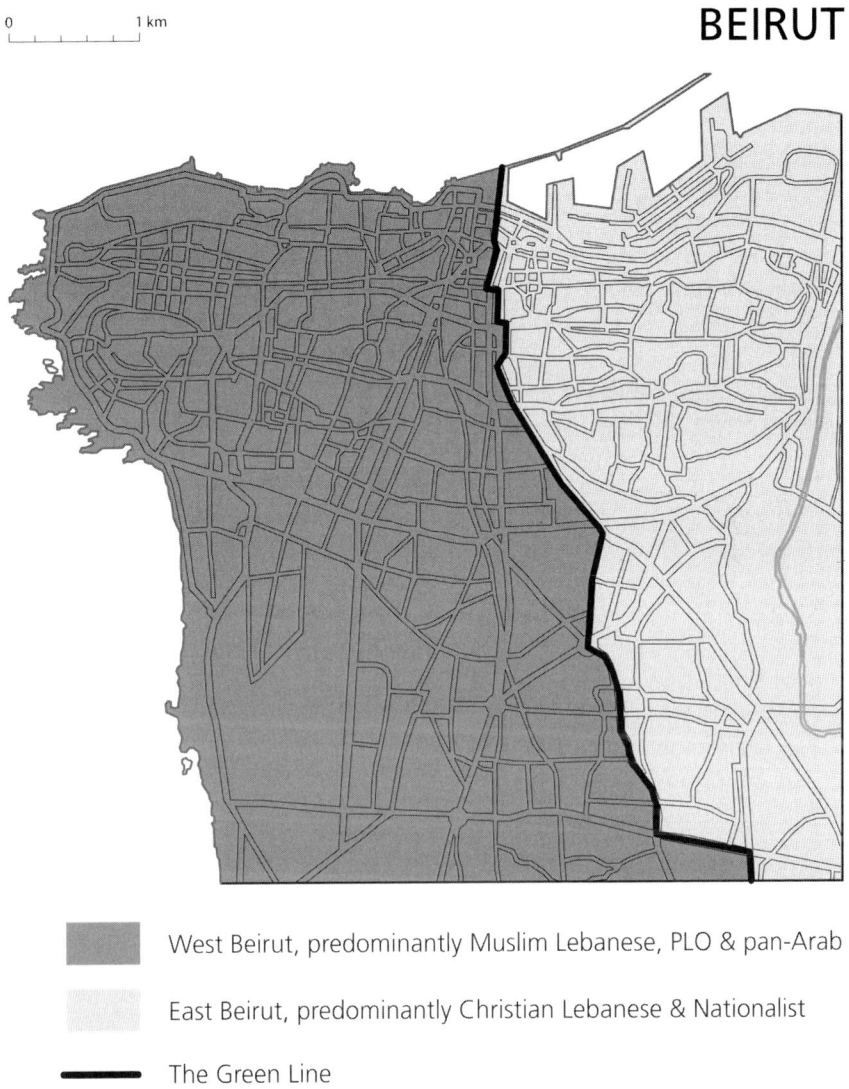

0 |___|___|___|___| 1 km

BEIRUT

West Beirut, predominantly Muslim Lebanese, PLO & pan-Arab

East Beirut, predominantly Christian Lebanese & Nationalist

The Green Line

Figure 12.2 Map of Beirut's Green Line.

hand, to develop a political strategy that would bind a multi-confessional society with 17 identifiable religious affiliations (most factions of major religions) and, on the other hand, to rebuild the country's economy. Yet, even a decade after violent armed conflict abated, many complex issues aggravating relationships among distinct groups before the Civil War remained unresolved. Lebanon continually suffered from political and humanitarian crises in Israel and Syria.

Political compromises structuring Lebanon's governance for the last half-century reveal entrenched religious divisions. National politics has been based on confessional groups, with parliamentary seats allotted on a sectarian basis: today every recognized religion has at least one seat and minority groups can hold high government positions. In mid-2008 there were four major parties, the largest parliamentary majority held by the Future Movement, led by Saad Hariri, who became Lebanon's Prime Minister in November 2009. Predominantly Sunni, Hariri's bloc included members of other sects. Yet Palestinian refugees had no political rights (Campaign for Good Governance in Lebanon 2008). In 1995, over 300,000 Palestinians remained in Lebanon, with 170,000 in refugee camps skirting Beirut (Partner 1995). Segregation and lack of widespread democratic power underlay the vulnerability of the Lebanese cultural heritage of Beirut to fall dangerously into the hands of one authority, leaving it at the mercy of exclusive judgements about what, how and why certain heritage would be preserved.

Makdisi (1997: 667–74) traces the history of the plans for reconstruction of the BCD which continued alongside the Civil War and caused even more damage. Initially, in 1977, an official Council for Development and Reconstruction (CDR) plan expressed a faithful reconstruction of the BCD, re-establishing its pre-war role as a central heart of the nation, as a transport hub, commercial and cultural centre, and a meeting place for different classes and sects. At the same time the plan was to improve its infrastructure and modernize it. However, a private engineering company, owned by billionaire Rafiq Hariri, took responsibility for the BCD's reconstruction. In contradiction to the prevailing CDR plan for rehabilitation, Makdisi points out that demolition involved 'some of the district's most significant surviving buildings and structures as well as Souk Al-Nouriyeh and Souk Sursuq and large sections of Saifi'.

A few years later, similar clearances occurred. In 1983, Hariri personally funded the partial reconstruction of central Beirut after it was destroyed by the Israeli invasion. By the late 1980s private building interests were effectively 'planning' the BCD. In 1991, only a 'huge public outcry' ended plans to almost totally clear the BCD for modern developments. In 1992, more demolition was ordered by the government, which prompted a group of concerned architects to challenge official action. Makdisi iterates that more damage eventuated as a result of clearing for 'reconstruction' than the 15 years of Civil War had inflicted.

Rafiq Hariri extended and deepened control of reconstruction once he became Prime Minister. In 1992 Hariri's government passed legislation allowing a select group of powerful private interests to establish Solidere, which was given responsibility for developing the city centre through the assumption of rights to real estate there. The continuing Haririan association with Solidere explains the politics of architecture, planning and cultural heritage in Beirut. Rafiq Hariri rose to political leadership by marketing an aggressive plan for Lebanon's economic recovery and contributed one-fifth of Solidere's capital (Martinez-Garrido 2008: 3).

The Taif Agreement, the National Reconciliation Accord, signed towards the end of 1989 was the lynchpin of formal negotiations to end the Civil War (that is, disarmament) and the Syrian presence, and aimed to set a framework for 'political normalcy'. The agreement reduced the Christian presidency to a ceremonial and consultative position and strengthened the Sunni Muslim prime ministerial role that Hariri later assumed. Committing $US5 million of his private fortune to a feasibility study for the BCD redevelopment further consolidated Hariri's power (Partner 1995).

Compensating for compulsory purchases of land and damaged buildings, some Solidere stock was held by previous owners, and the rest by investors. Prepared by the leading Middle East Planning and Development Bureau (Dar al-Handasah) and French architect Henri Eddeh, the original 1991 Solidere master plan financed by Hariri focused narrowly on the old city centre rather than the whole city or country. It gave no scope for integrating new developments on Beirut's periphery that had started to mushroom by the end of 1990. Yet this reflected Rafiq Hariri's personal perspective and particular financial and political interests in reconstructing Beirut.

Hariri's fortune was drawn from years of construction and development activities in Saudi Arabia. He was Lebanon's largest philanthropist, donating millions of dollars to education and health. But Rafiq Hariri had many critics. His *nouveau riche* style offended and the time that he had spent in Saudi Arabia was resented, in that 'many Lebanese consider him an outsider' (Beyhum 1992: 23). Once he became the largest single shareholder in Solidere, its concept for reconstruction was seen as his personal vision, closely resembling the skyscraper rise of Dubai, where Hariri made money in the 1970s.

When asked what his children thought of Beirut's reconstruction, Hariri responded:

> They love it ... I was born in Saida [Sidon, Saidon] to a poor family. So when I used to come to Beirut, I used to see everything different: I used to be amazed by everything ... They compare Beirut with Paris and I compare it with Saida ... They don't have the same feeling I have. (Interview with Rafiq Hariri, 10 June 2000)

In view of this nostalgia, it seems a paradox that in his visions for Beirut's future, Hariri had few concerns for either his Lebanese past or the poor who were ignored and trammelled in Solidere's activities. But then Hariri saw himself as a self-made man and internalized the divisions that characterized Lebanon. Beyhum (1992: 6) stresses that Hariri stood for cultural conservatism: 'a vision of a city broken up into segregated islands'. When we look at his ideas, his efforts to inspire and control national unity centred on recreating the Beirut Central District specifically to highlight its millennia-long mercantile and trading history. This narrow emphasis accorded with the state as an agent for private entrepreneurship and placed economic development as the driver and automatic answer to all challenges.

Solidere's vision

The development strategy proposed by Solidere, originally part of the national economic recovery project called Horizon 2000 created by the CDR, had the ambition of complete reconstruction and recovery by the year 2000, a symbolic beginning to the turn of the century (Fig. 12.3). Based upon the idea that a privatized real estate company could make compulsory purchases of land and damaged buildings, the original Solidere redevelopment plan was to restore the symbolic function of the centre by linking the metropolitan region through a series of sunken 'arteries', aiming to optimize waterfront assets and draw on the BCD's rich archaeological heritage.

The modern district was to spread over 180 hectares, one-third of it reclaimed from the sea. The goal of promoting social pluralism focused on the so-called 'neutral' city centre. The plan provided for superstructures and prescribed a mix of land uses covering 4.7 million square metres in offices, retail spaces, government buildings, leisure and cultural facilities (which were already substantially under way by 2003).

Major aspects of the central city plan involved:

- Redevelopment of the waterfront via a promenade, a continuous corniche.
- Preservation of 400 low-rise buildings, to protect the low-rise area.
- Limitation of, and scope of, intervention zones.
- International competitions for souks and associated housing projects (e.g. Safi village).

As such the plans included the rehabilitation of the ancient Souk (market) area. However, the creation of a new business district on reclaimed land at the northern tip of the original medieval city was the centrepiece. The three-phase reconstruction would take over twenty-two years: the first included preservation of the city's heritage, the second modernization of the city centre and, third, development and enhancement of road networks.

Critics

The main problem with the Solidere BCD vision was its narrow focus on commercial interests in modernization and the spatial exclusivity it expressed. This business 'island' was to be ringed by a major road effectively separating the reconstructed area from both the rest of the city and most of its residents. Though occupying only 2 per cent of Lebanon's land area, Beirut was home to half of Lebanon's population. Rapid postwar urbanization had been encouraged

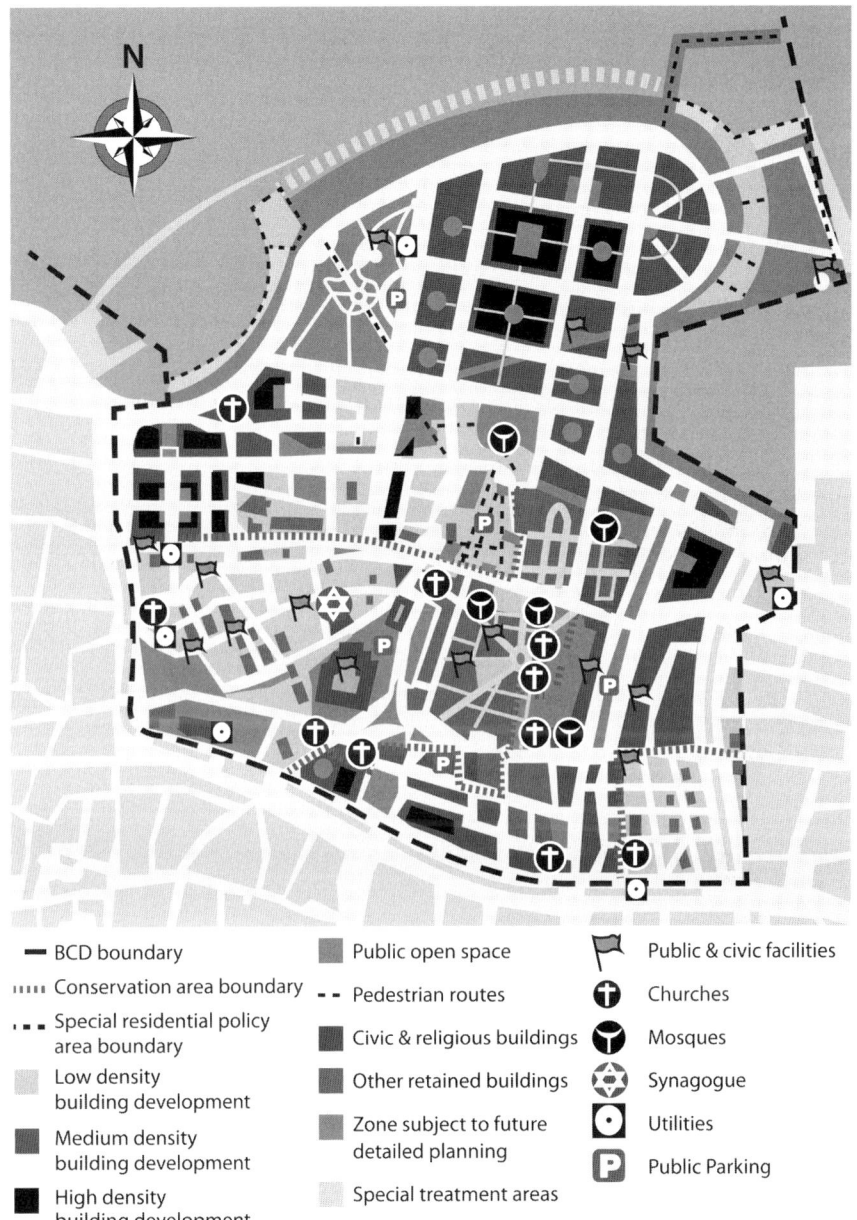

Legend		
▬ BCD boundary	▨ Public open space	⚑ Public & civic facilities
ⅢⅢⅢ Conservation area boundary	– – Pedestrian routes	✛ Churches
▪ ▪ ▪ Special residential policy area boundary	▨ Civic & religious buildings	☯ Mosques
▨ Low density building development	▨ Other retained buildings	✦ Synagogue
▨ Medium density building development	▨ Zone subject to future detailed planning	◉ Utilities
▨ High density building development	▨ Special treatment areas	Ⓟ Public Parking

Figure 12.3 Map of Beirut Central District.

by a centralist development policy (Khalaf 1993). But urbanization did not translate into more diverse and robust livelihoods for many of Beirut's new residents. Even as recently as 2009, the UNDP (2009: 11–12) has estimated that 29 per cent of Lebanese lived under the poverty line (of $US4 per day). The same report (37) pointed to 'significant health care challenges' and regional disparities in health statistics. In spatial terms Solidere focused on only 1.8 square kilometres, around 10 per cent of the destroyed city or 0.2 per cent of the nation's land. As such, Centre Ville ('Haririville') was bound to produce a segregated enclave to remind Lebanese of the immense and accelerating void between rich and poor.

A decade after the Civil War formally ended, the *Daily Star* (29 August 2001) reported a $US25 billion national debt and estimated unemployment at 45 per cent. The reconstruction timeline was continually revised following dramatic swings in Solidere's financial position. The Israeli withdrawal from the south of the country affected developments, as did increased Arab investment as a result of anti-Arab sentiments in the USA following the attacks in New York on 11 September 2001. These frustrations only highlighted the necessity for widespread consultation among the citizens of Lebanon to heal differences and forge a new built environment that expressed their diversity of backgrounds and needs.

Instead, American University of Beirut (AUB) Professor George Arbid (cited in Ouroussoff 2006) talks of Solidere 'marketing a nostalgia for a lost Lebanon'. Solidere saw the BCD combining the neo-rationalist Grand Design tradition strongly influenced by international market-driven urbanism (Saliba 2004: 197–200) while, in his detailed appreciation of the reconstruction of the port district (the Foch-Allenby and Etoile conservation areas), Saliba argues instead for a 'homegrown urbanism/synthesis'. Under the guise of preserving the BCD, archaeological remains were demolished in favour of new buildings and real estate, especially from 2004 (Shwayri 2008: 90–1). The souks (market places) are a case in point.

During reconstruction conservation of buildings was pursued by painstaking renovation and restoration, refurbishing, rebuilding according to original designs and remodelling, with contextual infill (Saliba 2004: Ch. 10). Despite careful restoration of exteriors, internal design was generally completely replaced with 'new functional cores' (Saliba 2004: Ch. 12). Unfortunately, these remarkable stone shells offer a metaphor for Beirut's reconstruction: expansive new urbanist façades, social masks and political clothes, empty of substance.

It is clear that the design of reconstruction was flawed and failed on the basis of several key criteria. The ownership of Beirut's remarkable architectural heritage was handed to narrow private interests who destroyed and preserved it to conform to their exclusive commercial vision and interests. Therefore, the opportunity to preserve and share Lebanon's cultural heritage as a basis for national unity and pride through common public ownership was lost. The crucial need for a city's layout, infrastructure and buildings to reflect and express openness, celebrate diversity and embrace it in strong public spaces and facilities, and to provide adequate infrastructure to support all its inhabitants was ignored.

Whose Cultural Heritage?

Cultural theorist Stuart Hall (2008) placed the question of 'Whose heritage?' at the centre of cultural heritage discourse. Whose remains? Whose past? Whose future? As Graeme Davison (2008) has pointed out, 'preserved for posterity' directs the attention of cultural heritage into the present and future, the 'unborn'. Most criticisms of the reconstruction process in Beirut over the past couple of decades focus on the dubious legal processes supporting Solidere's unbridled power, rather than aesthetic critiques of the results. The state's role was reduced to forming a development company and delineating its area of control. The planning process was not only undemocratic but privatized. Beirut failed because marginal groups were not empowered to participate in the reconstitution of their country and society.

Dispossession, segregation and suppression

In terms of domestic politics Hariri's role as patron exploited the idea of the divided city as a significant political opportunity (Bollens 1999: 67). Hariri was 'inventive' in the specific sense of the 'invention of tradition' (a phrase coined by Hobsbawm and Ranger) and explained by Palestinian cultural critic Edward Said as:

> a method for using collective memory selectively by manipulating certain bits of the national past, suppressing others, elevating still others in an entirely functional way. Thus memory is not necessarily authentic, but rather useful. (Said 2000: 179)

Solidere's direction was blatant. Much was destroyed, yet Solidere still saw ways of using Beirut's cultural heritage. According to Makdisi (1997: 681–2), a representative quoted in *Le Monde* said that Solidere had no interest in removing the city's archaeological or architectural 'patrimony' because 'it forms part of the marketing [program] of Solidere'. Ouroussoff (2006) concurs. Many critics, such as Makdisi (1997: 691), argue that Solidere attempted to 'spectacularize' history, using the capital's architectural heritage in a mercenary way as bait for tourists. At the same time the reconstruction aggravated social divisions and neglect.

An example of the divisive nature of the clearances in Beirut is indicated in a 2008 report (Hitti 2008) that Rafiq Hariri's son, Saad, had:

> Finally laid his hands on the last architectural gems of pre-war Beirut. Not to preserve them, turn them into a Museum ... But to demolish them and turn them into yet another disgusting skyscraper in which to house more corrupt businesses beholden to the Hariri empire and its company Solidere ...

Saad Hariri just tore down the last three standing Jewish buildings in Beirut's old Wadi Abu-Jmil district, gems of Beirut's 19th century architecture.

As architect Amine-Jules Iskandar describes the scene in a letter he sent to the Lebanese French-language daily *L'Orient Le Jour*, those three buildings were 'classified' (i.e. protected as historic landmarks) and are now no more than a pile of debris.

After Rafiq's assassination in 2005, Saad Hariri has gained more political and economic influence in Lebanon and became Prime Minister in 2009.

Certain countries have developed protocol for dealing with cultural heritage. Though controversial, the development of such protocol in Australia has been associated with establishing a multicultural society. Here, 'belonging' to a particular group (such as being an Indigenous Australian or Chinese Australian) gives a member rights and responsibilities associated with their specific cultural heritage (Schofield 2009: 176). This process not only allows space for a sense of 'ownership' of the heritage within broader shared public access but enriches records about and presentation of the findings for, in these cases, non-Indigenous and non-Chinese Australians. Disrespect for certain cultures in Beirut did not simply mean loss of architecture and ancient remains but also the loss of the opportunity to respect, understand and celebrate diverse backgrounds and interpretations.

Nagel (2002: 718) points out that 'like many texts, the built environment is significant not only for what it says, but for what it neglects to say about the past'. Even Beirut's Garden of Forgiveness, which has been erected in memory of the Civil War, reverberates as a form of suppression ('forgive and forget') rather than commemoration in a way that acknowledges diversity and the necessity of a continuous process of listening and reconciliation. Nagel (2002: 723) deplores the formal resistance to acknowledging the Civil War in memorials, especially given that the diverse cultures of the Lebanese are blatant outside the BCD: in Beirut's southern suburbs 'larger-than-life portraits of radical clerics and Iranian notables dominate the landscape'.

Similarly Makdisi (1997: 664) has stressed 'the extent to which this [Lebanese] identity, and even the very existence of an entity called Lebanon to which it supposedly corresponds, has been disputed', explaining how Solidere's approach contributed to confusion and suppression through:

a concerted effort to wipe the surface of central Beirut clean, to purify it of all historical associations in the form of its buildings, to render it pure space, pure commodity, pure real estate. The most obvious and striking potential war memorial (in a country that has all but forgotten its war), the shrapnel-scarred statue in Martyrs' Square, will be completely repaired

– its bullet holes erased and covered over just as the historical referents in the city center (and history itself) are being erased in the reconstruction. (Makdisi 1997: 692)

Exclusion

Hariri's island can be understood in the social-polarization lens of urban planning theorists such as Friedmann (1987), who describe cities as sites of society's winners/losers, the us/them of globalization. Solidere's vision of an 'instant city' ignored regional impacts or priorities of repairing immediate damage outside the city centre. As prominent Beirut architect Assem Salaam told one of the authors in an interview (10 June 2000), the approach should have been 'more timid', seeking areas 'to darn'.

Instead, the Solidere scheme took little account of how to accommodate the massive postwar demographic shifts of displaced persons across all Lebanon. Assuming travel in private cars, very little public transport was planned, reinforcing the enclave. Isolating the city centre from its wider metropolis – the heart from its body – further reinforced segregated Civil War patterns. Instead of returning the displaced, they were replaced. In fact Solidere displaced more when the BCD's original tenants were forced to give up property rights for shares – but had no say – in Solidere, which was controlled by rich Lebanese and foreigners.

In relation to Beirut's reconstruction, Davie (2002) has pointed out that a city 'is both *significant* and *signifié*, a coded object, which its societies continuously appropriate, territorialize, and re-territorialize according to numerous collective or individual stakes'. Following the vogue of 'new urbanism' (illustrated through gated residential developments such as 'Seaside' in the USA), the BCD does not encourage economically mixed neighbourhoods (Fig. 12.4). The majority of current residents are in upper income groups. Limiting mass access to the city centre prevented reviving one of the few areas where tolerant co-existence of diverse communities and groups had occurred in the past. In fact, private control of public space has been a challenge throughout Lebanon (Shwayri 2008: 90).

Martinez-Garrido (2008: 1–2) also points out how Solidere's mini-reconstruction worked against intercommunal contact and social cohesion. Shopping centres have become the main, and progressively exclusive, public spaces. Instead, cultural heritage, which is by definition 'public' (Davison 2008), was the natural complement to public space. Martinez-Garrido (2008: 3, 6) also deplores the practice of contracting foreign construction companies, which employ foreign workers and profit from low-cost subcontracts to Lebanese, rather than engage Lebanese to collaborate on reconstructions that enhance social reconciliation and integration, heal past conflict and create a unified future for Lebanon.

Using rebuilding as a tool for reconciliation required moving beyond the BCD, as Beirut architect Arrida proposed in 2001: 'a much more "fractal"

Figure 12.4 Beirut Central District, 2001.

boundary, taking Solidere beyond the ring, and bringing the "messy bits" inside the ring, thus obliging a higher degree of osmosis and of mutual catalysis of development' (Interview with Ayssar Arrida, 13 October 2001). Instead Beirut became an 'exclusionary city' (Boyer 1996).

The need for a privatized reconstruction model in Beirut might seem unique, but not according to Solidere's planning advisor:

> regeneration has moved on a long way from the public sector-led urban renewal disasters of the 1950s in the US and Europe ... Solidere has taken the trend towards public–private partnerships further than anywhere else in the world ... admired as the kind of framework that could be adapted to problems of inner-city regeneration in the developed world as well as other situations of postwar reconstruction. (Angus Gavin cited in Barnett 2002)

This statement indicates the implications of the Beirut experiment as a precedent, and raises issues about the responsibilities of professionals who are approached to work on projects that involve questionable policies, processes and practices.

The role of architects

Dutch archaeologist Hans H. Curvers (1997) reported discomfort working on the BCD because the 'ruthless' excavations demanded for new developments contradicted the conservation ethic of avoiding disturbing remains. The archaeologists were constrained by political policies and UNESCO was compromised through their lack of power to protect historic urban fabric. Curvers argued that neither private nor public property had been managed for future generations. While remains were removed and records made, Curvers feared a future in which the city would 'be dominated by haphazardly located monuments of high-tech and ruins of the past'.

All such development involved architects, foreign and national. In 2001 Arbid estimated that the latter totalled around 4,000–5,000 of four million Lebanese, alongside seven architecture schools (Interview with George Arbid, 1 August 2001). These architects and local planners had debated the Solidere reconstruction. In a public act of defiance (1992) one group raised a 'trenchant critique' of Solidere's vision (Khalaf 1993: 25). Late in 1997 the University of York held an international conference, on reconstructing war-torn cities, co-organized by the International Union of Architects and the Beirut Order of Engineers and Architects. Lebanese participants expressed concern over issues associated with 'traditional construction methods, globalization and their identity', concluding with a statement which included:

- A concern to preserve, as much as possible, the coherence of the social fabric as a basis for any reconstruction project.
- A concern to control the density and form of development and to restrain the rights of the individual to develop their own land in defiance of the interests of the community; the role of public authorities being to initiate,

follow up and control the implementation of reconstruction plans
entrusted to various actors.
• A call to launch public participation as an absolute necessity in any
planning process. Information, consultation and partnerships are major
elements of public participation, which should precede and accompany
each step of the reconstruction process so as to prevent any demagogic
distortion. (*Revival* 1998)

Solidere was a sponsor of the conference. Ironically these points contradicted
its everyday practices and none of its projects could have been realized
without many of the architects who had been involved in the University of
York forum.

It seems that the modernist influence on Lebanese architects in pre-Civil
War decades and reconstruction politics left little space to value heritage or
challenge Solidere's exclusionary practices. A characteristic lawlessness
emerged from the lack of planning regulations, the archaic zoning laws and an
elite in charge of development decisions. A stereotypical French *beaux-arts*
urban surgery approach was popular when planners did degrees in the 1990s,
which crowded out the development of a model more appropriate for the
climate and spatial typologies of Middle Eastern cities, such as internal
courtyards and small intimate streets. Physical dimensions of spaces were the
main real estate considerations in the BCD development, reinforcing a
development rather than design role for architects and planners.

Many Beirut architects interviewed in 2000 agreed that it would have been
preferable to use funds spent on the BCD to develop a metropolitan vision
strengthening the polycentric structure surrounding Beirut by renewing its
infrastructure connections and links. However, there were few opportunities
for them to voice such concerns, exert influence or assist in 're-stitching' or
re-visioning the divided communities of Beirut. A culture of elitism and a
tradition of importing foreign expertise that Solidere had perpetuated
pressured local talent to defer to non-Lebanese architects and work on projects
with which they were uncomfortable. In *Main Gate* (2004), a young local
architect heading up a small firm that had over a dozen projects in the BCD
explained the painful reality thus: 'The space is beautiful, but at what cost? ...
Hardly anyone can afford an office downtown, with the exception of the rich
and the rich from the Gulf.'

According to the same journal, however, a few younger-generation
architects, such as Simone Kosremelli's small firm, stuck doggedly to
rehabilitating and reconstructing traditional buildings. Kosremelli deplored
the tendency to seek foreign advice and leadership. Similarly, acclaimed local
architect Assem Salaam (2008) has pointed out that Lebanese vernacular
homes are highly functional, environmentally sensible and the typical design
is one that is shared across classes. If traditional architecture had been pursued
at a household level this characteristic alone had the potential to build cohesion

and an element of unitary identity for Lebanese residents. But Salaam argues that Beirutis have been 'throwing away their own heritage': the village architecture characteristic of Beirut just decades ago has been destroyed through real estate developments along with the 'ancestral know-how' of refining stonework.

Also, some new leaders have evolved. Eminent Lebanese architect Bernard Khoury (in Ouroussoff 2006) criticizes Solidere's 'pseudohistoric vision' as 'a saccharine image of the past' and deplores the neocolonialism of 'the big international stars' that dominate its recent BCD developments. His architecture responds critically to Solidere, aiming to be 'a truthful reflection of Beirut'. An example is Centrale restaurant (2001), which preserved destroyed aspects of its site to cradle a bold building intimating social disparities and discomfort in its interior.

In another project atypical not only for Beirut, Khoury asked each client of a multi-residential building to provide him with the number of levels and rooms of their choice, and a sketch of how they would like the interiors of their spaces and then how in an inside-out way he amalgamated them into a bizarre building that: 'beautifully reflects an aspect of the city's past', that is, its constant, higgledy-piggledy renovation. Thus, Ouroussoff (2006) argues: 'Khoury's approach suggests what Beirut might be if the arbitrary formulas created by developers suddenly dropped away, and the city became an honest expression of its competing histories'.

Such examples show exactly how architects can forge a defence against the activities of powerful agencies such as Solidere. Architects, like planners, can infuse their designs with respect for cultural heritage and integrate participatory processes for working with clients in their daily practice. Once professional associations set down standards for their everyday practice that include such ethical codes of professional practice, there is a stronger basis for architects, planners and archaeologists to work collaboratively in lifting broader ethical standards. Thus there is great potential for collective effort which would automatically flow into and become part of university training as well as better practices arising from academic criticism and challenge.

Conclusion

This chapter briefly outlined the Civil War in Lebanon and the destructive impacts on its urban fabric of reconstruction supervised by Solidere. A privatized model of rebuilding to achieve economic modernization meant 'destructive construction', destroying and contorting cultural heritage as well as failing to address social, cultural and religious divisions. This analysis of Beirut's reconstruction identified some interconnected major failings: lack of broad participation in planning strategies; singular power vested in a private company serving an economic and political elite which simply produced an island refuge for them; a neocolonial preference for foreign architects, which highlighted both a pervasive *politics of exclusion* and the general failure of professional conduct; in short, a failure to manage cultural heritage as a public resource.

Reconstructing the centre as the metaphorical heart of a destroyed city and nation through privatized fast-track development strategies resulted in an over-planned central urban area and a vastly under-planned greater Beirut metropolis. This plan failed to address critical inequities, poverty and religious differences. In fact the metaphor of city as spine, a backbone for the peace process, would have been more appropriate to guide the development of urban patterns linking communities. What the nation really called for was a holistic process of economic, political, spatial, social and cultural reconciliation. Instead Solidere's plans typified and exaggerated neglect of such challenges. Therefore the question remains whether Lebanon's still profoundly divided social fabric can be rewoven with its remaining cultural heritage intact.

References

Barnett, N. (2002) 'Beirut: The Phoenician Phoenix', *The Middle East* (July–August), 47.

Beyhum, N. (1992) *Rebuilding Beirut and Lost Opportunity*, Beirut: Rami al Khal.

Bollens, S. (1999) *Urban Peace-Building in Divided Societies: Belfast and Johannesburg*, Boulder: Westview Press.

Boyer, C. (1996) *Dreaming the Rational City: The Myth of American City Planning, 1893–1945*, Cambridge, MA: MIT Press.

Calame, J. and Charlesworth, E. (2009) *Divided Cities: Belfast, Beirut, Jerusalem, Mostar, and Nicosia*, Philadelphia: University of Pennsylvania Press.

Campaign for Good Governance in Lebanon (2008) 'Human Rights Report: Lebanon', Centre for Democracy and the Rule of Law. Online: www.cggl.org/scripts/document.asp?id=46305 (accessed 14 October 2009).

Charlesworth, E. (2006) *Architects Without Frontiers: War, Reconstruction and Design Responsibility*, Oxford: Architectural Press.

Curvers, H. H. (1997) 'Archeological Resource Management in the Beirut Central District', IPP University of Amsterdam. Online: http://almashriq.hiof.no/lebanon/900/930/930.1/beirut/hhc/resource-management.html (accessed 21 October 2009).

Davie, M. F. (2002) 'City as Excavation? Notes for the Excavation of Beirut: A Quest for National Identity?' Paper presented to City Debates Seminar, American University of Beirut, 3 June.

Davison, G. (2008) 'Heritage: From patrimony to Pastiche', in G. Fairclough, R. Harrison, J.H. Jameson Jr and J. Schofield (eds), *The Heritage Reader*, London: Routledge.

Friedmann, J. (1987) *Planning in the Public Domain: From Knowledge to Action*, Princeton: Princeton University Press.

Hall, S. (2008) 'Whose Heritage? Un-settling "The Heritage", Re-imagining the Post-Nation', in G. Fairclough, R. Harrison, J. H. Jameson Jr and J. Schofield (eds), *The Heritage Reader*, London: Routledge.

Hitti, J. (2008) 'Hariri's Solidere Demolishes Beirut's Last Jewish Buildings', *American Chronicle*, 19 March. Online: www.americanchronicle.com (accessed 10 October 2009).

Hourani, A. (1995) *The Emergence of the Middle East*, Berkeley: University of California Press.

Khalaf, S. (1993) *Beirut Reclaimed: Reflections on Urban Design and the Restoration of Civility*, Beirut: Dar an-Nahar.

Main Gate (2004) 'Behold Beirut Architecture's New Frontier', II (3 & 4) Summer. Online: http/staff.aub.edu.lb/~webmgate/summer04/feature1.html (accessed 20 October 2009).

Makdisi, S. (1997) 'Laying Claim to Beirut: Urban Narrative and Spatial Identity in the Age of Solidere', *Critical Inquiry* 23(3) (Spring), 661–705.

Martinez-Garrido, L. (2008) 'Beirut Reconstruction: A Missed Opportunity for Conflict Resolution', *Al Nakhalah: The Fletcher School Online Journal on Southwest Asia and Islamic Civilization*, Tufts University, Fall. Online: http://fletcher.tufts.edu/al_nakhlah/archives/Fall2008.asp (accessed 10 October 2009).

Nagel, C. (2002) 'Reconstructing Space, Re-creating Memory: Sectarian Politics and Urban Development in Post-War Beirut', *Political Geography* 21, 717–25.

Ouroussoff, N. (2006) 'Lebanese Architect Troubled by Soul-less Solidere', *New York Times*, 22 May.

Partner, P. (1995) 'The Rebirth of Beirut', *New York Times*, 25 May.

Revival (1998) 'Reconstruction of War-Torn Cities', University of York Post-War Reconstruction and Development Unit (February) 9.

Said, E. W. (2000) 'Invention, Memory, and Place', *Critical Inquiry* 26(2), 175–92.

Salaam, A. (2008) 'Lebanese architecture, Old Building Beirut', extract from C. Yazbeck, C. Corm, K. Mouzawak and C. Coroller, *A Complete Insiders' Guide to Lebanon*, Souk el Tayeb Press. Online: www.discoverlebanon.com/en/forum/viewtopic_t_112_sid_506a63b5a8812e 2ac031fb321c536a6b.html (accessed October 2009).

Saliba, R. (2004) *Beirut City Centre Recovery: the Foch-Allenby and Etoile Conservation Area*, Göttingen and London: Steidl and Thames & Hudson.

Salibi, K. (1998) *A House of Many Mansions: The History of Lebanon Reconsidered*, London: I. B. Tauris.

Schofield, J. (2009) *Aftermath: Readings in the Archaeology of Recent Conflict*, New York: Springer.

Shwayri, S. T. (2008) 'From Regional node to Backwater and Back to Uncertainty', in Y. Elsheshtawy (ed.), *The Evolving Arab City: Tradition, Modernity and Urban Development*, London: Routledge.

Tueni, G. (1992) 'Beirut Our City', *An Nahar*, 2 February.

UNDP (2009) *Millennium Development Goals Lebanon Report 2008*, New York: United Nations Development Program.

Index

Note: Page numbers in **bold** are for figures.